The Spirit of
Jewish Thought

The Spirit of
Jewish Thought

edited and with commentary by

Bernard Evslin

A Rutledge Book
published by
Grosset & Dunlap, Inc.
New York, New York

For some time now my wife, Dorothy, has practiced indispensability.
The research she did for this book is but one more of those
radiant and self-effacing performances which place themselves
beyond gratitude.

Bernard Evslin

Copyright © 1969 by Grosset & Dunlap, Inc., and Rutledge Books, Inc.
Prepared and produced by Rutledge Books
Published by Grosset & Dunlap, Inc.
Published simultaneously in Canada
All rights reserved
Library of Congress Catalog Card Number: 68–10736
Printed in the United States of America

The Spirit of
Jewish Thought

Contents

Introduction

As the slow blood-colored history of the Jews has unreeled like a dream from which the dreamer cannot awake, this people has been called many things and has called itself many things. Not often do the names given to the Jews and the names taken by them coincide. But there is one title—applied by Mohammed—which they have gladly adopted, and which has been accepted even by those who like them least. To themselves, to Christian, to Moslem, to the various groups of the nonreligious, they are recognized as "the People of the Book."

It is a good name. They have fed on the word and it has become flesh, and nonsymbolically. The claim of Jewish intellectual preeminence, however, is a sore subject for Jew as well as Gentile. Beneath all the words there is an unspoken dialogue going on between the Jews and their neighbors, and what each thinks he hears is more important than what is said. Christians think they hear the Jews saying, "We had to invent a form of monotheism simple enough for the goyim to understand." And the Jews think they hear, "It is not for killing our God that we hate you, but for giving him to us, along with all the responsibility for being civilized."

So the question of how these irritating People of the Book came by their intellectual preeminence is an incendiary one. But there are certain clues to their intellectual achievements which move the subject from the realm of racial mystique. In their long exile among people who loathed them, Jews were fused into family units of a strength that is unimaginable today. And the theme of the family was simple. It was the duty of the father to instruct the son, the duty of the son to be instructed. By instruction was meant all the accumulated knowledge and wisdom of those who went before. This was not a form of words; it was a form of conduct. Consider this passage from the Code of Education (page 113) drawn up by English Jews of the twelfth century to guide teachers in schools that had been set up by the community.

"From month to month," the Code directs, "you shall increase my son's task. If this month he can learn half the weekly portion of Scripture, next month he must go through the whole. From Tammus [June-July] to Tishri he must go through the weekly portion in Hebrew, and from Tishri to Nisan in the vernacular. Then the boy is six years old."

However, it must be emphasized that with all this passion for learning, the idea of the ivory tower was absolutely alien to Jewish thinking. The word of God, which was the beginning of all wisdom, expressed itself through the world He had created and in all its phenomena; learning was necessary for living, and the Code continues thus:

"The sages also say: 'The chief thing is not Learning but Action.' . . . But because the people are hunted away from Action they must console themselves with clinging to the faith. The Separated [very learned] however can combine both the Law and its fulfillment in Action."

Is there a unity to Jewish thought over the ages? The question on the face of it seems ridiculous. Nowhere does there seem more diversity. There are mystics, visionaries; there are uncompromising rationalists. There are those who see salvation only in a Jewish state and those who believe any such state is a heresy—that it must await the Messiah. There are those who created the religious consciousness of the western world. There are those, like Freud and Marx, who have done more than anyone else to smash the metaphysical God. What relationship except the disputed one of lineage can you trace between a Maimonides, for instance, and Lenny Bruce? Is not the process of lumping all these various kinds of minds together under the word "Jewish" a kind of ultimate vulgarization, a crude chauvinism?

These perfectly legitimate questions can best be answered if we accept the Jewish intellectual tradition as one which expresses the intellectual process itself, that is: hospitality, curiosity, investigation; an insistence that ideas must undergo a kind of validation no matter what the outcome. The mood engendered by these elements is twofold, expressing the ideal environment of the intellectual process: a hospitality for conflicting notions; the opportunity to dissent.

These are not latter-day concepts. In the Bible itself, undoubtedly the greatest gift of the Jews—or of any other people—to the world, there are creation myths, codes of personal and social conduct, erotic songs, battle hymns, prayers, tragic drama as in the book of Job, and even an exquisitely cadenced atheistic tract in Ecclesiastes.

Or take the second great book of Judaism, the Talmud, that vast book of civil and religious code based on syllable-by-syllable interpretation of the Scriptures. Here we see a curious thing. The Talmud has become the key statement of the religion, the pillar of its orthodoxy, superseding even that upon which it is based, the Bible itself. And yet as we study it we see that what is as sacred as the evolved content itself is the *process* of its evolution. That is, the process of disputation. Orthodoxy was wrought by the incessant dispute of thousands of scholars over a period of several hundred years. Psychologically, the dispute was enshrined, even if other shrines had to fall as the Question overflowed orthodoxies.

Question, investigation, dispute, dissent—these are bone and flesh of the tradition. That is why we find it natural to include all kinds of iconoclasts in this collection, which takes its primal inspiration from the adventures of that first idol-smasher, Abraham, who could neither deny the God Who was revealed to him nor forbear from questioning Him.

I
IN THE BEGINNING:
THE BIBLE

And the Lord God formed man of the dust of the ground
and breathed into his nostrils the breath of life; and
man became a living soul.

Genesis 2:7

Introduction

  The Jews are the People of the Book and the Bible is their Book of books. But not only Jews are concerned in the unfolding of its mighty rhythms. It is the great source book of western culture. Its terrain is the fatherland of contemporary theology, philosophy and ethics; ancient Greece is the motherland.

  Actually, the Bible is a whole library of books; its first tales were told long before the word Israel, or Hebrew, first appears in Egyptian records to describe the loose federation of tribes living in the hills of Palestine. In this library are history, mythology, tomes of law, tabulations of ancient customs, novels. There are all kinds of poetry—epic and lyric, love odes, hymnals, threnodies; there are prayers and prophecies and proverbs. Its moods run the whole range of human emotion from the stark wonder of the creation myths to the sophisticated and convoluted tragedy of Job, through the psalms of David, martial and joyous, and the bitter cynicism of Ecclesiastes, to the passionate love stories of Tamar and Ruth and Solomon. And behind it all is the reality of God's presence, a metaphysical reality so awesome, so magnificent, so all-pervasive, that human activity becomes a dance of midges in the great sunlight of His gaze.

Jacob's Farewell

Jacob has traveled down to Egypt to visit his abducted son, Joseph, and the terrible grief of the old man has been transmuted to rejoicing. After abiding in Egypt a space of years, Jacob comes to his last strength and gathers his sons about him to give them his blessing.

It must be remembered that the blessing of the patriarch was no mere form of words; it conveyed the actual passage of kingship. This is what Jacob does in our first selection as he apostrophizes Judah, passing on to him the leadership of that people who were finally to take their name from him, and whose unique ordeal was to make this endowment the very prototype of mixed blessing.

Then, in magical passages in which mingle a father's love and a wild spirit of augury, Jacob separately blesses his other sons, predicting for each of them and their tribes a destiny in the history of civilizations still to be born. He departs only once from prophecy, and that is when he comes to Joseph. Here all else is laid aside and his love bursts forth in a radiant fountain of poetry. It is father and son caught in a moment of time bathed in an eternal light.

To Judah

Judah, thou art he whom thy brethren shall praise; thy hand shall be in the neck of thine enemies; thy father's children shall bow down before thee.

Judah is a lion's whelp; from the prey, my son, thou art gone up: he stooped down, he couched as a lion, and as an old lion; who shall rouse him up?

The sceptre shall not depart from Judah, nor a lawgiver from between his feet, until Shiloh come; and unto him shall the gathering of the people be.

Binding his foal unto the vine, and his ass's colt unto the choice vine, he washes his garments in wine, and his clothes in the blood of grapes:

His eyes shall be red with wine, and his teeth white with milk.

16

To Joseph

Joseph is a fruitful bough, even a fruitful bough by a well; whose branches run over the wall:

The archers have sorely grieved him, and shot at him and hated him:

But his bow abode in strength, and the arms of his hands were made strong by the hands of the mighty God of Jacob; (from thence is the shepherd, the stone of Israel:)

Even by the God of thy father, who shall help thee; and by the Almighty, who shall bless thee with blessings of heaven above, blessings of the deep that lieth under, blessings of the breasts, and of the womb:

The blessings of thy father have prevailed above the blessings of my progenitors unto the utmost bound of the everlasting hills: they shall be on the head of Joseph, and on the crown of the head of him that was separate from his brethren.

Moses and God

The opening passages of the tremendous chronicle of Moses and the Exodus describes the lawgiver's first encounter with the living God. In the final words is the essence of Jewish monotheism.

And it came to pass in the process of time, that the king of Egypt died: and the children of Israel sighed by reason of the bondage, and they cried, and their cry came up unto God.

And God heard their groaning, and God remembered his covenant with Abraham, with Isaac, and with Jacob.

Now Moses kept the flock of Jethro his father in law, the priest of Midian: and he led the flock to the mountain of God, even to Horeb.

And the angel of the Lord appeared unto him in a flame of fire out of the midst of a bush: and he looked, and, behold, the bush burned with fire, and the bush was not consumed.

And God called unto him out of the midst of the bush, and said, Put off thy shoes from off thy feet, for the place whereon thou standest is holy ground. I am the God of thy father, the God of Abraham, the God of Isaac, and the God of Jacob.

And Moses hid his face; for he was afraid to look upon God.

And the Lord said, I have surely seen the affliction of my people which are in Egypt; and have heard their cry by reason of their taskmasters; and I am come down to deliver them out of the hand of the Egyptians. Come now therefore, and I will send thee unto Pharoah, that thou mayest bring forth my people the children of Israel out of Egypt.

And Moses said unto God, Behold when I come unto the children of Israel, and shall say unto them, The God of your fathers hath sent me unto you; and they shall say to me, What is his name? what shall I say unto them?

And God said unto Moses, I AM THAT I AM. . . .

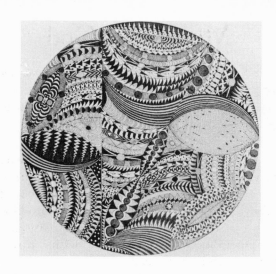

Leviticus

"Leviticus" means Law of the Priests. It is the third book of the Pentateuch, which comprises the five Books of Moses. For the most part, Leviticus consists of a recital of the Law given to Moses on Mount Sinai and lays down enormously detailed injunctions on ritual, personal habits and ethical behavior.

And the Lord spake unto Moses, saying,

Ye shall be holy: for I the Lord your God am holy.

Ye shall fear every man his mother, and his father, and keep my sabbaths: I am the Lord your God.

Turn ye not unto idols, nor make to yourselves molten gods: I am the Lord your God.

Ye shall not steal, neither deal falsely, neither lie one to another.

And ye shall not swear by my name falsely, neither shalt thou profane the name of thy God: I am the Lord.

Thou shalt not curse the deaf, nor put a stumbling block before the blind, but shalt fear thy God: I am the Lord.

Ye shall do no unrighteousness in judgment: thou shalt not respect the person of the poor, nor honour the person of the mighty: but in righteousness shalt thou judge thy neighbour.

Ye shall not . . . use enchantment, nor observe times.

Do not prostitute thy daughter, to cause her to be a whore; lest the land fall to whoredom, and the land become full of wickedness.

Ye shall keep my sabbaths, and reverence my sanctuary: I am the Lord.

Regard not them that have familiar spirits, neither seek after wizards, to be defiled by them: I am the Lord your God.

Thou shalt rise up before the hoary head, and honour the face of the old man, and fear thy God: I am the Lord.

And if a stranger sojourn with thee in your land, ye shall not vex him.

But the stranger that dwelleth with you shall be unto you as one born among you, and thou shalt love him as thyself; for ye were strangers in the land of Egypt: I am the Lord your God.

Deuteronomy

Deuteronomy is the last of the Books of Moses and continues a recital of the law. It also contains many chapters of Moses' last words to the Children of Israel, full of prophecy, menace and mandate.

Judges and officers shalt thou make thee in all thy gates, which the Lord thy God giveth thee, throughout thy tribes: and they shall judge the people with just judgment.

Thou shalt not wrest judgment; thou shalt not respect persons, neither take a gift: for a gift doth blind the eyes of the wise, and pervert the words of the righteous.

That which is altogether just shalt thou follow, that thou mayest live, and inherit the land which the Lord thy God giveth thee.

One witness shall not rise up against a man for any iniquity, or for any sin, in any sin that he sinneth: at the mouth of two witnesses, shall the matter be established.

When thou goest out to battle against thine enemies . . .

. . . The officers shall speak unto the people, saying, What man is there that hath built a new house, and hath not dedicated it? let him go and return to his house, lest he die in the battle, and another man dedicate it.

And what man is he that hath planted a vineyard, and hath not yet eaten of it? let him also go and return unto his house, lest he die in the battle, and another man eat of it.

And what man is there that hath betrothed a wife, and hath not taken her? let him go and return unto his house, lest he die in the battle, and another man take her.

And the officers shall speak further unto the people, and they shall say, What man is there that is fearful and fainthearted? let him go and return unto his house, lest his brethren's heart faint as well as his heart.

When a man hath taken a new wife, he shall not go out to war, neither shall he be charged with any business: but he shall be free at home one year, and shall cheer up his wife which he hath taken.

Thou shalt not deliver unto his master the servant which is escaped from his master unto thee:

He shall dwell with thee, even among you, in that place which he shall choose, in one of thy gates, where it liketh him best: thou shalt not oppress him.

When thou comest into thy neighbour's vineyard, then thou mayest eat grapes thy fill at thine own pleasure; but thou shalt not put any in thy vessel.

When thou comest into the standing corn of thy neighbour, then thou mayest pluck the ears with thine hand; but thou shalt not move a sickle unto thy neighbour's standing corn.

No man shall take the nether or the upper millstone to pledge: for he taketh a man's life to pledge.

The fathers shall not be put to death for the children, neither shall the children be put to death for the fathers: every man shall be put to death for his own sin.

When thou cuttest down thine harvest in thy field, and hast forgot a sheaf in the field, thou shalt not go again to fetch it: it shall be for the stranger, for the fatherless, and for the widow: that the Lord thy God may bless thee in all the work of thine hands. . . .

When thou gatherest the grapes of thy vineyard, thou shalt not glean it afterward: it shall be for the stranger, for the fatherless, and for the widow.

And thou shalt remember that thou wast a bondman in the land of Egypt: therefore I command thee to do this thing.

The Song of Deborah

*The Song of Deborah, from Judges, is not only
a song. It is the choreography for a wild war dance—and
like many primitive ritual dances, the song-story of a
military triumph. It tells how, in the dark days of defeat
when all the captains of the tribes of Israel were in hiding,
the prophetess Deborah arose from obscurity, gathered her
broken people, welded them into a fighting force, filled
them with the words of God, and led them to a great
victory over the invading kings of Canaan.*

Praise ye the Lord for the avenging of
Israel, when the people willingly offered themselves. . . .

In the days of Shamgar the son of
Anath, in the days of Jael, the highways were
unoccupied, and the travellers walked through
byways.

The inhabitants of the villages ceased,
they ceased in Israel, until that I Deborah arose,
that I arose a mother in Israel.

They chose new gods; then was war
in the gates: was there a shield or spear seen among
forty thousand in Israel? . . .

Awake, awake, Deborah: awake, awake,
utter a song: arise, Barak, and lead thy captivity
captive, thou son of Abinoam.

Then he made him that remaineth
have dominion over the nobles among the people:
the Lord made me have dominion over the mighty.

Out of Ephraim was there a root of
them against Amalek; after thee, Benjamin, among
thy people; out of Machir came down governors,
and out of Zebulun they that handle the pen of the
writer.

And the princes of Issachar were with
Deborah; even Issachar, and also Barak: he was
sent on foot into the valley. For the divisions of
Reuben there were great thoughts of heart.

Gilead abode beyond Jordan: and why
did Dan remain in ships? Asher continued on the
sea shore, and abode in his breaches.

Zebulun and Naphtali were a people that jeoparded their lives unto the death in the high places of the field.

The kings came and fought, then fought the kings of Canaan in Taanach by the waters of Megiddo; they took no gain of money.

They fought from heaven; the stars in their courses fought against Sisera.

The river of Kishon swept them away, that ancient river, the river Kishon. . . .

Then were the horsehoofs broken by the means of the prancings, the prancings of their mighty ones.

Curse ye Meroz, said the angel of the Lord, curse ye bitterly the inhabitants thereof; because they came not to the help of the Lord, to the help of the Lord against the mighty.

Blessed above women shall Jael the wife of Heber the Kenite be, blessed shall she be above women in the tent.

He asked water, and she gave him milk; she brought forth butter in a lordly dish.

She put her hand to the nail, and her right hand to the workmen's hammer; and with the hammer she smote Sisera, she smote off his head, when she had pierced and stricken through his temples.

At her feet he bowed, he fell, he lay down: at her feet he bowed, he fell: where he bowed, there he fell down dead.

The mother of Sisera looked out at a window, and cried through the lattice, Why is his chariot so long in coming? why tarry the wheels of his chariots?

So let all thine enemies perish, O Lord: but let them that love him be as the sun when he goeth forth in his might.

And the land had rest forty years.

Job

Job is the man God chose to torment for what seemed like His own amusement. The victim's anguished bewilderment, his questions piercing to the very quick of misfortune's meaning, the complacent advice of his more successful friends, make this unique among Bible stories.

The passages chosen are from Job's duologue with God wherein an idea was developed that lies at the heart of metaphysics—but which is largely rejected by today's rational religionists—that the roots of good, evil and justice are unknowable to man, that God's caprice is man's law.

Man that is born of a woman is of few days, and full of trouble.

He cometh forth like a flower, and is cut down: he fleeth also as a shadow, and continueth not.

And dost thou open thine eyes upon such an one, and bringest me into judgment with thee?

Who can bring a clean thing out of an unclean? not one.

Seeing his days are determined, the number of his months are with thee, thou hast appointed his bounds that he cannot pass:

Turn from him, that he may rest, till he shall accomplish, as an hireling, his day.

For there is hope of a tree, if it be cut down, that it will sprout again, and that the tender branch thereof will not cease.

Though the root thereof wax old in the earth, and the stock thereof die in the ground;

Yet through the scent of water it will bud, and bring forth boughs like a plant.

But man dieth, and wasteth away: yea, man giveth up the ghost, and where is he?

As the waters fail from the sea, and the flood decayeth and drieth up:

So man lieth down, and riseth not: till the heavens be no more, they shall not awake, nor be raised out of their sleep.

O that thou wouldest hide me in the grave, that thou wouldest keep me secret, until thy wrath be past, that thou wouldest appoint me a set time, and remember me!

If a man die, shall he live again? all the days of my appointed time will I wait, till my change come.

Thou shalt call, and I will answer thee: thou wilt have a desire to the work of thine hands.

For now thou numberest my steps: dost thou not watch over my sin?

My transgression is sealed up in a bag, and thou sewest up mine iniquity.

And surely the mountain falling cometh to nought, and the rock is removed out of his place.

The waters wear the stones: thou washest away the things which grow out of the dust of the earth; and thou destroyest the hope of man.

Thou prevailest for ever against him, and he passeth: thou changest his countenance, and sendest him away.

His sons come to honour, and he knoweth it not; and they are brought low, but he perceiveth it not of them.

But his flesh upon him shall have pain, and his soul within him shall mourn.

Shall any teach God knowledge? seeing he judgeth those that are high.

One dieth in his full strength, being wholly at ease and quiet.

His breasts are full of milk, and his bones are moistened with marrow.

And another dieth in the bitterness of his soul, and never eateth with pleasure.

They shall lie down alike in the dust, and the worms shall cover them.

Surely there is a vein for the silver, and a place for gold where they fine it.

Iron is taken out of the earth, and brass is molten out of the stone.

He setteth an end to darkness, and

searcheth out all perfection: the stones of darkness, and the shadow of death.

He putteth forth his hand upon the rock; he overturneth the mountains by the roots.

He cutteth out rivers among the rocks; and his eye seeth every precious thing.

He bindeth the floods from overflowing; and the thing that is hid bringeth he forth to light.

Whence then cometh wisdom? and where is the place of understanding?

Seeing it is hid from the eyes of all living, and kept close from the fowls of the air.

Destruction and death say, We have heard the fame thereof with our ears.

God understandeth the way thereof, and he knoweth the place thereof.

. . . He prepared it, yea, and searched it out.

And unto man he said, Behold, the fear of the Lord, that is wisdom; and to depart from evil is understanding.

Then the Lord answered Job out of the whirlwind, and said,

Who is this that darkeneth counsel by words without knowledge?

Gird up now thy loins like a man; for I will demand of thee, and answer thou me.

Where wast thou when I laid the foundations of the earth? declare, if thou hast understanding.

Who shut up the sea with doors, when it brake forth, as if it had issued out of the womb?

Hast thou commanded the morning since thy days; and caused the dayspring to know his place;

That it might take hold of the ends of the earth, that the wicked might be shaken out of it?

Hast thou entered into the springs of

the sea? or hast thou walked in the search of the depth?

Have the gates of death been opened unto thee? or hast thou seen the doors of the shadow of death?

Hast thou perceived the breadth of the earth? declare if thou knowest it all.

Knowest thou the ordinances of heaven? canst thou set the dominion thereof in the earth?

Canst thou lift up thy voice to the clouds, that abundance of waters may cover thee?

Shall he that contendeth with the Almighty instruct him? he that reproveth God, let him answer it.

Psalms

Countless books have been written about the psalms and their meaning. Modern Bible scholarship holds that they were written by many different people at many different times. But they are traditionally attributed to David, and there is a unity of style and of idea in them that could well belong to that greatest king of Judah.

For David, in the hugeness and color of his soul, lived many different kinds of lives. He was a shepherd boy, a fairy-tale vanquisher of giants, passionate friend to Jonathan, young acolyte to Saul, a harpist whose strains could bewitch the hardest-hearted; he was fugitive, avenger, warrior king, adulterer. Through it all he was constantly in touch with God, Whom he favored with what seemed like daily communications. These are the psalms.

They are unique in Bible literature, though they do not seem so now because of the prayers and hymns which they have fathered and which have become the common coin of religious service, Christian as well as Jewish. They are song-prayers in a tone at once exalted and intimate, a white-hot dialogue between King David and God, the Father. They describe his terror, loneliness, joy, his amazement at the sun and the stars, his love of hill and desert and the animals of earth. They form a kind of emotional log of David's stormy career.

Psalm 8

O Lord our Lord, how excellent is thy name in all the earth! who hast set thy glory above the heavens.

Out of the mouth of babes and sucklings hast thou ordained strength because of thine enemies that thou mightest still the enemy and the avenger.

When I consider thy heavens, the work of thy fingers, the moon and the stars, which thou hast ordained;

What is man, that thou art mindful of him? and the son of man, that thou visitest him?

For thou hast made him a little lower than the angels, and hast crowned him with glory and honour.

Thou madest him to have dominion over the works of thy hands; thou hast put all things under his feet:

All sheep and oxen, yea, and the beasts of the field;

The fowl of the air, and the fish of the sea, and whatever passeth through the paths of the seas.

O Lord our Lord, how excellent is thy name in all the earth!

Psalm 18

I will love thee, O Lord, my strength.

The Lord is my rock, and my fortress, and my deliverer; my God, my strength, in whom I will trust; my buckler, and the horn of my salvation, and my high tower.

I will call upon the Lord, who is worthy to be praised: so shall I be saved from mine enemies.

The sorrows of death compassed me, and the floods of ungodly men made me afraid.

The sorrows of hell compassed me about: the snares of death prevented me.

In my distress I called upon the Lord, and cried unto my God: he heard my voice out of his temple, and my cry came before him, even into his ears.

Then the earth shook and trembled; the foundations also of the hills moved and were shaken, because he was wroth.

The Lord also thundered in the heavens, and the Highest gave his voice; hail stones and coals of fire.

Yea, he sent out his arrows, and scattered them; and he shot out lightnings, and discomfited them.

Then the channels of water were seen, and the foundations of the world were discovered at thy rebuke, O Lord, at the blast of the breath of thy nostrils.

He sent from above, he took me, he drew me out of many waters.

He delivered me from my strong enemy, and from them which hated me: for they were too strong for me.

They prevented me in the day of my calamity: but the Lord was my stay.

He brought me forth also into a large place; he delivered me, because he delighted in me.

Therefore will I give thanks unto thee, O Lord, among the heathen, and sing praises unto thy name.

Great deliverance giveth he to his king; and sheweth mercy to his anointed, to David, and to his need for evermore.

Psalm 22

My God, my God, why hast thou forsaken me? why art thou so far from helping me, and from the words of my roaring?

O my God, I cry in the daytime, but thou hearest not; and in the night season, and am not silent.

Be not far from me; for trouble is near; for there is none to help.

Many bulls have compassed me: strong bulls of Bashan have beset me round.

They gaped upon me with their mouths, as a ravening and a roaring lion.

I am poured out like water, and all my bones are out of joint; my heart is like wax; it is melted in the midst of my bowels.

My strength is dried up like a potsherd; and my tongue cleaveth to my jaws; and thou hast brought me into the dust of death.

But be not thou far from me, O Lord: O my strength, haste thee to help me.

I will declare thy name unto my brethren: in the midst of the congregation will I praise thee.

Ye that fear the Lord, praise him; all ye the seed of Jacob, glorify him; and fear him, all ye the seed of Israel.

All the ends of the world shall remember and turn unto the Lord: and all the kindreds of the nations shall worship before thee.

For the kingdom is the Lord's: and he is the governor among the nations. . . .

Psalm 23

The Lord is my shepherd; I shall not want.

He maketh me to lie down in green pastures: he leadeth me beside the still waters.

He restoreth my soul: he leadeth me in the paths of righteousness for his name's sake.

Yea, though I walk through the valley of the shadow of death, I will fear no evil: for thou art with me; thy rod and thy staff they comfort me.

Thou preparest a table before me in the presence of mine enemies: thou anointest my head with oil; my cup runneth over.

Surely goodness and mercy shall follow me all the days of my life: and I will dwell in the house of the Lord for ever.

Psalm 73

Truly God is good to Israel, even to such as are of a clean heart.

But as for me, my feet were almost gone; my steps had well nigh slipped.

For I was envious at the foolish, when I saw the prosperity of the wicked.

For there are no bands in their death; but their strength is firm.

They are not in trouble as other men; neither are they plagued like other men.

Therefore pride compasseth them about as a chain: violence covereth them as a garment.

Their eyes stand out with fatness: they have more than heart could wish.

They are corrupt, and speak wickedly concerning oppression; they speak loftily.

They set their mouth against the heavens, and their tongue walketh through the earth.

Therefore his people return hither: and waters of a full cup are wrung out to them.

And they say, How doth God know? and is there knowledge in the most High?

Behold, these are the ungodly, who prosper in the world; they increase in riches.

Verily I have cleansed my heart in vain, and washed my hands in innocency.

For all the day long have I been plagued, and chastened every morning.

Nevertheless I am continually with thee: thou hast holden me by my right hand.

Thou shalt guide me with thy counsel, and afterward receive me to glory.

Whom have I in heaven but thee? and there is none upon earth that I desire beside thee.

My flesh and my heart faileth: but God is the strength of my heart, and my portion for ever.

For, lo, they that are far from thee shall perish: thou hast destroyed all them that go a whoring from thee.

But it is good for me to draw near to God: I have put my trust in the Lord God, that I may declare all thy works.

Psalm 84

How amiable are thy tabernacles, O Lord of hosts!

My soul longeth, yea, even fainteth for the courts of the Lord: my heart and my flesh crieth out for the living God.

Yea, the sparrow hath found an house, and the swallow a nest for herself, where she may lay her young, even thine altars, O Lord of hosts, my King, and my God.

Blessed are they that dwell in thy house: they will be still praising thee. Selah.

Blessed is the man whose strength is in thee; in whose heart are the ways of them.

Who passing through the valley of Baea make it a well; the rain also filleth the pools.

They go from strength to strength, every one of them in Zion appeareth before God.

O Lord God of hosts, hear my prayer: give ear, O God of Jacob. Selah.

Behold, O God our shield, and look upon the face of thine anointed.

For a day in thy courts is better than a thousand. I had rather be a doorkeeper in the house of my God, than to dwell in the tents of wickedness.

For the Lord God is a sun and shield: the Lord will give grace and glory: no good thing will he withhold from them that walk uprightly.

O Lord of hosts, blessed is the man that trusteth in thee.

Psalm 114

When Israel went out of Egypt, the house of Jacob from a people of strange language;

Judah was his sanctuary, and Israel his dominion.

The sea saw it, and fled: Jordan was driven back.

The mountains skipped like rams, and the little hills like lambs.

What ailed thee, O thou sea, that thou fleddest? thou Jordan, that thou wast driven back?

Ye mountains, that ye skipped like rams; and ye little hills, like lambs?

Tremble, thou earth, at the presence of the Lord, at the presence of the God of Jacob;

Which turned the rock into a standing water, the flint into a fountain of waters.

Psalm 137

By the rivers of Babylon, there we sat down, yea, we wept, when we remembered Zion.

We hanged our harps upon the willows in the midst thereof.

For there they that carried us away captives required of us a song; and they that wasted us required of us mirth, saying, Sing us one of the songs of Zion.

How shall we sing the Lord's song in a strange land?

If I forget thee, O Jerusalem, let my right hand forget her cunning.

If I do not remember thee, let my tongue cleave to the roof of my mouth; if I prefer not Jerusalem above my chief joy.

Remember, O Lord, the children of Edom in the day of Jerusalem; who said, Rase it, rase it, even to the foundation thereof.

O daughter of Babylon, who art to be destroyed; happy shall he be, that rewardeth thee as thou hast served us.

Happy shall he be, that taketh and dasheth thy little ones against the stones.

Proverbs

Proverbs belongs to the genre known as Hebrew Wisdom Literature, a form basically oriental. Its theme is that wisdom will be rewarded and ignorance punished. But the words wisdom and ignorance did not mean, in Bible times, what they mean today. For the authors of the Proverbs, wisdom meant fear of God; ignorance meant the ignoring of His law.

A wise son makes a glad father;
But a foolish son is a grief to his mother.

Hatred stirs up strife;
But love draws a veil over all transgressions.

Where words abound, sin will not be wanting;
But he who holds his tongue acts wisely.

As the whirlwind passes, so the wicked
man vanishes;
But the righteous one is rooted forever.

As vinegar to the teeth, and as smoke to the eyes,
So is the sluggard to those who send
him on an errand.

Like a golden ring in the snout of a sow
Is a beautiful woman lacking in taste.

Better a man of low rank, who works for his living,
Than he who puts on grand airs,
yet has nothing to eat.

Hope deferred makes the heart sick;
But desire fulfilled is a tree of life.

He who walks with wise men will become wise;
But the companion of fools will smart for it.

Every man knows his own bitterness,
And in his joy no stranger can share

The poor man is hated even by his neighbour;
But the rich has many friends.

A tranquil mind is health for the body;
But passion is a rot in the bones.

A soothing tongue is a tree of life;
But wild words break the spirit.

All the ways of a man are pure in his own eyes;
But the Lord weighs the motives.

A fickle man sows discord,
And a whisperer separates friends.

Better be met by a bear robbed of her cubs
Than by a fool in his folly.

A foolish man is his father's ruin;
And a quarrelsome wife is like a constant drip.

Ecclesiastes

Ascribed to Koheleth, a son of David, is the section of the Bible known as Ecclesiastes and perhaps less like other religious writing than anything else the Bible contains. These are bitter, bitter verses full of world-weariness and despair, and a pessimism so deep that it approaches humor. Indeed, the legendary Koheleth would seem to have been a very civilized man, and civilized in contemporary terms. He is subtle, ironic, clear-sighted, unafraid. If hope has disappeared from his universe, so has terror. He has seen it all, knows it all. There is possibly in the name Koheleth a clue to his identity. It means "one who speaks in assembly"; some authorities believe it was adopted as a pseudonym by Solomon. In any case, from a literary point of view there are no cadences in any language more exquisite than those of Koheleth.

Vanity of vanities, all is vanity.

What profit hath a man of all his labour which he taketh under the sun?

One generation passeth away, and another generation cometh: but the earth abideth for ever.

The sun also ariseth, and the sun goeth down, and hasteth to his place where he arose.

The wind goeth toward the south, and turneth about unto the north; it whirleth about continually, and the wind returneth again according to his circuits.

All the rivers run into the sea; yet the sea is not full; unto the place from whence the rivers come, thither they return again.

All things are full of labour; man cannot utter it: the eye is not satisfied with seeing, nor the ear filled with hearing.

The thing that hath been, it is that which shall be; and that which is done is that which shall be done: and there is no new thing under the sun.

Isaiah

Of all the superbly angry old men whom we know as the Prophets, Isaiah is the dominant figure. Here is a prophecy whose reverberations are as compelling now as when they were uttered more than 2,000 years ago.

. . . Behold, the Lord rideth upon a swift cloud, and shall come into Egypt: and the idols of Egypt shall be moved at his presence, and the heart of Egypt shall melt in the midst of it.

And I will set the Egyptians against the Egyptians: and they shall fight every one against his brother, and every one against his neighbour; city against city, and kingdom against kingdom.

And the spirit of Egypt shall fail in the midst thereof; and I will destroy the counsel thereof: and they shall seek to the idols, and to the charmers, and to them that have familiar spirits, and to the wizards.

And the Egyptians will I give over into the hand of a cruel lord; and a fierce king shall rule over them.

And the waters shall fail from the sea, and the river shall be wasted and dried up.

And they shall turn the rivers far away; and the brooks of defence shall be emptied and dried up: the reeds and flags shall wither.

The paper reeds by the brooks, and every thing sown by the brooks, shall wither, be driven away, and be no more.

The fishers also shall mourn, and all they that cast angle into the brooks shall lament, and they that spread nets upon the waters shall languish.

In that day shall Egypt be like unto women: and it shall be afraid and fear because of the shaking of the hand of the Lord of hosts.

And the land of Judah shall be a terror unto Egypt, every one that maketh mention thereof shall be afraid in himself, because of the counsel of the Lord of hosts, which he hath determined against it.

And the Lord shall smite Egypt: and they shall return to the Lord, and he shall be entreated of them, and shall heal them.

In that day shall there be a highway out of Egypt to Assyria, and the Assyrian shall come into Egypt, and the Egyptian into Assyria, and the Egyptians shall serve with the Assyrians.

In that day shall Israel be the third with Egypt and with Assyria, even a blessing in the midst of the land.

The Vision of Daniel

The book of Daniel is a strange one. It tells the famous story of the dissenters and the lions' cage and the thwarting of the wicked king of Babylon. Less well known is the vision of Daniel; the bestiary of its symbolism provided the inspiration for John's apocalyptic vision of the New Testament and has generated millions of paragraphs of commentary and interpretation. In itself, it is great poetry.

In the first year of Belshazzar king of Babylon Daniel had a dream and visions of his head upon his bed: then he wrote the dream, and told the sum of the matters.

Daniel spake and said, I saw in my vision by night, and, behold, the four winds of the heaven strove upon the great sea.

And four great beasts came up from the sea, diverse one from another.

The first was like a lion, and had eagle's wings: I beheld till the wings thereof were plucked, and it was lifted up from the earth, and made stand upon the feet as a man, and a man's heart was given to it.

And behold another beast, a second, like to a bear, and it raised up itself on one side, and it had three ribs in the mouth of it between the teeth of it: and they said thus unto it, Arise, devour much flesh.

After this I beheld, and lo another, like a leopard, which had upon the back of it four wings of a fowl; the beast had also four heads; and dominion was given to it.

After this I saw in the night visions, and behold a fourth beast, dreadful and terrible, and strong exceedingly; and it had great iron teeth: it devoured and brake in pieces, and stamped the residue with the feet of it: and it was diverse from all the beasts that were before it; and it had ten horns.

I considered the horns, and, behold,

there came up among them another little horn, before whom there were three of the first horns plucked up by the roots: and, behold, in this horn were eyes like the eyes of man, and a mouth speaking great things.

I beheld till the thrones were cast down, and the Ancient of days did sit, whose garment was white as snow, and the hair of his head like the pure wool: his throne was like the fiery flame, and his wheels as burning fire.

A fiery stream issued and came forth from before him: thousand thousands ministered unto him, and ten thousand times ten thousand stood before him: the judgment was set, and the books were opened.

I beheld then because of the voice of the great words which the horn spake: I beheld even till the beast was slain, and his body destroyed, and given to the burning flame.

As concerning the rest of the beasts, they had their dominion taken away: yet their lives were prolonged for a season and time.

I saw in the night visions, and behold, one like the Son of man came with the clouds of heaven, and came to the Ancient of days, and they brought him near before him.

And there was given him dominion, and glory, and a kingdom, that all people, nations, and languages, should serve him: his dominion is an everlasting dominion, which shall not pass away, and his kingdom that which shall not be destroyed.

I Daniel was grieved in my spirit in the midst of my body, and the visions of my head troubled me.

I came near unto one of them that stood by, and asked him the truth of all this. So he told me, and made me know the interpretation of the things.

These great beasts, which are four, are four kings, which shall arise out of the earth.

But the saints of the most High shall take the kingdom, and possess the kingdom for ever, even for ever and ever.

Then I would know the truth of the fourth beast, which was diverse from all the others, exceedingly dreadful, whose teeth were of iron, and his nails of brass; which devoured, brake in pieces, and stamped the residue with his feet;

And of the ten horns that were in his head, and of the other which came up, and before whom three fell; even of that horn that had eyes, and a mouth that spake very great things, whose look was more stout than his fellows.

I beheld, and the same horn made war with the saints, and prevailed against them;

Until the Ancient of days came, and judgment was given to the saints of the most High; and the time came that the saints possessed the kingdom.

Thus he said, The fourth beast shall be the fourth kingdom upon earth, which shall be diverse from all kingdoms, and shall devour the whole earth, and shall tread it down, and break it in pieces.

And the ten horns out of this kingdom are ten kings that shall arise: and another shall rise after them; and he shall be diverse from the first, and he shall subdue three kings.

And he shall speak great words against the most High, and shall wear out the saints of the most High, and think to change times and laws: and they shall be given into his hand until a time and times and the dividing of time.

But the judgment shall sit, and they shall take away his dominion, to consume and to destroy it unto the end.

And the kingdom and dominion, and the greatness of the kingdom under the whole heaven, shall be given to the people of the saints of the most High, whose kingdom is an everlasting kingdom, and all dominions shall serve and obey him.

Hitherto is the end of the matter. As for me Daniel, my cogitations much troubled me, and my countenance changed in me: but I kept the matter in my heart.

Amos

Amos was the earliest of the Prophets. His indict-
ments were leveled at two prosperous reigns: that of Uzziel,
King of Judah, and Jeroboam, King of Israel. Amos was
the first to enunciate the stern proposition that of all
nations Israel was the most likely to attract the wrath of
God because of its high condition of "chosen-ness"; and so
its people had to conduct themselves more ethically than
others.

I will send a fire upon Judah, and it shall devour the palaces of Jerusalem.

. . . Because they sold the righteous for silver, and the poor for a pair of shoes;

That pant after the dust of the earth on the head of the poor, and turn aside the way of the meek. . . .

And they lay themselves down upon clothes laid to pledge by every altar, and they drink the wine of the condemned in the house of their god.

Behold, I am pressed under you, as a cart is pressed that is full of sheaves.

Therefore the flight shall perish from the swift, and the strong shall not strengthen his force, neither shall the mighty deliver himself:

Neither shall he stand that handleth the bow; and he that is swift of foot shall not deliver himself: neither shall he that rideth the horse deliver himself.

And he that is courageous among the mighty shall flee away naked in that day, saith the Lord.

Hear ye this word which I take up against you, even a lamentation, O house of Israel.

They hate him that rebuketh in the gate, and they abhor him that speaketh uprightly.

. . . Ye have built houses of hewn stone, but ye shall not dwell in them; ye have planted pleasant vineyards, but ye shall not drink wine of them.

Hear this word, ye kine of Bashan . . . which oppress the poor, which crush the needy, which say to their masters, Bring, and let us drink.

The Lord God hath sworn by his holiness, that, lo, the days shall come upon you, that he will take you away with hooks, and your posterity with fishhooks.

And ye shall go out at the breaches, every cow at that which is before her; and ye shall cast them into the palace.

I hate, I despise your feast days, and I will not smell in your solemn assemblies.

Though ye offer me burnt offerings and your meat offerings, I will not accept them: neither will I regard the peace offerings of your fat beasts.

Take thou away from me the noise of thy songs; for I will not hear the melody of thy viols.

But let judgment run down as waters, and righteousness as a mighty stream.

II
DESTROYERS
IN THE RUINS

This world is only the vestibule to another; you must
prepare yourself in the vestibule so that you may
enter the banquet hall.

The Talmud

Introduction

During the centuries reflected in the early books of the Bible, a ceaseless shifting power struggle among the petty chieftains of the Mesopotamian region battered the Jewish tribes and weakened them before invaders. By the first millennium B.C. these tribes had been dispersed— some to disappear into the Caucasus, some to be scattered on all the shores of the Mediterranean basin, others exiled to the Babylonian cities between the Tigris and Euphrates. The ones who were taken to Babylon survived as Jews and, miraculously, developed and refined their religion while in exile. Somehow they managed to retain their tribal heritage, their monotheistic worship and their belief that they had been chosen from among the peoples of the earth by the one true God—that, in fact, He had announced his unique godhead through them, and that His survival was linked to theirs. This faith allowed them to retain their identity until the Persian, Cyrus, having conquered Babylon, permitted the Jews to return to Judea in 538 B.C.

The Temple was rebuilt in Palestine, and a fairly autonomous Jewish state established. But internal strife and the infiltration of alien habits worked toward its destruction. Hellenization, which swept over the whole known world with Alexander, attracted large numbers of the most sophisticated Jews. But the un-Hellenized made thunderous efforts to reclaim their brothers for orthodoxy, denying any authority in religious matters except the Torah. The Apocryphal expansions of Bible material, most of which had been handed down orally and finally achieved written status in Greek, were frowned on by the authoritarian elders. Cultivated Jews like Philo, valued for their acceptance in the outside world, were nevertheless suspect within the walls.

As Roman power succeeded Greek, there was frequent opportunity for ambitious Jews to live as Josephus did—half in the Jewish world, half in the Roman—and many must finally have opted, as he did, for Rome. In Josephus' own report on the fall of Masada, which closed the Jewish-Roman wars, the zealot Eleazar bitterly condemns his followers for having incurred God's wrath and their own destruction by falling away from the old fierce single-minded devotion to the precepts of the Torah—even maintaining that indifference to the apostasy of others was as great a sin as apostasy itself.

From the Apocrypha

Oddly enough, the Christian Church is responsible for preserving a critically important body of Jewish writing. These works, written over a four-hundred-year span between the second century B.C. and the second century A.D., are known as the Apocrypha (secret) and Pseudepigrapha (under false title). They are actually outlawed parts of the Bible, prevented from entering the Scripture because they were set down too late for the tastes of the zealots who arbitrarily declared that God's book was closed.

Much of this work is in no way inferior to what is contained in the Bible; in fact it enjoyed immense popularity among the Jewish people and has indeed become part of Jewish religious thinking. Yet if it had not been preserved by the early Christian fathers, it would have disappeared from our knowledge.

The primitive richness of the Apocrypha is typified by Enoch, who tells a marvelous story of the angels when the world was new—how they lusted after the daughters of earth, and the terrors that were born of their lust.

This passage was so influential in Christian thinking that at one time it rivaled the story of Adam and Eve as the key event in the concept of original sin. Certain theologians maintained that original sin flowed not from Adam's disobedience but from this illicit hunger of angels for the daughters of earth.

Enoch: The Lust of the Angels

And it came to pass when the children of men had multiplied that in those days were born unto them beautiful and comely daughters. And the angels, the children of the heaven, saw and lusted after them, and said to one another: 'Come, let us choose us wives from among the children of men and beget us children.' And Semjaza, who was their leader, said unto them: 'I fear ye will not indeed agree to do this deed, and I alone shall have to pay the penalty of a great sin.' And they all answered him and said: 'Let us all swear an oath, and all bind ourselves by mutual imprecations not to abandon this plan but to do this thing.'

And all the others together with them took unto themselves wives, and each chose for himself one, and they began to go in unto them and to defile themselves with them, and they taught them charms and enchantments, and the cutting of roots, and made them acquainted with plants. And they became pregnant, and they bare great giants, whose height was three thousand ells: Who consumed all the acquisitions of men. And when men could no longer sustain them, the giants turned against them and devoured mankind. And they began to sin against birds, and beasts, and reptiles, and fish, and to devour one another's flesh, and drink the blood. Then the earth laid accusation against the lawless ones.

And then Michael, Uriel, Raphael, and Gabriel looked down from heaven and saw much blood being shed upon the earth, and all lawlessness being wrought upon the earth. And they said to the Lord of the ages: 'They have gone to the daughters of men upon the earth, and have slept with the women, and have defiled themselves, and revealed to them all kinds of sins. And the women have borne giants, and the whole earth has thereby been filled with blood and unrighteousness.'

Then said the Most High, the Holy and Great One, 'Go to Noah and tell him in my name "Hide thyself!" and reveal to him the end that is approaching: that the whole earth will be destroyed, and a deluge is about to come upon the whole earth, and will destroy all that is on it. And now instruct him that he may escape and his seed may be preserved for all the generations of the world.'

The Killing of Abel

The familiar Bible version of the story of Cain and Abel is simply a recital of events. But in the Apocrypha, the oldest murder becomes a full-blooded narrative that goes zestfully into character, relationships, even sensations. And in this story is implicit one of the great Bible mysteries, a puzzle that has been discussed by generations of religious philosophers. What really is the first sin of Cain? Why, when he complies with God's directive to bring his offering, is it refused, without explanation?

This turnabout seems to us like caprice. But it contains a fundamental religious premise: the inscrutability and mystery of God's design. The Jews recognized that there was injustice on this earth that could not be rationalized in any way. Certainly their own later experience proved this—and so does the common human condition. How many of us encounter similar rejection? We come with our most beautiful offerings, our greatest gifts; we do our best. And somehow, incomprehensibly, we are refused. We fail, while others, who offer less, are accepted and rise to their desired goals. Can we grow so angry that we murder?

The Bible says No, and the no is repeated in this Apocryphal version. No matter how great the injustice, how shattering the misfortune, there is no justification for the sin of taking another human life. To the great Biblical question, "Am I my brother's keeper?", God replies, "You are—even if your brother prospers and you do not."

Abel, at the age of twenty years, became a keeper of sheep, and Cain was a tiller of the ground. And Adam said unto them: "From the produce of your labour, ye shall take out one tenth for God's portion." And the sheep of Abel brought forth one with numberless speckles; Abel chose it for God's portion; but for love of his brother, he would not offer it. He said within himself: "When the crops of my brother are ripe, then we will offer up together the portion to God."

When Cain's crops of corn were ripe, he cut down his corn, he made bunches of that which was beaten by the wind, fastened it up in sheaves, and put them apart for God's portion.

And Abel brought his lamb that he had chosen, and had promised unto God as his portion. And Cain stood up in prayer to God, saying: "Know, thou, O Lord, Creator of all, that from everything that I worked for and produced, I took out a portion and a tenth part of my substance and offered unto thee. And now let thy will be done, as it pleases thee."

And the Lord was wroth with Cain, and as a handful of dust is carried away by the wind, so he scattered all his harvest of corn, and destroyed all his riches so that not even an ear of corn could be found. He beat Cain's face with hail, which blackened like coal, and thus he remained with a black face.

But Abel offered unto God the first-born lamb, and stretching out his hands, prayed unto the Lord, saying: "Lord God, Creator and maker of all good things, I beseech thee, accept my offering."

Immediately a gentle breeze blew, and a light came down from heaven, and Abel's face became shining, and a voice came from heaven, saying: "Thy prayer is heard, and thine offering is accepted."

And Cain nourished a hatred against Abel, and would have killed him, but knew not how, for as yet no murder had taken place. And Abel knew not the wicked intention of his brother, and they did always eat and drink, and walk together.

But on a certain day Cain said unto his brother: "Let us go and take a walk in the field." So they arose and went into the field, and Cain wished to bind his brother; but Abel was more vigorous than Cain, and therefore Cain could not reveal his intention unto him. Then he began to play with his brother, and wrestle with him, but in trying to take hold of him in flank, he fell down, and could not overcome Abel. Then Cain getting up, looked around and saw a very long shoot of a vine, and said: "Come brother, let us play with this shoot. Throw your arms around this tree, and with these three shoots I will bind thee, and see whether thou canst break them, and set thyself free. Then will I embrace the tree, and thou shalt bind me; and so will we see who shall be able to break free."

Then Abel approached the tree, and Cain took the shoot of the vine, and with it he bound him around three times, body and hands. Then Abel understood his brother's wickedness, and entreated him, "Brother, let me loose from the bond." But Cain would not release him; he bound him stronger, and walked about and looked for something with which he could kill his brother.

And Satan the wicked one, at the close of the day, showed him a stone sharp as a razor. Cain took the sharp stone and came unto Abel.

And Abel wept, but Cain had no pity upon him. And as the stone was a small one, hardly could Cain in an hour slay him.

When he had slain his brother, and was going away cheerfully, the Lord appeared and said to him: "Where is thy brother?"

And Cain boldly said: "Who made me his guardian that thou askest me?"

The Testaments of
the Patriarchs

*The twelve patriarchs were the sons of Jacob,
who later became the fathers of the tribes of Israel. They
were: Simeon and Levi, the violent brothers; Judah, who
was to inherit the blessing and give his name to the Jews;
Reuben, Zebulon, Issachar, Dan, Gad, Asher, Naphthali;
and the two sons of Rachel, the beloved Joseph and the
youngest, Benjamin.*

*It was Joseph's elder brothers, jealous of their
father's love for Joseph, who sold him into slavery in Egypt
and commenced his mighty saga. Later, after they had gone
down into Egypt and been forgiven by Joseph and had
settled there and lived their lives—founding the Israelite
tribes—they were stricken by conscience on their deathbeds
and delivered themselves of remarkable confessions. These
confessions are not part of the Bible story but come to
us through the Apocrypha. They are the Testaments of the
Twelve Patriarchs, parts of which follow.*

Reuben

For evil are women, my children; and
since they have no power or strength over man,
they use wiles by outward attractions that they
may draw him to themselves. And whom they cannot bewitch by outward attractions, him they
overcome by craft. For an angel of the Lord told
me that women are overcome by the spirit of
fornication more than men, and in their heart
they plot against men; and by means of their
adornment they deceive first their minds, and by
the glance of the eye instil the poison, and then
through the accomplished act they take them
captive. Flee, therefore, fornication, my children,
and command your wives and your daughters that
they adorn not their heads and faces to deceive
the mind; because every woman who useth these
wiles hath been reserved for eternal punishment.

56

Simeon

For envy maketh savage the soul and destroyeth the body; it causeth anger and war in the mind, and stirreth up unto deeds of blood, and leadeth the mind into frenzy, and causeth tumult to the soul and trembling to the body. For even in sleep some malicious jealousy gnaweth, and with wicked spirits disturbeth and causeth the body to be troubled, and waketh the mind from sleep in confusion.

Levi

Fear the Lord your God with your whole heart,/And walk in simplicity according to all His law.

And do ye also teach your children letters,/That they may have understanding all their life,/Reading unceasingly the law of God.

For every one that knoweth the law of the Lord shall be honoured,/And shall not be a stranger whithersoever he goeth.

For though there be a leading unto captivity,/And cities and lands be destroyed,/And gold and silver and every possession perish,/The wisdom of the wise nought can take away.

Judah

My children, the love of money leadeth to idolatry; because, when led astray through money, men name as gods those who are not gods, and it causeth him who hath it to fall into madness.

Be not drunk with wine; for wine turneth the mind away from the truth, and inspires the passion of lust, and leadeth the eyes into error. For if a man drink wine to drunkenness, it disturbeth the mind with filthy thoughts leading to fornication, and heateth the body to carnal union.

Zebulon

And now my children, I bid you to keep the commands of the Lord, and to show mercy to your neighbours, and to have compassion toward all, not toward men only, but also toward beasts.

Oversee the waters and know when they flow together, they sweep along stones, trees, earth, and other things. But if they are divided into many streams, the earth swalloweth them up, and they become of no account. So shall ye also be if ye be divided. Be not ye, therefore, divided into two heads, for everything which the Lord made hath but one head.

Issachar

The single-minded man coveteth not gold,
He overreacheth not his neighbour,
He longeth not after manifold dainties,
He delighteth not in varied apparel,
He doth not desire to live a long life,
But only waiteth for the will of God.
And the spirits of deceit have no power
   against him.

Dan

Understand ye the power of wrath, that it is vain. For it first of all giveth provocation by word; then by deeds it strengtheneth him who is angry, and with sharp losses disturbeth his mind, and so stirreth up with great wrath his soul. Therefore, when any one speaketh against you, be not ye moved to anger, and if any man praiseth you as holy men, be not uplifted; be not moved either to delight or to disgust. For first it pleaseth the hearing and so maketh the mind keen to perceive the grounds for provocation; and then being enraged, he thinketh that he is justly angry.

Gad

Hatred is evil, for it constantly mateth with lying, speaking against the truth; and it maketh small things to be great, and causeth the light to be darkness, and calleth the sweet bitter, and teacheth slander, and kindleth wrath, and stirreth up war, and violence and all covetousness; it filleth the heart with evils and devilish poison. For he that is just and humble is ashamed to do what is unjust, being reproved not of another, but of his own heart, because the Lord looketh on his inclination.

Asher

Ye see, my children, how that there are two in all things, one against the other, and the one is hidden by the other: in wealth, covetousness, in conviviality, drunkenness, in laughter, grief, in wedlock, lechery. Death succeeds to life, dishonour to glory, night to day and darkness to light; and all things are under the day, just things under life, unjust things under death; wherefore also eternal life awaiteth death. But it may not be said that truth is a lie, or that right is wrong; for all truth is under the light, even as all things are under God.

Naphthali

Be ye, therefore, not eager to corrupt your doings through covetousness or with vain words to beguile your souls; because if ye keep silence in purity of heart, ye shall understand how to hold fast the will of God, and to cast away the will of Beliar. Sun and moon and stars change not their order; so do ye also change not the law of God in the disorderliness of your doings. The Gentiles went astray, and forsook the Lord, and changed their order, and obeyed sticks and stones, spirits of deceit. In like manner the Watchers also changed the order of their nature, whom the Lord cursed at the flood, on whose account He made the earth without inhabitants and fruitless.

Joseph

Do ye, therefore, love one another, and with long-suffering hide ye one another's faults. For God delighteth in the unity of brethren, and in the purpose of a heart that takes pleasure in love.

If ye walk in the commandments of the Lord, my children, He will exalt you there, and will bless you with good things for ever and ever. And if any one seeketh to do evil unto you, do well unto him, and pray for him, and ye shall be redeemed of the Lord from all evil.

Benjamin

The good mind hath not two tongues, of blessing and of cursing, of contumely and of honour, of sorrow and of joy, of quietness and of confusion, of hypocrisy and of truth, of poverty and of wealth; but it hath one disposition, uncorrupt and pure, concerning all men. It hath no double sight, nor double hearing; for in everything which he doeth, or speaketh, or seeth, he knoweth that the Lord looketh on his soul. And he cleanseth his mind that he be not condemned by men as well as by God.

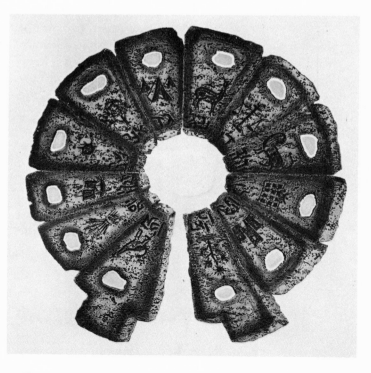

Jewish Legends

To read these stories is to journey through a marvelous terrain, full of haunting echoes and strange lights—the magical landscape of Jewish folklore and legend.

The characters and situations in the Bible are the great fountainhead of these legends, whose tone differs radically from their exalted source. The Bible is told in very stark terms; its form is inherently dramatic—there is almost no background material, no description of person, place, clothing. It is as though the white-hot dialogue between God and man, which is the theme of the Old Testament, had burned away appearance, leaving us only with essences. But alongside these stark tales another literature arose, almost unknown now. The characters of the Bible—the patriarchs, judges, heroes, villains, prophets, sinners—had woven themselves so deeply into the fabric of Jewish experience that the imagination of the people could not put them aside. But the Bible lore was played with, embroidered; incidents were added, whole episodes. All of which exfoliated into the luxuriant growth of Jewish legend.

There are no official versions of these stories. They have been shaped by the imagination of hundreds of generations, and are retold for this collection by the editor.

Let us begin in the beginning with stories of the Creation . . . not quite in the beginning, but on the fifth and sixth days when God made the creatures of the deep and the animals of the land.

The Fifth Day

On the fifth day God mixed fire and water and made the fishes of the sea—and set a king over them named Leviathan. At first there were two, male and female, but they were so large and strong that God feared they might devour the earth, and he killed the female. So great is the Leviathan's thirst that he drinks up all the waters of the Jordan each day. When he is hungry he blows a hot breath that makes the sea boil. Brilliant light flashes from his fins and his eyes are so huge and radiant that they light the waters. This marvelous beast is known as God's toy.

The Sixth Day

The fish were made of water, and the birds of mud, but mammals were made of solid earth. The king of the mammals was named Behemoth. So huge is he that the leaves of the trees that grow on 1,000 mountains are needed for his food each day, and all the water of ten rivers he swallows in one gulp. In the world to come the savory flesh of the Behemoth is to be served to the pious, along with the flesh of the Leviathan. But before they are served this meal, those who have been obedient to God will enjoy the spectacle of a gigantic earthshaking combat between Leviathan and Behemoth. This will be their reward for having denied themselves in life the pagan delights of the circus and the gladiatorial ring.

A remarkable animal known in the beginning of time was the Adne Sadeh. He looks like a man, but his navel cord is rooted in the earth. When the cord is broken, he dies. They say that he was a man once, but envied the peace of vegetables, and so God granted him his wish in such a way as to teach other creatures not to wish for anything they had not been given.

A marvelous bird is the Phoenix. When Eve picked the apple she gave all the animals and birds in the Garden a bite of the forbidden fruit. The Phoenix alone refused, and was rewarded with eternal life.

On the sixth day, when animals were first made, they were all friends; enmity came later. The mouse appeared before God and said: "I am hungry, and the cat deserves to be eaten." The Lord announced: "You are an intriguer. You should have learned from the example of the Moon, who spoke ill of the Sun to me, and so was deprived of the larger part of her light. Now I shall punish you likewise, by having done unto you what you would have done unto the cat." Since that time cats eat mice.

Lilith

There are hundreds of these charming tales about the fish and the birds and the animals in the dawn of Creation, but let us pass now to the most important thing God made—Man.

The story of Adam and Eve is very fertile in legend. One of the most fascinating of these is the story of Lilith, who was said to have been Adam's wife before the creation of Eve.

The word Lilith means Night. Some say it means Dark Spirit. She had long black hair, her eyes were black pits, and when she wanted to fly her arms turned into beautiful black wings. She was quarrelsome, and tormented Adam about the names he had given to the animals, and sometimes at night she changed their names so that there was great confusion. Then one night she flew away. Adam complained to God, who sent forth three angels to capture her. They found her on the shores of the Red Sea, but she refused to return, and since then amuses herself by stealing the breath of newborn children so that they die.

Then God decided to make another wife for Adam, but he puzzled how to make her. "I will not make her out of man's head," he said, "lest she be proud and arrogant. Nor from the eyes, lest she be a spy. Nor from the ear, lest she eavesdrop. Nor from the mouth, lest she tattle and scold. Nor from the foot, lest she be footloose. I will form her from a modest part of the body, the rib." And He did. Nevertheless, woman has always been full of pride, has been eavesdropper, tattler and gadabout.

However, after Cain murdered Abel, Adam abstained from Eve, because, as he said, "Why should I father children who kill each other?" And Lilith, seeing her chance, visited him in lustful dreams at night, and the fruit of those nights are all the demons that tease man and turn him to sin.

Hanina, Son of Lilith

*However, one of these sons of Lilith gave rise
to a very different kind of story, a veritable jewel among
Jewish legends.*

Once upon a time there lived in Jerusalem a very learned and pious man who knew
all of the Torah by heart, word for word, but his
son, Hanina, was no man of books and this grieved
his father. One day he sent for his son and said:
"O Hanina, I have had a dream. In seven days I
shall die, and at the very same hour my wife, your
mother, will die. I am not rich. I have only a small
sum of money to leave, and you must spend this
money all at once. As soon as you bury us take the
money to the market and buy the very first thing
that is offered you."

Hanina obeyed. After the death of his
parents he went to market and there met an old
man who offered him a wooden bowl, and asked
the whole sum Hanina's father had left. The young
man knew he was being cheated, but followed his
father's last instructions and gave the old man the
money and took the wooden bowl. When he came
home he put it on a table and a frog jumped out
and said, "I am hungry." Hanina fed him and the
frog became as big as a dog and said: "I am hungry

still." Hanina fed him all the food in the house and the frog grew as big as a man. And so great was his appetite that poor Hanina had to sell everything he owned to buy food to feed the frog, even his house. . . .

How the Animals Lost Their Speech

The Great Flood has watered the fancy of fabulists ever since the first storm clouds of God's reprisal began to darken the sky. The Noah story is the best known but there are flood myths in every mythology. Here is a charming little story from the Noah cycle, one which is almost never told.

Once upon a time, long, long ago, when the world was very new, animals could speak the language of man. But then the world grew very wicked and God sent a flood of waters to drown the sinful race of man, allowing only Noah to escape on his wooden ark with two each of all the animals of the world.

It was a long journey and the animals grew discontented. They gathered together, the birds and the beasts, and decided that the world's wickedness would persist so long as man did. So they planned to kill Noah and his family so that the race of man would disappear forever from earth and innocence would return.

But this solution was unsatisfactory to God, Who had his own plans, and He decided to strip his beasts of language lest they parley together toward the destruction of man.

He wiped their wild mouths of speech then, and a great silence fell upon the ark. God, hearing the emptiness of this silence, relented, and permitted some beasts to imitate speech without comprehension and others to understand human speech without being able to utter it.

And so it has been.

Noah's Vineyard

After the Flood, Noah's descendants spread all over the earth, and so did the stories about him. The great navigator of the Flood is one of the figures about whom legends cluster. There are many, many stories about disputes among the animals and why the dove was chosen instead of the raven, and about Noah's sons who were a very mixed litter indeed. But here is a story about what happened after the Flood.

When Noah began to fall away from the word of God, the occasion of his downfall was that he found the vine which Adam had taken with him from Paradise. Noah tasted the fruit of this vine and was immediately seized with a great desire to plant a vineyard.

Soon Noah became a gardener. All in one day he planted the vine, and saw it bear fruit, and pressed the grapes into wine, and drank of it. Satan appeared and said: "What fruit is this you have planted?" "The grape," said Noah. "And I have drunk of the juice of the grape and it gladdens my heart." Satan said: "I am pleased, let us tend the vineyard together and grow a profusion of fruit, and press out the juice for all men to drink."

So Noah and Satan tended the vine together and pressed out the juice of the grape. Satan killed a lamb, a lion, a pig and a monkey, and blood flowed over the vine, and gave their qualities to the grape—which was Satan's plan. Therefore it is that before man drinks wine he is innocent as a lamb; when he drinks somewhat he feels strong as a lion; when he drinks more he resembles a pig, swilling, and if he drinks still more he becomes a monkey, tottering around and gibbering obscenely.

Abraham

Now we are confronted with stories on a somewhat different plane. All the giant figures of the Bible before Abraham are, in fact, pre-Judaic. Since they did not enter so literally the great ethical testament which is Judaism, the imagination of the Jews felt more free to deal with them. When it came to the patriarchs, however, the people felt more awe, more reverence. There were stories, to be sure, but they do not flourish so boldly, they are not quite so wild in fancy, there is less playfulness. However, the great Father of the patriarchs, Abraham, transcends these inhibitions. He is such a tremendous figure, and so antique, that he still looms gigantically in the mists of time, like a mountain whose face is wreathed in clouds. So there are many legends about Abraham— some very beautiful ones. Stories attend him from the time of his birth to when he was laid to rest in the Cave of the Patriarchs.

The Birth of Abraham

The wicked king Nimrod knew how to read the stars and he read one night that a baby was to be born who would destroy his gods, and whose offspring would be conquerors. He thereupon ordered a great prison house built where all the pregnant women in the kingdom should abide until they gave birth. Whoever bore a son would see that son slain before her eyes. Whoever gave birth to a daughter would receive gifts.

70,000 men-children were so slain by order of the king. But then a woman named Emtelai knew herself with child and was told in a dream that it would be a man-child, and she hid her pregnancy from her husband, Terah. One day Terah said to her, "Why is your face so pale and your body so swollen?" She said, "It is a malady I suffer from. My mother suffered from it, my grandmother, and all the women of my family." But Terah said, "Wife, do not seek to mislead me. You

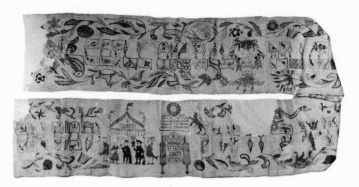

are big with child and you must obey our king, Nimrod, and go to his prison house." But then a miracle happened. When he put his hand on his wife's body, the child rose and it lay under her breasts, and Terah felt nothing, and said: "You have spoken the truth," and the baby remained invisible until the day it was born.

When her pains became strong Emtelai left the city and went into the desert and hid in a cave, where she gave birth to a son. The whole cave was filled with light. Light poured from the baby's face as if it were a star, and a voice said, "Be Not Afraid."

The Idol-Smasher

The young Abraham went back to the house of his father and there grew to manhood. Nimrod was still king and the people of Ur worshipped idols made of stone. Abraham's father, Terah, kept a shop where he sold these idols and his sons worked in the shop, too.

One day when Abraham was 20 years old Terah felt sick and left Abraham in charge of the shop.

A man came in and said to Abraham, "I would buy this idol. Tell me the price." Abraham said: "I will tell you the price if you will tell me your age." "I am 30 years old," the man said. "30 years old," said Abraham, "and yet you would buy this idol, which I made this morning!"

The man left the shop. Then Abraham put a rope about the necks of two idols and dragged them into the street, crying, "See what you worship, it has a mouth but it speaks nothing; eyes, but it sees nothing; feet but it does not walk; ears, but it does not hear."

Terah heard what his son was doing and feared for his life. He rose from his bed and hurried to the shop. In the meantime Abraham had smashed the idols with a mallet. Then, hearing his father come, he put the mallet in the hands of the largest idol, who stood unhurt. Terah entered the shop and reproached Abraham, saying, "What have you done, you have broken the idols. Just so will the king destroy us." Abraham said, "Father, I did not smash the idols, it was the largest idol who smashed the smaller ones, to give an example of cruelty to the king."

But the king heard that his stone gods had been smashed and he ordered Abraham to be burned alive.

So the executioner put a torch to the fire and made the flames leap. This was the fire that was to receive Abraham, but a small rain came and put out the flames.

Another fire was lighted. Again rain fell from a cloudless sky and put out the flames, and Nimrod was afraid. Then Satan appeared to Nimrod and said: "I will build a roof over the flames to stop the rain, but you are to put Abraham into a catapult to cast him swiftly into the flames."

Thereupon Abraham was bound hand and foot and placed into the catapult and slung into the flames. Nimrod shouted with joy, saying, "Can your God save you now?"

And Abraham said: "I trust in Him, He is the God of heaven and earth and will rescue me." Whereupon it was seen that the wood piled around Abraham had burst into bud like the living tree from which it had been cut, and that the flames were red flowers growing, and Abraham was unharmed. When the king saw this he cried: "Witchcraft! Fire cannot harm you. You stand among the flames as in a garden." But all the court of Nimrod and the people were gathered and cried in one voice: "No, King, it is not witchcraft, but the great God, God of Abraham, the living God."

And when Abraham left the land of Ur, many followed him.

Sarah's Beauty

Abraham journeyed from Ur to Canaan, and there spoke to God and entered the covenant. Then when famine struck Canaan he was sent to Egypt. According to a remarkable legend it was on this journey from Canaan to Egypt that Abraham first noticed how very beautiful his wife was. Apparently he had been so steeped in his negotiations with God that he had never really looked at Sarah, although they had lived together some twenty years by this time.

Abraham and Sarah were crossing a river. All at once he saw her reflection in the water, beautiful as the moon when she trembles in a mirror of waters. And Abraham said, "The Egyptians are men of wild lust. When they see your beauty they will steal you from me. Therefore, I must hide you in a casket."

When he came to the Egyptian border the customs officials asked him what was in the box.

"Barley," said Abraham.

"You lie," they said. "It must contain wheat."

"Very well," said Abraham, "I will pay the tax on wheat."

"Aha. It is something more valuable than wheat. Pepper, perhaps."

"I will pay the tax on pepper."

"It is all very suspicious," the customs officials said. "You have gold in there, or jewels."

"I will pay whatever tax you ask," said Abraham.

Now the suspicions of the customs officials were terribly inflamed and they made him open the casket. When Sarah stepped out they exclaimed in amazement.

"Truly," one said, "here is a treasure more precious than gold or jewels. The Pharaoh will pay a mighty price for her. Compared to her all our women look like apes. She is more beautiful than Eve herself."

They reported the matter to the Pharaoh who sent soldiers to bring her to the palace. Abraham spoke to God, saying, "Is this my reward for believing in you? Do you rob me of my wife and put me to shame?" And Sarah prayed, saying, "O, Lord, deliver me from the hands of the Pharaoh for I am afraid." An angel appeared to Sarah while she was in the king's chamber. The angel was visible. He told her, "Fear nothing. God has heard you."

The Pharaoh asked Sarah who the man was who had brought her to Egypt, and Sarah, knowing that Abraham would be killed if he was known to be her husband, said that he was her brother. Pharaoh was so smitten with love for Sarah that he promised to make Abraham rich and powerful. He sent him gold, diamonds, slaves, oxen and gave him rooms in the palace. To Sarah he gave a great treasure and his own daughter Hagar as her servant.

But it all came to nothing. That night when the Pharaoh came to Sarah, an angel appeared, carrying a club. Each time the Pharaoh tried to touch Sarah the angel smote him on the head. At the same time the whole court was infected with leprosy. Terrified, the Pharaoh sent for his soothsayers who told him that he was being cursed because of his desire for Sarah. He then returned her to Abraham and allowed them to keep all that he had given them, for he feared Abraham's God.

While Abraham stayed in Egypt he preached the one God, and many changed their belief.

The War Horses
of Pharaoh

This story in its basic irreverence and rather bestial beauty resembles Greek myth more than it does Hebrew. But it concerns itself with a theme from Exodus —the pursuit of the Israelites by the Egyptians—so we must assume it was first concocted by a Hebrew fabulist more pagan-minded than his fellows.

It will be recalled that when the children of Israel were fleeing the Egyptian host, God parted the waters of the Red Sea so that they might pass.

But Pharaoh's captains followed the children of Israel on to the bed of the sea. Their great war chariots were of brass, whose wheels were armed with great knives capable of winnowing a rank of armed men as wheat is cut by scythes in the field. And these fierce chariots were drawn by stallions—towering white fire-maned horses whom the Egyptians called the horses of the sun.

When the Israelites, fleeing across the narrow path of dry land that divided the waters, saw the pursuing chariots, they raised their voices in lament, crying:

"Oh Moses, once again we are betrayed. Once again the God Whom you worship and bid us worship has delivered us into the hands of the enemy. When the sea parted we believed ourselves safe. But lo, the Egyptians follow and overtake us, and soon we must die."

Moses said: "Have faith. The Lord God Who has parted the waters will bear you safely across if you maintain your trust in Him."

When God heard these words of Moses He decided to help the Israelites once again even though He was angered by their mistrust and constant complaining. So He changed Himself into a white mare which appeared between the Israelites and the pursuing chariots. It was a beautiful mare. Sleek and sumptuous, afire with life. White as the snows on Mt. Lebanon with jet-black hoofs and brilliant black eyes and coral-pink nostrils and a flowing black mane. The beautiful mare frisked about arousing the stallions of Pharaoh to such a storm of desire that their trumpeting cries were heard in far Babylon. Then the mare plunged off the road into the green billows which towered above the strip of land, taut as silk, held by the miracle of God's command. The mare plunged into the water and the stallions plunged after her dragging their chariots behind them. The mare swam away but the brass chariots sank to the bottom of the sea, and horses and drivers were drowned.

The Israelites gained the opposite shore and resumed their long journey. But they were to anger God again and again before they reached the promised land.

Solomon and Sheba

The reign of Solomon was a climax of splendor in the complex, bloody pageant of Jewish history. Under this son of David the kingdom of Judah reached its apogee of military triumph; the small monarchy became an empire. And the personality of King Solomon radiates with that splendor. He is warrior, sage and lover; loins and brain rival each other in potency. He husbands a thousand wives, fathers innumerable children, and two proverbs for every child. Legends, of course, swarm about him. Here is one which tells of his first encounter with his dusky paramour, the Queen of Sheba.

Solomon was king of men—but also of beasts, birds, fish, devils and ghosts. He spoke all languages—bestial, devilish and spectral; he could twitter with the birds and speak the bubble-language of fish. One day, feeling specially magnificent, he summoned all the beasts and the birds to his court to admire him. Everyone was there except the white crow, a great spy whom Solomon counted on for gossip. The King was furious.

"Find him," he roared. "Pluck his feathers—prepare him for the pot."

No sooner had Solomon said these words than the crow appeared and said:

"Almighty King, Lord of all that man knows and other things as well—hearken to your servant and be not wroth. I was absent only on your own service. You may not realize it, Oh King, but I labor day and night to expand your realms. I do not pause to eat or drink but fly here and there over the world to see if I can find a place which does not own Solomon as King."

"All this busy flying about produces very small results," said Solomon. "You have yet to locate a speck of territory wherein my name is not hailed."

"But hearken," said the crow. "I have found a wondrous city all aglitter with gold and jewels. The very dust is silver and when sunlight falls upon the city, it thickens into ingots of gold.

Such trees you have never seen, Oh King. They sink to the very Garden of Eden and suck up those crystal waters. The men are fat with easy living. They do not hunt, they do not fight. But their Queen—their Queen, Oh Lord, is such a one as you have never had for all your thousand wives. Her name is Sheba. She is dark and comely. Her shoulders are sleek. Her eyes are large enough to drown in. Her legs are pillars of yielding muscle, great pincers to kill a man with pleasure. She cannot find a husband among her fat feeble men. She needs a potent king. I think she should welcome an invitation to come to your court. Write it out now and I will fly there without rest for I am tireless in your service."

Thereupon the crow bore King Solomon's letter to the Queen of Sheba. He flew into her chamber whose walls were of gold. There the Queen sat before a mirror that was one great sheet of flawless crystal. She was trying perfumes, specially made for her by slaves who had been blinded so that their noses would grow more keen.

"Leave off your primping, Queen," cried the crow in his hoarse voice. "I bear a message from Solomon the magnificent."

The Queen read the letter. It said:

"I, Solomon, King of men, beasts, birds, devils and ghosts greet you Sheba, Queen of Beauty. It is time that we two met. I shall expect you when the year turns. Quarters will be provided to suit your state and your attendants to the number of six thousand."

The Queen sent word by the crow that she was pleased to accept the invitation. Solomon thereupon had a palace of glass constructed so that he might watch for her approach from every room therein. She came to him at the turn of the year with six thousand youths and maidens all exactly the same size, all clothed in purple and hung with jewels. Solomon was amazed with her beauty and troubled by her feet which were tufted with hair. For the first time in his life he was confused by a woman. The Queen saw his confusion and pressed her advantage saying:

"Oh Solomon, all the world speaks of your wisdom. But I have learned to discount views too widely held. May I test your wisdom for myself?"

"Surely, Oh Queen. Ask me what you will."

"I will riddle you a riddle. When seven goes, nine comes. Two give drink to one."

Solomon said:

"It is a woman's riddle and this is the answer: Seven days of a month she answers the moon's demands with bloody issue—which ceases when she is quickened by seed and begins her nine months of pregnancy. The drink is given by her two breasts which suckle one child. Riddle me another."

"Who was not born and has not died?"

"I may not say his name," said Solomon. "But it is the Lord God, blessed be He."

"What land is it that has known the sun but once?"

"The land is the bottom of the Red Sea on the day that the waters parted."

"The grave moved, the dead arose and prayed."

"Jonah it was who was swallowed by a whale which became his living grave. When he was given up by the whale, Jonah spoke his thanks to the Lord which is prayer."

"You are wise as men say, Oh King!" cried Sheba, "and wiser yet. Four things a maiden dreams of in a man but as she grows and her dreams pale, she counts herself lucky if she finds a man who owns one of these virtues. And it is the lot of most women to settle for the man around with no virtues at all and count herself lucky still. How lucky am I then, how showered with the Lord's blessing to find a man like you. At once beautiful, wise, strong and rich."

Hearing these words, Solomon forgot all the misgivings he had felt at the sight of Sheba's ape-like feet and thought she was the most beautiful and perceptive woman in the whole world. And he made her his chief wife.

Solomon's Daughter

This rare story of Solomon's daughter—perhaps the only time a daughter of his is mentioned anywhere—is a very good example of how the great Bible protagonists were humanized in the legends. For here is Solomon, the uniquely wise, making all the mistakes with his daughter that fathers have always made. The tale is interesting also in its resemblance to the beginning of the Greek myth of Perseus—whose mother was also imprisoned by a father-king and entertained a secret lover.

Among Solomon's huge family given to him by his thousand wives was one daughter, a very beautiful girl whom he favored above all the others.

One night Solomon sat reading the stars to learn how things were to be in time to come. And there in the patterns of light he read that this daughter was fated to become the wife of the poorest boy in the whole world. Now Solomon, for all his wisdom, sometimes behaved very much like other fathers and he flew into a fury upon learning of his daughter's poor match.

"I'll teach that little slut," he said to himself. "I had it in mind for her to marry the next most powerful king on earth and provide me with a powerful ally, as well as an illustrious son-in-law. But no. The little fool has to marry some beggar she does not even know about yet. I'll teach her. I'll teach destiny, too. After all, the future is the future only so long as men are passive and do not dare to change it. I'll lock her away in a stone tower which I shall have specially built, so that no one can come in or go out. And I shall not release her until I have arranged for her wedding with the powerful prince of the East."

He issued orders then and five thousand slaves were set to work building a stone tower upon a tiny island twenty miles out to sea. They worked night and day until it was finished. There Solomon imprisoned his lovely daughter who could not understand why she was being treated so. At night she went out to the roof of the tower and looked at the blazing stars and wept. And she prayed saying:

"I have sinned. I have worshipped my father as a God but he is only a man, I see, with all a man's cruelty and injustice. So I'll seek favor from a greater King, the King of the Universe. Almighty God, hear my prayer and save me from this dungeon."

Her prayer flew straight to heaven and was heard. She fell asleep.

The next morning on a desert beyond the sea a young camel driver was trudging the white-hot waste of sand trying to urge his old camel to the next well which was miles away. This camel was the only thing the boy owned—his only means of livelihood and his only friend.

"Please don't collapse, oh camel," he said. "If you fall, you die and if you die I might as well die, too, because I will be the poorest human in all the world."

But the camel was too old and the sun was too hot. He collapsed and the boy could not rouse him. Then a voice as of the wind spoke softly to the boy saying:

"Borrow your friend's cloak and wrap yourself well and trust me."

The boy thought and thought. "My friend's cloak. What can that mean? This dead camel is my only friend. His cloak, his cloak? Why that must be his skin. But must I skin him then and wrap himself in the bloody pelt, hot as it is? That would be terrible. I won't do it."

But even as he was thinking this, the words of the wind acted upon him with such authority that he found himself pulling out his knife and beginning to skin the dead camel. When he had it done, he wrapped himself in the hide. Night had fallen and the chill desert wind had sprung up so he was grateful for the warmth. He fell asleep. As he slept a vulture swooped, devoured the dead camel and then flew away with its hide with which he meant to line his nest. But a strange strong wind blew, forcing him off his course, over the sea. The only perch he could find was the roof of a stone tower. There the vulture landed, rested a bit, then flew away leaving the hide behind.

Solomon's daughter climbing to the roof found a strange furry bundle. She unfolded it and there by the light of the moon saw a boy fast asleep. At the sight of that pale young face glimmering in the weird light, her heart turned over and she said to herself, "When he awakens, I will marry him."

Some time later, Solomon was rowed upon his golden barge to the island and there commanded that his daughter be brought before him. The guards fetched her.

"God in heaven," cried Solomon. "She is pregnant."

"Yes, father."

"Only how did it happen? How can it be?"

"May I introduce to you my husband?"

The boy came out of the tower and bowed low before Solomon.

The King said, "How did you get here?"

"I do not know," said the lad. "My camel perished upon the desert and a voice bade me to take his skin and wrap myself in it. And I did and fell asleep and when I awoke I was here on the roof of this tower in the arms of your lovely daughter."

"Plainly," said Solomon "it is the will of God which surpasses the will of kings. Nevertheless, I have still outwitted destiny. They said my daughter would wed the poorest boy on earth. Not at all, for I shall make him rich beyond greedy dreams."

Solomon's daughter bore a boy who later became a great king.

The Catechism of the Two Ways

The Catechism of the Two Ways is contained in an ancient codex now in the British Museum. It is believed to have been a product of the Essene community, that band of desert-dwelling Jewish ascetics whose teachings became widely known with the publication of the Dead Sea scrolls.

There is some evidence that Christ belonged to the Essene sect, whose doctrine is considered a link between Judaism and Christianity. Be that as it may, this Catechism of the Two Ways served as a model for early Christian catechism.

There are two ways, one of life and one of death, but there is a great difference between the two ways. Now, the way of life is this: first, Thou shalt love God who made thee; secondly, thy neighbour as thyself, and all things whatsoever thou wouldest not should be done to thee, do thou also not to another. Thou shalt not kill, thou shalt not commit adultery, thou shalt not corrupt boys, thou shalt not commit fornication, thou shalt not steal, thou shalt not use witchcraft, thou shalt not use enchantments, thou shalt not kill an infant whether before or after birth, thou shalt not covet thy neighbour's goods.

But thou shalt seek out day by day the faces of the saints, that thou mayest rest in their words.

Thou shalt not desire division, but shalt make peace between those at strife; so thou shalt judge justly. Thou shalt not respect a person in rebuking for transgressions.

Thou shalt not be of two minds whether it shall be or not.

Be not one that stretcheth out his hands to receive, but shutteth them close for giving.

Thou shalt not turn away from him that needeth, but shalt share all things with thy brother, and shalt not say that they are thine own; for if ye are fellow-sharers in that which is imperishable, how much more in perishable things.

Thou shalt not take away thine hand from thy son or from thy daughter, but from their youth up shalt thou teach them the fear of God.

Thou shalt not in thy bitterness lay commands on thy man-servant or thy maid-servant, who hope in the same God, lest they should not fear him who is God over you both; for He cometh not to call men according to the outward appearance, but to those whom the Spirit hath prepared.

But ye, servants, shall be subject to your masters as to a figure of God in reverence and fear.

Thou shalt not forsake the commandments of the Lord, but shalt keep what thou hast received, neither adding thereto nor taking away from it.

Thou shalt confess thy transgressions, and shalt not come to thy prayer with an evil conscience. This is the way of life.

But the way of death is this. First of all, it is evil and full of curse; murders, adulteries, lusts, fornications, thefts, idolatries, witchcrafts, sorceries, robberies, false witnessings, hypocrisies, double-heartedness, deceit, pride, wickedness, self-will, covetousness, filthy talking, jealousy, presumption, haughtiness, flattery.

Persecutors of the good, hating truth, loving a lie, not knowing the reward of righteousness, not cleaving to that which is good nor to righteous judgment, watching not for the good but for the evil, far from whom is meekness and patience, loving vain things, seeking after reward, not pitying the poor, nor toiling with him who is vexed with toil, not knowing Him that made them, murderers of children, destroyers of the image of God, turning away from him that is in need, vexing him that is afflicted, advocates of the rich, lawless judges of the poor, wholly sinful.

Take heed that no one make thee to err from this way of teaching, since he teacheth thee not according to God.

Philo Judaeus (c. 20 B.C.–A.D. 50)

Philo Judaeus was a Hellenized Jew who lived in Alexandria during the lifetime of Christ. A member of a wealthy and influential family, he was able to pursue an intensive interest in philosophy—a pursuit which, then as now, is considerably abetted by an independent income. He also had some part in the political life of the time, becoming in about A.D. 40 a member of a deputation that traveled to Rome to persuade the bloodthirsty Caligula against wholesale slaughter of the Jews—a mission that achieved temporary success through a combination of soft words and hard cash.

Philo is best known for his Bible commentary, in which he insisted that the Scriptural tales are nonliteral—meaningless unless read as pure allegory.

Commentary

Moses lays down a general command, "Do not remove the boundary stone of thy neighbour, which thy ancestors have set up." This, methinks, does not refer merely to inheritances and the boundary of land, but it is ordained with a view to the preservation of ancient customs. For customs are unwritten laws engraved upon the souls of the generations who through the ages maintain the chosen community. Children should accept the ancestral customs as part of their inheritance, for they were reared on them, and lived on them from their swaddling days, and they should not neglect them merely because the tradition is not written. The man who obeys the written laws is not, indeed, worthy of praise, for he may be constrained by fear of punishment. But he who holds fast to the unwritten laws gives proof of a voluntary goodness and is worthy of our eulogy.

He who flees from God, flees unto himself. For there are two kinds of mind, the mind of the universe, and that is God, and the mind of individual man. And the one flees from his own mind to the mind of the universe—for whoever leaves his own mind, avows therewith that the works of the mortal mind are as nothing, and ascribes everything to God. But the other flees from God, and declares that not God is the cause of anything at all, but that he himself is the cause of all that comes to pass.

Thus there are many who believe that all the things in the world go their own course by themselves, without a guide, and that it is the spirit of man that has invented the arts, crafts, laws, customs, state institutions, and the rights of the individual and the community, both in regard to men and to beasts, that are without reason.

But you, O my soul, see the difference between these two points of view. For the one leaves the perishable mortal mind, which has been created, and chooses for its true aid the primordial and immortal mind of the universe. But the other, which sets aside God, foolishly courts as its ally the human mind, which is not even able to help itself.

Flavius Josephus (c. A.D. 38–A.D. 100)

Apparently there is no better way to gain a balanced view of history than switching sides in the middle of a war—for the man who stands out as one of the worst traitors in the history of the Jews also happens to be its outstanding historian. He was born Josef Ben Matthias ha-Cohen, but like many other Jews after him who have tried to join the winners, he changed his name, romanizing it to Flavius Josephus. Under that name he wrote his great work The Jewish War.

The career of Josephus was astounding. A successful politician who went from Palestine to Rome on an embassy, he later became governor of Galilee. Revolutions were stirring in Palestine at that time and Galilee was a hotbed of resistance to Roman rule. As governor he attempted to calm the hotheads and at the same time stop the Romans from mounting a punitive expedition. When Roman legions were sent into Galilee, Josephus for a time led the Jewish defenders. But when the city of Jotapata was besieged, his antirevolutionary sympathies reinforced his eager appetite for survival and he went over to the Romans.

From then on he conducted himself like a full-fledged traitor. When Vespasian laid siege to Jerusalem, Josephus actively attempted to persuade the city's defenders to lay down their arms and open the gates. After the revolt was crushed he moved to Rome and turned from politics to history.

The Jewish War is a superb piece of historical narration, an account of the turbulent period in the first century of the Christian era when Palestine was the only Roman colony to defy the conquerors, arising again and again in bloody revolt. Perhaps the best-known episode in the saga of siege and massacre is the story of the final fall of Masada, held until almost the last days of the war by a fanatic band of zealots under Eleazar.

The fate of the Jews never lost its fascination for Josephus. He has also dealt eloquently with other aspects of Jewish history, and several episodes are presented here.

The Fall of Masada

Against Eleazar and the Sicarii who with him held Masada came the Roman general Silva at the head of his forces. He established his own headquarters at a place that seemed most opportune for directing the siege, where the rocks on which the fortress stood were linked to the mountain near by.

A tower was erected 90 feet high and covered all over with iron plates: on this the Romans mounted a number of quick-loaders and stone-throwers which pelted the defenders, driving them from the battlements and forcing them to keep under cover. A great ram was swung continuously against the wall till at long last a breach was made and a small section collapsed.

Inside however the Sicarii had lost no time in building a second wall. Huge baulks were laid lengthwise and fastened together at the ends:

these were in two parallel rows separated by the width of a wall and with the space between filled with earth. The blows of the engines falling on yielding earth were absorbed.

Seeing this Silva instructed his men to direct a volley of burning torches at it. Being made mostly of wood it soon caught fire. Just as the fire broke out a gust of wind from the north blew back the flame. Then all of a sudden as if by divine providence the wind swung to the south and flung the flames against the wall. God was indeed on the side of the Romans.

Eleazar could think of no other means of escape or heroic endeavour; death seemed to him the right choice for them all. He collected the toughest of his comrades and urged it upon them in a speech of which this was the substance:

"My loyal followers, long ago we resolved to serve neither the Romans nor anyone else but only God, who alone is the true and righteous Lord of men: now the time has come that bids us prove our determination by our deeds.

"From the very first, we ought perhaps to have read the mind of God and realised that His once beloved Jewish race had been sentenced to extinction. We hoped that of all the Jewish race we alone would come through safe, still in possession of our freedom, as if we had committed no sin against God and taken part in no crime—we who had taught the others!

"God himself without a doubt has taken away all hope of survival. The fire that was being carried into the enemy lines did not turn back of its own accord towards the wall we had built; these things are God's vengeance for the many wrongs that in our madness we dared to do to our own countrymen.

"For those wrongs let us pay the penalty not to our bitterest enemies, the Romans, but to God—by our own hands. It will be easier to bear. Let our wives die unabused, our children without knowledge of slavery.

"But first let our possessions and the whole fortress go up in flames. One thing only let

us spare—our store of food. It will bear witness
when we are dead to the fact that we perished, not
through want but because, as we resolved at the
beginning, we chose death rather than slavery."

Such was Eleazar's appeal. Some were
eager to do as he said, others less heroic were
moved by pity for their wives and families, and
certainly too by the prospect of their own end.
When he saw them playing the coward Eleazar,
bursting with ardour, began: "Ever since primitive
man began to think, the words of our ancestors
have constantly impressed on us that *life* is the
calamity for man, not death. Death gives freedom
to our souls.

"Sleep will provide you with the clear-
est proof of what I say. In sleep souls left to themselves and free from bodily distractions enjoy the
most blissful repose, and consorting with God
whose kin they are they go wherever they will and
foretell many of the things to come. Why, pray,
should we fear death if we love to repose in sleep?
And isn't it absurd to run after the freedom of
this life and grudge ourselves the freedom of
eternity?

"God's will and sheer necessity doom
us to death. Long ago God issued this warning to
the whole Jewish race together, that life would be
taken from us if we misused it. Do not fasten the

blame on yourselves or give the Romans the credit for the fact that we are all ruined by the war against them. What Roman weapons slew the Jews who lived in Caesarea? Why, they had no thought of rebelling against Rome, but were in the middle of their seventh-day ceremonies when the Caesarean mob rushed at them, and though they offered no resistance butchered them with their wives and children. What are we to say of the Jews in Scythopolis? They had the effrontery to make war on us to please the Greeks, and would not join with us, their own kith and kin, to drive out the Romans. Much good they got from their faithful support of the Greeks! They were brutally massacred by them.

"It would take too long to speak now about every individual case: you know that of all the towns in Syria there isn't one that hasn't exterminated its Jewish inhabitants, though they were more hostile to us than to the Romans.

"All those who on their own took up arms against Rome were mastered; all came into the enemy's hands. Those who died in battle we may well congratulate. But the masses who are now under the thumb of Rome, who would not hasten to die rather than share their fate? Some of them have been broken on the rack or tortured to death at the stake or by the lash; some have been half-eaten by savage beasts and then kept alive to be their food a second time.

"Where is the mighty city, the mother-city of the whole Jewish race, secure within so many encircling walls, defended by thousands and thousands of determined men? Where now is the city that was believed to have God for her Founder? She has been torn up by the roots, and the only memorial of her that is left is the camp of her destroyers that still occupies her ruins!

"Which of us, realizing these facts, is such an enemy to his country, who so unmanly and so wedded to life as not to be sorry he is alive today? Let us at once choose death with honour and do the kindest thing we can do for ourselves, our wives and children, while it is still possible to show ourselves any kindness. After all we were born to die, we and those we brought into the world. So let us deny the enemy their hoped-for pleasure at our expense, and without more ado leave them to be dumbfounded by our death and awed by our courage."

Eleazar had many more arguments to urge, but all his listeners cut him short. As if possessed they rushed off, everyone anxious to be quicker than the next man, and not to be found among the last. In the end not a man failed to carry out his terrible resolve—with their own hands they murdered their wives and children and felt it to be the lightest of evils.

Thus these men died supposing that they had left no living soul to fall into the hands of the Romans; but an old woman escaped, along with another who was related to Eleazar, and five little children. They had hidden in the conduits that brought drinking-water underground while the rest were intent upon the suicide-pact. These numbered 960, women and children included. The tragedy was enacted on the 15th April.

The Jewish Sects

The Jews of the first century were a far from homogeneous group. In the extraordinarily detailed Jewish War, *Josephus noted the habits and attitudes of three of the major sects -the Pharisees, the Sadducees and the Essenes.*

The Pharisees hold all souls to be imperishable, but contend that only the souls of the good migrate into other bodies and that the souls of the wicked suffer eternal punishment.

The Pharisees live simply, despise delicacies, and are guided by their tradition; what that prescribes as good, they do. They think they ought earnestly to strive to observe the school's dictates, respect those advanced in years; and are not so bold as to oppose anything these have initiated. They love one another and foster harmony and esteem for the community.

The Sadducees disregard fate entirely and place God beyond the commission or the very sight of evil. God and evil, they contend, are man's choice, and everyone is free to embrace one or the other according to his will. The soul's permanence after death and the punishments and rewards of Hades, they reject.

The Sadducees hold that souls die with the bodies. Their views are received by only a few, but these few are of the highest rank.

The Essenes are reputed to cultivate peculiar sanctity. Jews by birth, they love each other more than do the other sects. Pleasures they reject as evil: continence and control of the passions they deem a special virtue.

They disdain marriage, but adopting the children of others, while yet pliant to instruction, they treat them as kin and mold them in accordance with their own principles. Wedlock, indeed, and the progeny arising from it, they do not on principle condemn; but they guard against the levity of women and are convinced that none of them stay faithful to but one man.

They hold riches in contempt; the community of goods among them is to be admired. No one among them has more than another. It is their law that whoever joins the sect relinquishes his fortune to the order. They regard oil as defiling; if one of them accidentally comes in contact with it, he wipes his body, for they consider a dry skin to be good, and clothe it always in white.

The property of the brethren is at the disposal of any member coming from another place as though it were his own; they enter the homes of people they have never seen as though they were the most intimate of friends. They therefore carry nothing with them on a journey save arms for protection against brigands. They renew neither clothing nor shoes until these are in shreds or worn out from long use.

A simple affirmation is more valid among them than an oath; they avoid swearing, regarding it as worse than perjury. He who cannot be believed without an appeal to God is, they say, already condemned.

The Story of Nehemiah

Now there was one of the Jews that had been carried into captivity, who was cup-bearer to king Xerxes, whose name was Nehemiah. As he was walking about in the suburbs of Susa, the metropolis of the Persians, he heard some strangers that were entering the city after a long journey, speaking to one another in the Hebrew tongue, so he went to them and asked them whence they came? And when their answer was, that they came from Judaea, he began to inquire of them again in what state the multitude was? and in what condition Jerusalem was? And they replied that they were in a bad state, for their walls were thrown down to the ground, and the neighbouring nations did a great deal of mischief to the Jews, for in the day time they overran the country and pillaged it, and in the night did them mischief, insomuch that not a few were led away captive out of the country and from Jerusalem itself, and the roads were every day found full of dead men.

At this Nehemiah shed tears, commiserating the calamities of his countrymen: and looking up to heaven, he said, "How long, O Lord, wilt thou allow our nation to suffer such great miseries, for we are made the prey and spoil of all men."

And while he stayed at the gate and lamented thus, one told him that the king was going to sit down to supper; so he made haste, and went at once as he was, without washing himself, to minister to the king in his office of cup-bearer. And as the king was very pleasant after supper, and more cheerful than usual, he cast his eyes on Nehemiah, and seeing him looking sad, he asked him why he was sad?

Whereupon he prayed to God to give him favour, and persuasion to his words, and said, "How can I, O king, appear otherwise than sad and in trouble of mind when I hear that the walls of Jerusalem, the city where are the sepulchres of my fathers, are thrown down to the ground, and that its gates are consumed by fire; but do thou grant me the favour to go and build its wall, and to finish the building of the temple."

And the king gave him a sign that he freely granted him what he asked, and told him to carry a letter to the satraps, that they might pay him due honour, and afford him whatever assistance he wanted for what he pleased. "Leave off thy sorrow, therefore," added the king, "and be cheerful henceforth in the performance of thy office."

Then Nehemiah worshipped God, and gave the king thanks for his promise, and cleared up his sad and cloudy countenance in the pleasure he had at the king's promises. And the king called for him the next day, and gave him a letter to carry to Adaeus, the governor of Syria and Phoenicia and Samaria, wherein he gave him injunctions to pay due honour to Nehemiah, and to supply him with what he wanted for the building.

Now when he had gone to Babylon, and had taken with him thence many of his countrymen who voluntarily followed him, he arrived at Jerusalem in the twenty-fifth year of the reign of Xerxes: and when he had shown the letters to God, he gave them to Adaeus and the other governors. He also called together all the people to Jerusalem, and stood in the midst of the temple, and made the following speech to them.

"You know, O Jews, that our forefathers, Abraham, Isaac, and Jacob, kept God in mind continually; and for the sake of their righteousness, he has not left off the care of you: indeed he has assisted me in gaining this leave from the king to raise up our wall, and finish what is wanting of the temple. I desire you therefore (who well know the ill-will the neighbouring nations bear to us, who, when once they perceive that we are in earnest about building, will come upon us, and contrive many ways of obstructing our work), in the first place to put your trust in God, as in one who will assist us against their hatred, and next to intermit building neither night nor day, but to use all diligence, and to hasten on the work, now we have this especial opportunity for it."

When he had said this, he gave order that the rulers should measure the wall and divide the work of it among the people, according to their villages and cities, and according to every one's ability. And when he had added the promise, that he himself with his servants would assist them in the building, he dissolved the assembly. So the Jews prepared for the work. They have been called Jews from the day that they came up from Babylon, after the tribe of Judah, which came first to those places, and so both they and the country gained that appellation.

Now when the Ammonites and Moabites and Samaritans, and all that inhabited Coele-Syria, heard that the building of the walls went on apace, they took it ill, and proceeded to lay snares for them, and to hinder their intention. They also slew many of the Jews, and sought to destroy Nehemiah himself, by hiring some of the foreigners to kill him. They also put the Jews in fear and alarm, and spread abroad rumours, as if many nations were going to make an expedition against them, by which means they were alarmed, and almost left off the building. But none of these things could deter Nehemiah from being diligent about the work, only he kept a number of men about him as a body-guard, and unweariedly persevered therein, and was insensible of any toil in his desire to perfect the work. And thus did he take care of his own safety attentively and with great forecast, not that he feared death, but because he was persuaded that if he were dead, the walls for his fellow-citizens would never be raised.

He also gave orders that the builders should keep their ranks, and have their armour on while they were building. Accordingly, the mason had his sword on, as well as he that brought the materials for building. He also ordered that their shields should lie very near them, and he placed trumpeters at intervals of five hundred feet, and charged them if their enemies appeared, that they should give notice of it to the people, that they might fight in their armour, and that their enemies might not fall upon them when they were unarmed.

He also went about the rounds of the city by night, being never discouraged, either about the work itself, or about his own diet and sleep, for he made no use of those things for pleasure, but only out of necessity. And he underwent this toil for two years and four months: for in so long time was the wall built, in the twenty-eighth year of the reign of Xerxes in the ninth month.

And when the walls were finished, Nehemiah and the multitude offered sacrifices to God for the building of them, and continued feasting for eight days. But when the nations which dwelt in Syria heard that the building of the walls was finished, they were indignant at it. Now when Nehemiah saw that the city was thinly peopled, he exhorted the priests and Levites to leave the country and remove to the city and live there and he built them houses at his own expense, and he commanded those of the people who were employed in cultivating the land to bring the tithes of their fruits to Jerusalem, that the priest and Levites, having perpetually whereon they might live, might not leave the divine worship. And they willingly hearkened to the orders of Nehemiah, so the city of Jerusalem came to be fuller of people than it was before.

And when Nehemiah had finally done many other excellent things worthy of commendation, he died at a good old age. He was a man of a good and righteous disposition, and very ambitious to make his own nation happy; and he left the walls of Jerusalem as his eternal monument. They were built in the days of Xerxes.

The Infant Moses

The king had a daughter, Thermuthis. Playing by the river bank and spying the basket being borne down the stream, she sent off some swimmers with orders to bring that cot to her. When these returned from their errand with the cot, she, at sight of the little child, was enchanted at its size and beauty; for such was the tender care which God showed for Moses, that the very persons who by reason of his birth had decreed the destruction of all children of Hebrew parentage were made to condescend to nourish and tend him. And so Thermuthis ordered a woman to be brought to suckle the infant.

But when, instead of taking the breast, it spurned it, and then repeated this action with several women, Mariam, who had come upon the scene, apparently without design and from mere curiosity, said, "It is lost labour, my royal lady, to summon to feed the child these women who have no ties of kinship with it. Wert thou now to have one of the Hebrew women fetched, maybe it would take the breast of one of its own race." Her advice seemed sound, and the princess bade her do this service herself and run for a foster-mother. Availing herself of such permission, the girl returned bringing the mother, whom no one knew. Thereupon the infant, gleefully as it were, fastened upon the breast, and, by request of the princess, the mother was permanently entrusted with its nurture.

It was indeed from this very incident that the princess gave him the name recalling his immersion in the river, for the Egyptians call water móu and those who are saved eśes; so they conferred on the infant this name compounded of both words. And all agreed that, in accordance with the prediction of God, for grandeur of intellect and contempt of toils he was the noblest Hebrew of them all. (He was the seventh from Abraham, being the son of Amaram, who was the son of Caath, whose father was Levi, the son of Jacob, who was the son of Isaac, the son of Abraham.) His growth in understanding was not in line with his growth in stature, but far outran the measure of his years: its maturer excellence was displayed in his very games, and his actions then gave promise of the greater deeds to be wrought by him on reaching manhood.

When he was three years old, God gave wondrous increase to his stature; and none was so indifferent to beauty as not, on seeing Moses, to be amazed at his comeliness. And it often happened that persons meeting him as he was borne along the highway turned, attracted by the child's appearance, neglected their serious affairs to gaze at leisure upon him; indeed childish charm so perfect and pure as his held the beholders spellbound.

Such was the child whom Thermuthis adopted as her son, being blessed with no offspring of her own. Now one day she brought Moses to her father and showed him to him, and told him she had been mindful for the succession, were it God's will to grant her no child of her own, by bringing up a boy of divine beauty and generous spirit, and by what a miracle she had received him of the river's bounty, "and methought," she said, "to make him my child and heir to thy kingdom."

With these words she laid the babe in her father's arms; and he took and clasped him affectionately to his breast and, to please his daughter, placed his diadem upon his head. But Moses tore it off and flung it to the ground, in mere childishness, and trampled it underfoot; and this was taken as an omen of evil import to the kingdom. At that spectacle the sacred scribe who had foretold that this child's birth would lead to the abasement of the Egyptian empire rushed forward to kill him with a fearful shout: "This," he cried, "O King, this is that child whom God declared that we must kill to allay our terrors; he bears out the prediction by the act of insulting thy dominion and trampling the diadem under foot. Kill him then and at one stroke relieve the Egyptians of their fear of him and deprive the Hebrews of the courageous hopes that he inspires." But Thermuthis was too quick for him and snatched the child away; the king too delayed to slay him, from a hesitation induced by God, whose providence watched over Moses' life.

He was accordingly educated with the utmost care, the Hebrews resting the highest hopes upon him for their future, while the Egyptians viewed his upbringing with misgiving. However, since even if the king slew him, there was no one else in sight, whether relative by adoption or by other, in whom they could put more confidence to act in the interest of the Egyptians through his foreknowledge of the future, they refrained from slaying him.

From the Talmud

The Talmud is a singular work, stemming from eight centuries of scholarly disputation by Jewish theologians in the academies of Palestine and Babylon. Indeed, there are two versions of the Talmud—the Babylonian and the Palestinian. What they do is to elucidate, organize and codify the entire written and oral tradition of the Jews into a comprehensive body of religious and civil law.

A greater part of the religious law is derived from interpretations of the Bible. These interpretations are hammered out through incessant argumentation among scholars, much of it devoted to a kind of legalistic quibbling that tends to suffocate the original Bible passages and to dehydrate those majestic utterances. The arguments develop into a species of casuistry that is unmatched anywhere else in religious literature; the nuances of interpretations are so subtilized that they produce an overwhelming impression of the letter of law wholly superseding the human spirit.

Nevertheless, the intense and painful quibbling that went into the making of this massive legal code was inspired by a burning zeal. Its purpose was to translate God's will, as revealed through Scripture and interpreted by specialists, into a practical routine of living. These rabbinical scholars believed that every syllable and even every stylistic mannerism of the Torah expressed some aspect of God's multitudinous purpose. Therefore they subjected the Torah to an examination so agonizingly detailed that several different possible meanings were squeezed out of every passage.

However, the Talmud is many things. In the desert of legalisms one finds an oasis, a richly fertile section containing folktale, parable, aphorism, sophisticated comment on man's psychology and behavior. This is the section known as Aggadah, and these nuggets have become part of the furniture of the modern intellect—consummate examples of the Jewish mind working at its top bent.

The Offering of the Law

God did not offer the Law to Israel until he had asked other nations to accept it. He went to the wild desert-dwellers, the sons of Esau, and asked if they would accept the Torah.

"What is it?"

"The Book of the World. The manifold World of the Law."

"Tell us one Law."

"Thou shalt not kill."

"Impossible. We are warriors. We must kill. It is our occupation."

He went to the Ishmaelites asking them to accept the Torah.

"What does it say?"

"Thou shalt not steal."

"You are taking the bread from our mouths. We are thieves."

God went to all the other nations of the world and offered them the Torah and was refused. Finally, he went to the Israelites.

"What is written in this Book?"

"The Law, which is my will. Divided into six hundred and thirteen statutes."

"Your will is our desire. All that you speak we will do. In fact, we have already begun. Our father Abraham smashed the stone gods and recognised You. . . . Isaac honoured his father when he submitted to the knife on Mount Moriah. . . . Judah saved his brother Joseph from death observing thy commandment, 'Thou shalt not kill.' . . . Joseph walked in Thy ways and forbade himself lust for the Egyptian. . . . We accept the Torah, Oh Holy One, blessed be Thy Name, and will live according to Thy will forever."

Selections

God loves three kinds of men: One who does not fall into a rage; one who does not fall into drunkenness; and one who does not stand on his dignity. . . .

God's love is stronger than his hatred. He cursed the snake but it thrives. He cursed woman but man cannot live without her.

A man of means who does not share his wealth with a scholar will not enjoy his wealth.

Of these things a portion is very good; too much is very bad: money, marriage, labour, strong drink, sleep, medicine.

He who commits usury breaks every Commandment. His sin is as evil as murder.

Revere the sages of the Talmud but do not take their words too literally for this degrades the sacred utterance. You must seek the kernel of hidden sense; if you cannot find it do not play with the shell.

There is a phrase in Hebrew, "Za'ar Ba'ale Hay-yim," meaning "compassion toward all living creatures." The Jew was commanded to feed his pets and barnyard animals before himself eating.

It is written concerning serpents, rats, roaches and other vermin that they, too, have a place in creation.

It is said that Adam was created first and alone to teach the lesson that the life of one man is as valuable as the life of all. Saving the life of one person is like saving the whole world.

Concerning charity, do not give to a man publicly or to a woman privately.

The cow and the calf have equal desires—the calf to suckle, the cow to give suck.

If you wound your horse with spurs, you will be ridden in the afterworld by demons whose heel-bones are sharpened to spurs.

He whose argument is unsound seeks to cover it with many words.

Penitence is worthless if it eases your conscience.

Books are the best wealth; they are also easier to borrow and to lend than money.

Four shall not enter Paradise: the scoffer, the liar, the hypocrite, and the slanderer.

The sun will go down all by himself, without thy assistance.

In Palestine it was considered a sign of descent from a good family if any one first broke off in a quarrel. The greatest of heroes is he who turneth an enemy into a friend.

Oftentimes a man praises his fellow in a low voice but derides him in a loud.

This world is only the vestibule to another; you must prepare yourself in the vestibule so that you may enter the banquet hall.

To the aged man a small mound is comparable to a tall mountain.

An old man in a house is a burden, but an old woman is a treasure.

The angry man's speech is like the water which overflows from a boiling kettle.

Better one bird that is tied than a hundred birds that are flying.

If you do not teach the ox to plow in his youth, it will be difficult to teach him when he is grown.

All beginnings are difficult.

Let a man be generous in his charities, but let him beware of giving away all that he has.

If thou must strike a child, strike it with the string of a shoe.

The world itself rests upon the breath of the children in the schoolhouse.

A man should not enter a house suddenly, without ringing or knocking.

If you go to a certain place, conduct yourself in conformity with local usage.

Beware of him who gives thee advice according to his own interests.

A man should destroy nothing of his property of which he may later be able to make use.

People say: before a man is dead, his successor is ready.

A man cannot say to the Angel of Death: I wish to arrange my affairs before I die.

In the day of death, a man considers that he has lived but a single day.

Food is better for a man up to the age of forty; after forty drink is better.

More people die from overeating than from under-nourishment.

When the wicked are in trouble, they are submissive; but when their trouble is ended, they return to their evil ways.

Thou hast done good to the evil? Thou hast done evil.

The Evil Impulse seduces in this world and accuses in the next.

Anger in a home is like rottenness in fruit.

If a man sin against those of his own household, he will inevitably come to sin against his neighbour.

He who rebukes not his son leads him into delinquency.

He who entreats aid for his comrade, though he himself is in need, is answered first.

He who passes judgment on fools is himself judged to be a fool.

Run not too far, for thou must then return the same distance.

If a man has no money, he should not bid.

When the time comes for an accounting of a man's deeds, it is too late to do anything.

A man should be pliable as a reed, and not stiff as a cedar.

If a man combats the wave, it overpowers him. If he permits it to roll over him, the wave passes on.

Hypocrisy is like a woman who is in the apartment of her lover, and swears by the life of her husband.

Prohibit not something to others which you permit to yourself.

Judge a man not according to the words of his mother, but according to the comments of his neighbours.

When the year has been prosperous, people become brotherly toward each other.

He who does not teach his son an occupation is as one who has taught his son to rob.

If thou hast been hired to do work, do what thou art told, even though thou hast distaste for it.

A man does not lie about that which is certain to be revealed.

Before I was elected to head the court, I would have thrown to the lions anyone who would have suggested to me to become a candidate. After my election, I would throw boiling water on anyone who would suggest that I resign.

The Rabbis have said: "Be rather a tail to a lion than the head of a fox."

He who loves without jealousy does not truly love.

Woe will come to me from my Creator if I hearken to my impulses! Woe will come to me from my impulses if I obey my Creator!

Why is it easier to appease a male than a female? Because a male was created from soft dust, but a female from hard bone.

He who buys a Jewish serf buys a master for himself.

If a man merits it, his wife is his helpmate; if
    not, she is his antagonist.

The sweetest of poems does not enter into the
    ears of those troubled in heart.

Three things take in profusion and give in pro-
    fusion: the sea, the earth and the government.

He who strives to attain that which is not for him
    loses that which was intended for him.

A physician who takes no fee is worth no fee.

They say to fruit-bearing trees: "Why do you not
make any noise?" The trees reply: "Our fruits are
    sufficient advertisement for us."

If one man says to thee: "Thou art a donkey," do
not mind; if two men speak thus, purchase a
    saddle for thyself.

For every evil, silence is the best remedy.

Offer not pearls for sale to those who deal in
    vegetables and onions.

False friends are like migratory birds; they fly
    away in cold weather.

One who thinks he can live without others is mistaken. One who thinks others cannot live without
    him is more mistaken.

One who believes anything can be accomplished
    by money is likely to do anything for money.

Among those who stand, do not sit, and among
those who sit, do not stand. Among those who
laugh, do not weep; and among those who weep,
    do not laugh.

More flesh, more worms;
More wealth, more worry;
More women, more witchcraft;
More concubines, more lechery;
More slaves, more thievery.
But more law, more life;
More study, more wisdom;
More counsel, more enlightenment;
More righteousness, more peace.

The Zaddikim [holy men] held regular sessions with their followers on Sabbath afternoons. At one of these a sceptic who happened to be present, thinking to make sport of the holy man at the head of the table, asked him: "Rebbe, if you know all things, tell us what Eve did whenever Adam returned home late."

"She counted his ribs," replied the Zaddik.

The wife of a Zaddik said to him: "Your prayer was lengthy today. Have you succeeded in bringing it about that the rich should be more generous in their gifts to the poor?"

The Zaddik replied: "Half my prayer I have accomplished. The poor are willing to accept them."

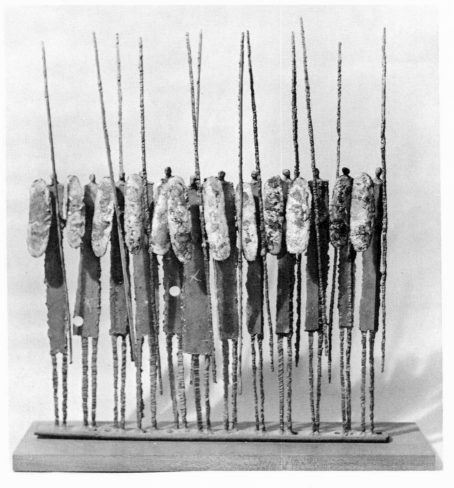

III
THE YEARS OF EXILE

The more we strive after that which is superfluous,
the less strength we have to grasp that which is
truly needed.

Maimonides

Introduction

When the Roman legions wrested the fertile areas of Europe from whoever happened to live there, they were followed by adventuring Jews who, protected by the Pax Romana, established themselves as artisans, merchants, farmers. Then, when Roman power drained from Europe, it left the broken provinces of Empire under the sway of Frank, Vandal, Visigoth and Ostrogoth, and in each of these territories lived pockets of Jews who had been there for hundreds of years. Thus, these self-conscious, affluent, literate communities were left intact among half-savage Teutonic tribes, and the Jews immediately began to wield an influence far beyond their scant numbers. And, by and large, for the first eight centuries after the Dispersion, the Jews of Europe were left in peace by their neighbors and flourished greatly, gaining in wealth and influence, and acknowledged as cultural leaders of a society they could never fully enter.

In one unique case, they managed to create a state of their own—the kingdom of Chazaria.

It is useful to note certain customs of the era which acted to strengthen their intellectual preeminence. Service to the community was held a high honor, and the highest service was some form of teaching. But honor was the only payment; no money could pass hands—because, according to ancient precept, "The Torah can not be used as a spade to dig with." Therefore the leader of the community became the man in whom learning most effectively coincided with the ability to work without pay. In other words, knowledge and success became interchangeable concepts in the little Jewish towns of Europe during the sullen dawn of the "dark" ages.

By the year 900, Provence in the south of France had developed into an important center of Jewish learning. One of these young scholars,

Gershom of Mayence, became so illustrious for his wisdom that he was known as Meor ha-Golah, "Light of the Dispersion." His great work was the updating of Jewish tradition through a series of brilliant interpretations which adapted the Bible teachings to the conditions of contemporary life. These were of enormous importance. It must be remembered that the day-to-day routine of Jewish living was controlled by religious edict. Thus Gershom's work was not addressed to doctrinal hair splitting but to such robust practicalities as the prohibition of polygamy—sanctioned by the Bible—and establishing the rights of women in divorce action. One of his *takhanot,* or instructions, might still prove useful today. It expressly forbade changes in the wording of any book, except by the author.

Nothing of Gershom's work is included in this volume because he is already so profusely anthologized. But his method is cited because it so strikingly illustrates the infusion of practical concern by spiritual teaching, the reexamination and reevaluation of the most sacred text in the light of man's evolving experience—which, a thousand years ago, had already become the heart of academic Jewish technique, and which can be epitomized thus: "Knowledge is sacred but there is nothing too sacred for investigation."

The Kingdom of Chazaria

It is not generally known, even by informed Jews, that two Jewish states existed between the destruction of the second Temple and the reestablishment of the State of Israel. One was in Yemen, where Jews ruled for more than a century; their suzerainty ended with the kingdom of Dhu Nuwas. The other, the kingdom of the Chazars in southern Russia, stands as one of the most striking oddities in Jewish history.

In the middle of the eighth century this area was overrun by pagan Turks, whose chieftain suddenly became converted to Judaism. No one knows why or how this occurred, though the conversion—which soon encompassed all his followers—is sometimes attributed to a possibly legendary prince named Obadiah. Other legends claim that the Chazars belonged to the ten lost tribes of Israel.

These warlike Turks spread their dominion from the shores of the Black Sea to the western banks of the Volga, and westward to the mouth of the Danube, taking in those vast reaches now known as the southern Ukraine. Their descendants ruled this enormous territory for more than four hundred years. While the Chazars are said to have followed the teachings of the Torah, they conducted themselves much more like biblical rather than Diaspora Jews, their displaced, and in most of the world homeless and helpless, brothers. They were fierce warriors and never allowed themselves to be captured alive in battle.

Though Chazaria is now barely a historical footnote, it was a recognized national entity in its time. This curious and rather touching document is a letter from Hasdai Ibn Shaprut, a tenth-century Jewish dignitary of the Spanish court, to Joseph, the last king of the Chazars.

I, Hasdai, son of Isaac, a son of Ezra, belonging to the exiled Jews of Jerusalem in Spain, a servant of my lord the King, bow to the earth before him and prostrate myself towards the abode of your Majesty from a distant land. I rejoice in your tranquility and magnificence and stretch forth my hands to God in heaven that He may prolong your reign in Israel. . . .

Praise be to the beneficent God for His mercy towards me! Kings of the earth, to whom (my lord the King's) magnificence and power are known, bring gifts to him, conciliating his favour by costly presents, such as the King of the Franks, the King of the Gebalim, who are Germans, the King of Constantinople, and others. All their gifts pass through my hands, and I am charged with making gifts in return.

I always ask the ambassadors of these monarchs who bring gifts about our brethren the Israelites, the remnant of the captivity, whether they have heard anything concerning the deliverance of those who have languished in bondage and have found no rest.

At length mercantile emissaries of Khorasan told me that there is a kingdom of Jews which is called Al-Chazar. But I did not believe these words for I thought that they told me such things to procure my goodwill and favour. I was therefore wondering, till the ambassadors of Constantinople came with presents and a letter from their king to our king, and I interrogated them concerning this matter.

They answered me: "It is quite true, and the name of that kingdom is Al-Chazar. It is a fifteen days' journey by sea from Constantinople but by land many nations intervene between us; the name of the king now reigning is Joseph; ships sometimes come from their country to ours bringing fish, skins, and wares of every kind. The men are our confederates and are honoured by us; there is communication between us by embassies and mutual gifts; they are very powerful; they occasionally engage in expeditions."

When I heard this report I was encouraged, my hands were strengthened and my hope was confirmed. Thereupon I bowed down and adored the God of heaven.

Aaron the Mystic

*This story within a story is an account of a
confrontation between Aaron ben Samuel Ha-Nasi, the
master mentioned in the tale, and a young man of the
congregation of the town of Benevento in southern Italy.
Aaron of Bagdad was a mystic and wonder-worker who was
well known to Jews on both shores of the Mediterranean
during the latter part of the ninth century. This legend
is rather characteristic of the mystical practices and beliefs
of that period.*

There came from Bagdad from our beloved ones an esteemed man of distinguished family, an illustrious scholar who made use of his
wonder-working wisdom to do very difficult and
astonishing things. When he reached Benevento the
entire community came out as one man to welcome him.

On the Sabbath, an esteemed young
man arose to read the prayers before Him that
dwelleth on high. He chanted with pleasing voice.
When he reached the words "Praise ye the Lord
who is to be praised," his voice lingered on the
sound, but he did not pronounce God's name. The
master at once realized that the reader was actually
a dead man, and it is known that the dead do not
praise God. "Stop," he at once commanded in a
loud voice. "Do not give praise, for thou art
not permitted to recite prayer before God."

Then he began to question the youth,
to plead with him in the name of his Maker,
saying: "Tell me and do not fear, do not conceal
from me what thou hast done, confess the truth
before the Creator of the Spirit. . . ."

Immediately he answered, "I have indeed sinned, and trespassed against God; I have
rebelled and transgressed and done wrong . . . I
will tell you plainly all that happened.

"In my time there was a Jew named
Rabbi Ahimaaz who went to Jerusalem, the glorious city, three times, to fulfill his vow. On each
pilgrimage he took one hundred pieces of gold

with him, as he had vowed to the Rock of his salvation, to give aid to those who mourned the ruined house of His glory.

"As he set out on his third pilgrimage, he asked my mother for me, saying: 'Let him go with me, to keep me company and help me on the way. I will bring him back to thee.'. . . Then we set out on our journey rejoicing, without a thought of sadness.

"As we were sitting at the table of the scholars in study . . . the head of their school turned to them and said: 'Let the young man in our midst, who has come with our colleague Rabbi Ahimaaz, cheer us and delight our heart with the flow of his knowledge and the utterance of his thoughts.' Then I began reverently to give praise in psalm and song to Him that putteth on light as a garment.

"There sat one of the elders in meditation, intently listening to my chanting. He began to weep bitterly. Rabbi Ahimaaz . . . arising from the company, went over to him and begged him to tell why he wept. The elder simply told him that God had decreed that, in a little while, the young man would surely die. When the good man heard this his eyes filled with tears, he rent his clothes and tore out his hair, and exclaimed before them all: 'I have no place among the living; I have sworn to his mother that I would bring him back to her, without mishap or harm; how can I return to my house, if the lad is not with me?'

"Seeing his affliction and his bitter weeping, they wrote the Holy Name that was written in the Sanctuary; they made an incision in the flesh of my right arm, and inserted the Name where the flesh had been cut. So I came away in peace and returned home to my mother. While Rabbi Ahimaaz was alive, I wandered from land to land. Living since that time, I can live forever if I so desire, for no man can know the place of the Name unless I reveal it; but I will show it to you; I am in your hands; deal with me as seems right in your eyes."

So they brought the grave clothes; he approached and put them on; he showed them where the master had made the incision and took the Name out of it. His body became lifeless; the corpse crumbled in decay as from the dissolution of many years, the flesh returned to the dust.

A Code of Education

American Jews have been conspicuously active among those who advocate "progressive" education; as parents they have been criticized for being overpermissive with their children.

It was not always so. This is a code of education drawn up by the leaders of the Jewish community in twelfth-century England.

From month to month you shall increase my son's task. If this month he can learn half the weekly portion of Scripture, next month he must go through the whole. From Tammus [June-July] to Tishri he must go through the weekly portion in Hebrew, and from Tishri to Nisan in the vernacular. Then the boy is six years old. In his seventh year he must learn the Aramaic version from the book and not by heart and translate it into the vulgar tongue. In his eighth and ninth year he must take the Prophets and Hagiographa.

The teachers shall instruct the lads to translate the Aramaic version (Targum) of the Scripture into the vernacular, so that they be practised in the language of the Talmud (Aramaic), and can be easily introduced to the study of Halacha (Rabbinic Law).

At ten years to the Mishnah. Then the lad is to be introduced to the Talmud at first in the Tractate Beracoth (or Benedictions) and the smaller tractates which belong to the order Moed (Festivals). For all this a space of three years is appointed. In the fourth he is "holy to the Eternal"; for then the lad is thirteen years old.

At thirteen the practice of religion. The father shall then take the son set apart and win him by friendly words, saying "Hail to thee that hast shown thyself worthy of partaking in the holy work," and then taking him to the house for the Separated. But the duty of separation only comes to the lad with his sixteenth year. Then he is taken to the rector, who lays his hand on him and says, "This is holy to the Eternal." Then the youngster remains there seven years to learn the greater tractates [of the Talmud].

There shall be an overseer for the scholars to fix their tasks and to notice their ability or laziness. For teachers are like day labourers that only wait till it is eve. Therefore teachers must not teach at home, but only in the school. This is called the small school. When the overseer notices one of the lads to be of slow intellect, he shall lead him to his father and say to him, "God grant thy son power to do noble deeds, but for the study of the Law he is too slow of intellect." Otherwise the talented boys would be kept back by the more backward ones. Besides the lad may go to another teacher to see if he has better luck with him.

The teachers shall not take more than ten students in one subject. For though our Sages have fixed 25 as the proper number of students for one teacher, that applied only to Palestine where the climate favoured the development of the mind, and for the time of political independence, for in freedom the mind is lofty, strong, clear and light, and takes up wisdom and knowledge easier than in a state of subjection.

The Sages used to go through the weekly readings on Sabbath twice in the original and once in translation, twice in the original for we always read anything we love twice over, and once in translation to make God's word understood of the women and the vulgar so that perchance the fear of God might enter their hearts. So too the French Jews have the custom of going through the weekly portion on Sabbath twice in the original and once in the vernacular.

Maimonides (1135–1204)

No anthologist of Jewish thought would dream of omitting selections of the vast work of Moses ben Maimon, commonly known as Maimonides. His Fundamentals of the Law *and* Guide for the Perplexed *are towering pillars of Jewish theology.*

The "Gate of Instruction" is a letter believed to have been written to his children and belonging to a unique and magnificent Jewish tradition whose memory has almost disappeared, except among specialists: the tradition of the Ethical Will. From the twelfth century to the seventeenth, it was the custom of Jewish fathers to leave explicit directions for the guidance of their children in the form of a last testament. The earliest of such written documents is placed about 1050. However, the tradition of the verbal testament goes right back to Abraham, of whom God said, "I have known him to the end that he may command his children and his household after him, that they may keep the way of the Lord."

Perhaps the most remarkable of these ethical testaments is this "Gate of Instruction," an obscure document attributed to Maimonides because its style has all his vigor and clarity. Its content is consistent with the noble purpose displayed in his other work.

The Gate of Instruction

Hear me, my children! Be strong and show yourselves men! Fear the Lord, the God of your father, that God of Abraham, Isaac and Jacob; and serve Him with a perfect heart, from fear and from love. For fear restrains from sin and love stimulates to virtue.

Accustom yourselves to habitual goodness, for habit and character are closely interwoven, habit becoming as it were second nature.

The perfection of the body is an antecedent to the perfection of the soul, for health is the key that unlocks the inner chamber. When I bid you to care for your bodily and moral welfare, my purpose is to open for you the gates of heaven.

115

Conduct yourselves with gravity and decency; avoid association with the wanton; sit not in the streets, sport not with the young, for the fruit thereof is evil. Be found rather in the company of the great and learned, but behave modestly in their presence, occupying the lower seats. Be not supercilious or conceited when with them; be not ashamed to ask explanations, but do so at the right moment and in fitting terms.

Love wisdom, seek her as silver, search for her as for hidden treasures. Emulate those who seek knowledge, despise those who have no intellectual curiosity. Whether you ask a question or answer one, speak without haste or obscurity, softly and without stammering. Use refined phrases, let your utterance be clear, tranquil, and apt to the point. Behave as one who wishes to learn and to discover the truth, not as one whose aim is to dispute and win a wordy victory.

Learn in your youth, when ye eat what others provide; while your mind is still free, and unencumbered with cares; ere the memory lose its vigor. For the time will come when ye will wish to learn but will be unable.

When you find in the Law or the Prophets, or the books of the Sages, a deep text or an obscure saying, which you cannot understand nor can penetrate into its secret; which appears subversive of the corner-stones of the Torah or altogether absurd; do not budge from your faith, let not your mind be confounded. Stand fast in your stronghold, and attribute the fault to yourselves. Place it "in a corner" and do not abominate the whole of your faith because you are incompetent to solve a single problem of philosophy.

Love truth and righteousness, and cleave to them. Prosperity so obtained is built on a sure rock. Hate falsehood and injustice, lust not after their dainties, for such happiness is built on sand.

Eat that ye may live, and lay a ban on excess. By taking the little food which is easily digested by the natural heat, a man's vigor and health increase, but if he eat more than enough, overtaxing his digestion, his intellect is dulled, his purse emptied. Overeating is, in fact, the cause of many maladies. Eat not in the public ways, do not incessantly nibble like mice, take your meals at fixed hours in your homes.

Beware of wine, which destroys the strong and degrades the honoured. I have not accustomed you to complete abstinence from wine from your earliest years. But break the strength of the wine with water, and drink it as food, not as a pastime.

Enjoy life in the society of your friends and the wife of your young manhood. Remember the warnings of Scripture against unchastity: "She hath cast down many wounded, yea a mighty host are her slain." Never excite desire, and when in the course of nature it comes upon you, satisfy it in the manner ordained by moral rule, to raise up offspring, and perpetuate the human race. Though it is not meet that ye should be dominated by your wives or reveal to them secrets placed in your keeping, you must honour your wives, for they are your honour. "All glorious is the King's daughter within the palace." Serve those who love you, and those near unto you, with your person and your substance, according to the good hand of the Lord upon you. But take heed lest ye serve them with your soul, for that is the divine portion!

The Aim of Learning

This discussion of teacher and scholar is from Maimonides' Commentary on the Mishnah, *"For The Sake of Truth."*

Imagine that they are bringing a little boy to the teacher, so that he teach him the Torah. This is of great benefit to the boy, because he will attain something of perfection. But because he is young in years, and his ability to comprehend is still weak, he cannot understand the degree of this benefit. And so his teacher, who is more mature than he, needs must goad him on to learn with things that are dear to him according to his tender age. He will say to him: "Read, and I shall give you nuts, or figs"; or "I shall give you some honey." And so he reads and makes an effort, not for the sake of the reading itself, whose worth he does not know, but so that his teacher will give him the promised things to eat.

As he grows older and his ability to comprehend becomes stronger and things that were important to him before grow slight in his eyes, and he desires something else, his teacher must goad him on and rouse his pleasure in learning through something that he now considers beautiful. And so his teacher will say to him, "Read, and I shall buy you fine shoes or fine garments." And every piece of apparel is, in his eyes, more important than the Torah; it is the aim of his reading.

But when his ability to comprehend becomes more mature, and these things also seem insignificant in his eyes, then his master will say to him: "Learn this paragraph or this passage, and I shall give you a dinar." And he reads and strives in order to receive the money.

As his knowledge increases he will desire something of more importance, and his master will say to him, "Learn, so that you may become an elder and a judge." Thus he reads and strives in order to attain this step: and his aim is to have people show him honour, to have them praise and exalt him.

All this is contemptible. But since man's ability to comprehend is small, he must needs set up another thing than wisdom as the goal of wisdom. Thus did the sages caution that wisdom must not be pursued with a motive. A man should have no purpose in the learning of wisdom save only this—to learn to know wisdom itself. Similarly, no purpose must be connected with truth, save that one should know what is true. And the Torah is truth and the purpose of knowing it is to live by it.

How A Wise Man Should Behave

In Guide for the Perplexed *Maimonides counsels the devout and prudent Jew on the application of his principles in both action and thought.*

A wise man should not shout or be noisy when he speaks, but his conversation with all people should be quiet. He should judge every man leniently, praising his friends, and not disparaging anyone. If he perceives that his words are helpful and listened to, he should continue talking; otherwise he keeps silent.

He does not enter the presence of his friend at the time of the latter's disgrace, but averts his eyes from him. He does not depart from his word, neither adding to it nor subtracting from it, except when peace is involved. He does not converse with a woman in a public place, even if it be his wife, sister or daughter.

A wise man should not walk with a haughty demeanour; nor should he walk with slow and measured gait like women and proud people; nor run about in public roads like madmen; nor stoop like a hunchback; but he should gaze downward as though standing in prayer, and walk in the street like a man occupied in business. From the manner of a man's walking, it may be perceived whether he is wise and learned, or foolish and ignorant.

119

The dress of a wise man should be suitable and clean. It is forbidden that stains or grease marks should be found on his garment. He should not wear the apparel of princes nor the clothes of paupers. His garments should be of a medium character and suitable for him. His flesh should not be visible through his apparel, like the very fine linen garments made in Egypt; nor should his dress drag along the ground like that of the haughty, but should only reach to the heel, and the sleeves to the tips of his fingers. He should not wear a conspicuously long prayer shawl save on the Sabbath, and then only if he has no other in its place. He should not wear patched shoes in Summer, but if he is a poor man he may wear them in Winter.

He should not go out into the street perfumed, nor with scented garments, nor use any perfume for his hair, but it is allowable if he anoint his body with perfume to remove the bad odor.

The course adopted by a man of intelligence is first to determine upon a means of livelihood, then to purchase a dwelling-house and then to marry. But fools marry first, then if they can afford it acquire a dwelling-house, and afterward, when advanced in years, go about to find a trade, or have to be supported from charity.

Some people assume that the Universe was created solely for the sake of man's existence, that he might serve God. Everything that is done they believe is done for man's sake; even the Spheres move only for his benefit, in order that his wants might be supplied.

Even if the Universe existed for man's sake and man existed for the purpose of serving God one must still ask: What is the end of serving God? He does not become more perfect if all His creatures serve Him. Nor would He lose anything if nothing existed beside Him.

It might perhaps be replied that the service of God is not intended for God's perfection, but for our own. Then, however, the question arises: What is the object of being perfect?

Pressing the inquiry as to the purpose of the Creation, we must at last arrive at the answer: It was the will of God. And this is the correct answer. Logic as well as tradition proves clearly that the Universe does not exist for man's sake, but that all things in it exist each for its own sake.

The evils which befall men are of three kinds:

The first kind of evil is that which comes to man because he is subject to birth and death, being possessed of a physical body. Now, it is in accordance with the divine wisdom that there can be no birth without death, for unless the individuals die, how can the species continue? If man were never subject to change, there would be one single being, but no individuals forming a species.

The second class of evils comprises such as people cause to each other: e.g., when some of them use their strength against others.

The third class of evils, however, comprises those which a man causes to himself by his own action. This is the largest class, and originates in man's vices, such as excessive desire for eating, drinking and love. Indulgence in these things in undue measure, or in improper manner, brings disease and affliction to body and soul alike. The soul, when accustomed to superfluous things, acquires a strong habit of desiring things which are neither necessary for the preservation of the individual nor for that of the species. This desire is without a limit. For example, you desire to have your vessels of silver, but golden vessels are still better; others have even vessels of sapphire.

How many trials and tribulations are due to the lust for superfluous things! In our frantic search for them, we lose even those which are indispensable. For the more we strive after that which is superfluous, the less strength have we left to grasp that which is truly needed.

Joseph Karo (1488–1575)

Joseph Karo was the great medieval codifier of Jewish law. His Shulchan Arukh *(The Prepared Table) examines all previous codes of the law and mediates among points of dispute. Despite much early opposition, Karo's views prevailed, and his code became the authoritative one. Orthodox Jews all over the world are still guided by its precepts.*

The Prepared Table

If a man cannot learn without sleeping at noon, then let him sleep. But not too long, for it is forbidden to sleep by day longer than a horse who sleeps as long as it takes him to draw sixty breaths. And even in so brief a sleep, man shall not be intent upon his pleasure, but upon restoring his body to serve the name of God.

And so shall it be with all that brings enjoyment to man in this world, so that even optional acts like eating, drinking, walking, sitting, standing, talking—and all the matters requisite for living—shall all be done in the service of the Creator.

And thus shall it also be when he sits in the circle of the upright or stands in the place where the righteous stand, or goes to the council of worthy men. If he does these things for his pleasure, if he is satisfying his desires or his longings, then it is not praiseworthy, for it is praiseworthy only if he does them in the name of heaven.

And it is the same with speaking. Even when he speaks about things bound up with wisdom, he must be intent upon serving the Creator, or upon something that leads to serving him.

Taken all in all: it is the duty of a man to turn his eyes and his heart to his path, and to weigh all his doing in the balance of reason. If he sees something that will lead to serving the Creator, let him do it; if not, let him not do it.

On Purim a person should drink until he does not know the difference between "Cursed be Haman," and "Blessed be Mordecai."

Every Jew is commanded to get married at eighteen, and he who gets married earlier is observing the commandment in the very best way. But no one ought to get married before thirteen, for this would be lust. Under no circumstances should one pass his twentieth birthday without getting married, and if a person passes his twentieth birthday and doesn't care to get married, the court shall compel him to marry in order that he may fulfill the command of propagation. However, if he is busied with the Torah and concerned about it, and is afraid to get married lest he be troubled too much about making a living, and therefore have to neglect his study of the Torah, he is permitted to delay.

A Jew is forbidden to say that he is a Gentile in order to avoid being killed. But he is allowed to put on different clothes during a period of persecution in order that they should not recognize that he is a Jew, inasmuch as he does not say that he is a Gentile.

If a man wants to become a Jew, they say to him: "What has prompted you to come to convert yourself? Don't you know that Jews are now oppressed, prostrate, mistreated, undergoing suffering?" If he answer, "I know, and I am not worthy to join you," then they accept him without further delay and inform him of the principles of Judaism, namely, the unity of God, and the prohibition of idolatry.

Amatus Lusitanus (1511–1568)

Perhaps one of the noblest statements on medical ethics since Hippocrates is this by Amatus Lusitanus, a sixteenth-century Portuguese Jew. Like many Jews in Spain and Portugal at that time, Lusitanus turned Christian in order to save himself from the executioners of the Inquisition. These converted Jews were called Marranos; many of them were Christians publicly but remained Jews privately, practicing their ritual in secret. However, Amatus grew weary of his double life and went to Rome where he studied medicine and became a noted practitioner, enjoying the patronage of Pope Julius III. Backed by these powerful connections, he was able to return to Judaism safely. In his later years he became a student of religious philosophy and did considerable writing.

The Oath of Amatus

I have at all times earnestly striven after this one thing, namely, that benefit might spread forward to mankind; that I have praised no one, and censured no one, merely to indulge in private passions.

Concerning the remuneration commonly given to physicians, I have not been anxious for this, but I have treated many, not only zealously, but even without pay. All men have been considered equal by me of whatever religion they were, whether Hebrews, Christians, or the followers of the Moslem faith. [The Church law that Jews must not treat Christian patients was not always observed.]

As regards loftiness of station, that has never been a matter of concern to me, and I have accorded the same care to the poor as to those born in exalted rank. I have never brought about sickness. In diagnosis I have always said what I thought to be true. I have unduly favoured no vendors of drugs, except perhaps those whom I knew to surpass the others by reason of their skill in their art or because of their natural qualities of mind. In prescribing drugs I have exercised moderation in proportion as the powers of the sick man allowed. I have revealed to no one a secret entrusted to me; I have given no one a fatal draught. No woman has ever brought about an abortion by my aid; nothing base has been committed by me in any house where I was practising.

I have published my books on medical matters with no desire for profit, but I have had regard for this one thing, namely, that I might, in some measure, provide for the health of mankind. Whether I have succeeded in this, I leave to the judgment of others. At all events, I have held this always before me, and have given it chief place in my prayers.

Baruch Spinoza (1632–1677)

In 1656, the Sephardic community of Amsterdam went through the formal rites of excommunication. The object of this rare exclusion proceeding was a descendant of Portuguese Jews by the name of Baruch Spinoza, whose unorthodox views of religion had infuriated the rabbinate.

It was a serious matter to be barred from participation in the Jewish community, since even an excommunicated Jew could not find acceptance among the Christians. It meant that this brilliant young philosopher could make his living only by menial tasks; he worked as a lens grinder. But indeed his labors were symbolic, for the body of his true work has served to sharpen the intellectual eye of mankind for all time.

What were these views that roused such murderous rancor? Spinoza was the father of modern Bible criticism, a great student of the Scriptures. He would not allow the ways in which the Bible contradicts itself to escape rational judgment. He insisted on rationalism even in the sanctioned unreason of religion. He challenged the authority of priests and the authority of revelation, and championed free thought. He attempted to apply the process of scientific inquiry, especially Euclidian methods, to metaphysics, and produced the theory of God as infinite substance, creator and created, present in every phenomenon and physical object. Virtue, to him, is the freedom of the sage to think and therefore to apply his wisdom to an informed love of God.

His philosophical writing is thorny and technical, but much of his correspondence, while impregnated with his philosophy, is less grueling to read. He carried on an argument by correspondence with a Dutch merchant named Willem de Blyenberg, and one of these letters contains the essence of his system.

A Letter to Blyenberg

In order to make the best of the present opportunity, I will at once proceed to answer your question. This seems to turn on the point "that it seems to be clear, not only from God's providence, which is identical with his will, but also from God's co-operation and continuous creations of things, either that there are no such things as sin or evil, or that God directly brings sin and evil to pass."

For my own part, I cannot admit that sin and evil have any positive existence, far less that anything can exist, or come to pass, contrary to the will of God. On the contrary, not only do I assert that sin has no positive existence, I also maintain that only in speaking improperly, or humanly, can we say that we sin against God, as in the expression that men offend God.

As to the first point, we know that whatsoever is, when considered in itself without regard to anything else, possesses perfection, extending in each thing as far as the limits of that thing's essence: for essence is nothing else. I take for an illustration the design or determined will of Adam to eat the forbidden fruit. This design or determined will, considered in itself alone, includes perfection in so far as it expresses reality. Sin, which indicates nothing save imperfection, cannot consist in anything that expresses reality, as we see in the case of Adam's decision and its execution.

Again, we cannot say that Adam's will is at variance with the law of God, and that it is evil because it is displeasing to God; for besides the fact that grave imperfection would be imputed to God, if we say that anything happens contrary to his will, or that he desires anything which he does not obtain or that his nature resembles that of his creatures in having sympathy with some things more than others; such an occurrence would be at complete variance with the nature of the divine will.

The will of God is identical with his intellect; in other words, anything which should come to pass against his will must be of a nature to be contrary to his intellect, such, for instance, as a round square.

Hence the will or decision of Adam regarded in itself was neither evil nor, properly speaking, against the will of God: it follows that God may—or rather, for the reason you call attention to, must—be its cause.

However, in order to make the way still plainer, and remove every doubt, I deem it necessary to answer the two following difficulties: First, why Holy Scripture says that God wishes for the conversion of the wicked, and also why God forbade Adam to eat of the fruit when he had ordained the contrary? Secondly, that it seems to follow from what I have said, that the wicked, by their pride, avarice, and deeds of desperation, worship God in no less degree than the good do by their nobleness, patience, love, etc., inasmuch as both execute God's will.

In answer to the first question, I observe that Scripture, being chiefly fitted for and beneficial to the multitude, speaks popularly after the fashion of men. For the multitude are incapable of grasping sublime conceptions. Hence I am persuaded that all matters, which God revealed to the prophets as necessary to salvation, are set down in the form of laws. With this understanding, the prophets invented whole parables, and represented God as a king and a lawgiver. They constantly speak of God as resembling a man, as sometimes angry, sometimes merciful, now desiring what is future, not jealous and suspicious, even as deceived by the devil.

Thus the command given to Adam consisted solely in this, that God revealed to Adam, that eating of the fruit brought about death; as he reveals to us, through our natural faculties, that poison is deadly. If you ask, for what object did he make this revelation, I answer in order to render Adam to that extent more perfect in knowledge.

As to the second difficulty, it is true that the wicked execute after their manner the will of God: but they cannot, therefore, be in any respect compared with the good. The more perfection a thing has, the more does it participate in the Deity, and the more does it express perfection. Thus, as the good have incomparably more perfection than the bad, their virtue cannot be likened to the virtue of the wicked, inasmuch as the wicked lack the love of God, which proceeds from the knowledge of God, and by which alone we are, according to our human understanding, called the servants of God. The wicked, knowing not God, are but as instruments in the hand of the workman, serving unconsciously, and perishing in the using; the good, on the other hand, serve consciously, and in serving become more perfect.

On Persecution

In Spinoza's view it was necessary for philosophy to irradiate all man's activities, if society were to become just and rational. His critique of authoritarianism, taken from his treatise Theology *and* Politics, *was remarkably courageous for the seventeenth century.*

What greater misfortune for a state can be conceived than that honourable men should be sent like criminals into exile, because they hold diverse opinions which they cannot disguise?

He that knows himself to be upright does not fear the death of a criminal, and shrinks from no punishment. His mind is not wrung with remorse for any disgraceful deed. He holds that death in a good cause is no punishment, but an honour, and that death for freedom is glory.

What purpose, then, is served by the

death of such men, what example is proclaimed? The cause for which they die is unknown to the idle and the foolish, hateful to the turbulent, loved by the upright. The only lesson we can draw from such scenes is to flatter the persecutor, or else to imitate the victim.

If formal assent is not to be esteemed above conviction, and if governments are to retain a firm hold of authority and not be compelled to yield to agitators, it is imperative that freedom of judgment should be granted, so that men may live together in harmony, however diverse, or even openly contradictory their opinions may be. We cannot doubt that such is the best system of government and open to the fewest objections, since it is the one most in harmony with human nature. In a democracy (the most natural form of government) everyone submits to the control of authority over his actions, but not over his judgment and reason; that is, seeing that all cannot think alike, the voice of the majority has the force of law; subject to repeal if circumstances bring about a change of opinion. In proportion as the power of free judgment is withheld we depart from the natural condition of mankind, and consequently the government becomes more tyrannical.

Nathan Hannover (?–1683)

*Between the massacre of Jews by the Crusaders
and the Hitler holocaust, the worst ordeal suffered by
European Jews was the series of Chmielnicki pogroms in
1648, when Bogdan Chmielnicki led hordes of Cossacks
and Ukrainian peasants in a three-way drive against Polish
landowners, the Catholic clergy and every kind of Jew
they could find. The Jews, as usual, were the worst sufferers.
Hundreds of communities were wiped out and hundreds of
thousands of Jews were slaughtered.*

*Much of Jewish thought is concerned with the
rationalization of such periodic outbreaks of Gentile cruelty.
Out of massacre, out of despair and the conviction that
this world held nothing for them grew a mood of horror
and depression that drove the Jews of Eastern Europe deep
into the wild mysticism of Hasidism, preparing the way for
premature messianic hopes and the rise of a number of
false messiahs—the most notorious of whom was Shab-
batai Zvi—who spread hysteria among adherents during
this period.*

*The best account of those events is found in a
graphic chronicle by Nathan Hannover, a rabbi, cabalist
and historian. He was killed by the Turks in Moravia
when he was only thirty-five, but during his short life he
wrote several beautiful prayers as well as this splendid
history. One of the most effective chapters of* The Miry
Depths *tells how the town of Nemirov was destroyed.*

The Fall of Nemirov
(June 10, 1648)

The oppressor Chmielnicki heard that
many Jews had assembled in the holy community
of Nemirov, and that they had a great deal of silver
and gold with them. (Because of the Cossacks,
many Jews came from the countryside to the fortress of Nemirov.) He knew also that the congregation of Nemirov itself was distinguished for its
riches.

Accordingly Chmielnicki sent a certain

leader, an enemy of the Jews, and about 600 swordsmen with him against this honored congregation. In addition he wrote to the magistrates of the city that they should help this band; to this the citizens readily responded that they would help them with all their might and main, not so much because of their love of the Cossacks, but because of their hatred of the Jews. The Greek Catholic townspeople hated the Jewish merchants, their competitors.

It came to pass on a Wednesday, the 20th of Siwan, that the Cossacks drew near to the city of Nemirov. On the anniversary of this day, June 10th, elegies are still recited in Poland. When the Jews saw the troops from afar they were frightened, though as yet they did not know whether they were Polish or Cossack. Nevertheless all the Jews went with their wives and infants, with their silver and gold, into the fortress and locked and barred its doors, ready to fight them. What did those scoundrels, those Cossacks, do? They made flags like the Poles, for there is no other way to distinguish between the Polish and the Cossack forces except through their banners. Now the people of the town, although they knew of this trick, nevertheless called to the Jews in the fortress: "Open the gates. This is a Polish army which has come to save you from your enemies, should they appear."

The Jews immediately opened the gates. No sooner had the gates been opened than the Cossacks entered with drawn swords, lances, and scythes, and some only with clubs, and they killed the Jews in huge numbers. They raped women and young girls; but some of the women and maidens jumped into the moat near the fortress in order that the Gentiles should not defile them and were drowned in the water. Many of the men who were able to swim also jumped into the water and swam, thinking they could save themselves from slaughter. The Russians swam after them with their swords and their scythes and killed them in the water.

The president of the rabbinical college

of Nemirov was also there . . . Rabbi Jehiel Michael, the son of his excellency, our teacher, Rabbi Eliezer, of blessed memory.

Jehiel also jumped into the water to save himself by swimming when a Russian seized him and wanted to murder him; but the scholar besought him not to kill him, for which he would give him a great deal of silver and gold. The Russian agreed and took him to his house, to the place where his silver and gold were hidden, and the Cossack then let him go alive. The scholar then left that place with his mother, and they hid themselves in a certain house there, all that night until the morning dawn.

On the morrow the Russians also searched the houses, thinking perhaps some Jew might be hidden there. The scholar then fled with his mother to the cemetery so that if they should kill them they would be in the cemetery and would thus receive burial. But it happened as he approached the place that one of the men of that city, a Russian, a shoemaker, ran after the scholar with a club in his hand and wounded him with it. The mother of the rabbi begged the Russian to kill her instead of her son, but he paid no attention to her and killed first the sage and then his mother. May God avenge their blood.

Three days after the massacre the wife of the scholar buried them; for in all the towns where the persecutions took place they allowed most of the women to live, except the old and sickly, whom they killed.

It happened there that a beautiful girl of a fine and rich family was taken captive by a certain Cossack who married her. But before they lived together she told him in guile that through a magic power that she possessed, no weapon could harm her. "If you don't believe me," she said to him, "just test me in this matter. Shoot at me with a gun and it won't hurt me at all." The Cossack, her husband, thought she was telling the truth, and in his simplicity, shot her with his gun and she fell, dying for the glorification of the Name to avoid being defiled by a Gentile.

It also happened that there was a certain beautiful girl who was to be wedded to a Cossack. She asked him to marry her in one of the Christian churches which stood on the other side of the bridge. He fulfilled her request and with timbrels and flutes led her to the marriage in regal dress. As soon as she came to the bridge she jumped into the water and was drowned as a martyr. May God avenge her blood. There were many such cases, too numerous to record.

The number of all those murdered and drowned in the holy community of Nemirov was about 6000; these met all sorts of terrible deaths, as has already been described. Those of the holy congregation of Nemirov who escaped the sword fled to the honored community of Tulchin, for there, outside the city, was a very strong fortress. But in Tulchin the Jews were betrayed into the hands of the Cossacks by the Polish nobles. The Cossacks then turned and killed the Poles.

IV
THE
ENLIGHTENMENT

I see now that the Greeks were only handsome youths,
whilst the Jews were always men—powerful, indomitable
men—who have fought and suffered on every battlefield
of human thought.

Heinrich Heine

Introduction

By the 14th century the Jews had become the pariahs of Europe, a role they were to play in varying degrees of intensity the next 500 years. Among other things they were hated for their indispensability. Forbidden to hold land or to bear arms, they had turned their energies and ingenuity to commerce. They invented banking; their chain of trading stations and counting offices, where Jew met Jew and spoke a common language although living on different continents, became the pivotal points of international trade. Kings and nobles allowed them to amass wealth, took what they had and then granted them enough freedom to start filling their treasuries again. But often Jew hatred flared out of control and the half-savage peasants, eager to find a scapegoat for their own misery, fell upon the Jewish villages and slaughtered everyone they could find.

This hatred, of course, confirmed the Jew in his own contempt for the gentile. Traits and attributes that added up to the reality—Jew—were enormously exaggerated. The more he was punished for being himself, the more unlike anyone else he became, and that fatal distinction, nourished by bloodshed, was his pride. In one sense this may have strengthened the Jewish spirit and reinforced its weird stubbornness. In another way it began to weaken the Jew's intellectual authority by making his outlook provincial. In his passion for survival, in his determination to maintain his identity, in his own fear and hatred of the gentile, the Jew ghettoized his perspectives.

But in the 15th century there was a ferment of ideas abroad. The ice floe of feudalism was breaking up. The authority of the Church was being questioned. Scholars were rediscovering the classic thinkers and beginning to reinvestigate natural phenomena in defiance of Papal edict. The seeds of the Renaissance were quickening in medieval Europe. This activity exerted a magnetism on Jewish scholarship. In joyful excitement brilliant young Talmudists began to question their own traditions and to challenge the processes by which they felt their own life style being condemned to obsolescence.

They were attacked from all sides, by Jewish traditionalist and by Christian academician. They flourished in solitude. And through them the Question was revived, Jewish thinking revitalized and powerful wattage given to that rational light that was piercing the mists of medievalism.

Moses Hayyim Luzzato
(1707–1747)

This eighteenth-century Italian Jew is one of the most remarkable figures in Jewish literature. Mystic, cabalist, poet, in his short forty years he produced works that electrified his generation and helped create the whole era of modern Jewish literature. He began his career by announcing that the spirits of the patriarchs had come to earth to seek him out and to initiate him in sacred mysteries, and became the leader of a cult practicing secret rituals. Forbidden these activities by the Italian rabbinate, he left Italy, went to Germany, then to Holland and finally to Palestine. Four years after his arrival he was caught in an outbreak of plague and died in Acre.

Luzzato's great work is Mesillat Yesharim *(The Path of the Righteous). Herein is a remarkable blend of the two currents of Jewish thought, the mystic and the ethical. In it, revelation is disciplined by moral principle, and the Law is illumined by vision.*

The Path of the Righteous

If you will observe the present state of affairs, you will note that most of those who possess quick mental grasp and keen intellect concentrate all their study and thought upon the subtleties of the sciences, each according to the bent of his mind and natural taste. Some devote themselves to the physical sciences; others turn all their thoughts to astronomy and mathematics; others, again, to the arts. Finally, there are those who penetrate into the innermost sanctuary of knowledge, which is the study of the holy Torah. Of these latter, some pursue the study of dialectics, some study *Midrash,* and others study the Codes. There are but few who study the nature of the love and the fear of God, of communion, or any other phase of saintliness.

Yet the neglect of these studies is not due to their being regarded as inessential. On the contrary, everyone would admit that these subjects are of cardinal importance. The reason they are neglected is that they are regarded as so familiar and commonplace as not to deserve that anyone should spend much time on them. Consequently, the pursuit of these studies is confined to people of limited mentality. Indeed one who is saintly is inevitably suspected of being a dullard.

This fact has its evil consequences both for the learned and the unlearned. It will be exceedingly hard to find saintliness among us, since neither the learned nor the ignorant are likely to cultivate it. The learned will lack saintliness because they do not give it sufficient thought; the ignorant will not possess it because their powers of understanding are limited, so that the majority of men will conceive saintliness to consist in reciting numerous Psalms and long confessionals, in fasting and ablutions in ice and snow. Such practises fail to satisfy the intellect, and offer nothing to the understanding.

Although saintliness is latent in the character of every normal person, yet without cultivation it is sure to remain dormant. Bear in mind that such qualities of character as saintliness, fear and love of God, and purity of heart are not so innate as to enable men to dispense with the effort needed to develop them. They can be developed only by means of special effort.

Should we not, therefore, devote some time to this study in order to find out all that is to be known about the virtuous traits of character, and learn how to acquire and cultivate them? How shall a man obtain wisdom if he does not look for it? What shall we answer for ourselves on the Judgment Day, if we are too indolent to engage in this study, and so neglect one of the principal duties prescribed to us by God?

If we make no effort to understand what true fear of God means, or to comprehend its various aspects, how can we acquire it, or how can we escape the worldly vanities that distract us from it? How can we discover the love of God within us? How can our thinking be pure, if we do not strive to cleanse it of the impurities with which our physical nature taints it?

If, however, we shall apply ourselves earnestly to this subject, we shall not only master it ourselves, but we may also be able to teach others. In speaking of wisdom, Solomon said, "If thou seekest her as silver and searchest for her as for hidden treasures, then shalt thou understand the fear of the Lord" (Proverbs 2:4,5). He did not say, "then shalt thou understand philosophy, astronomy, medicine, the codes, the *halakot*," but "then shalt thou understand the fear of the Lord." We infer from that verse that to understand what the fear of God is, one must search for it as for hidden treasures.

We read in Scripture, "The fear of the Lord, that is wisdom." The truth is that the fear of God, to be properly understood, requires profound study. Whoever pursues this inquiry realises that saintliness has nothing to do with what foolish pietists consider to be essential, but rather with wisdom and true perfection.

This is the teaching of Moses in the following verse, "And now, Israel, what doth the Lord thy God require of thee, but to fear the Lord thy God, to walk in all His ways and to love Him, and to serve the Lord thy God with all thy heart and with all thy soul, to keep the commandments of the Lord and His statutes which I command thee this day for thy good."

To fear God is to be moved by a sense of awe. In every move that one makes, one ought to feel self-abased before the greatness of God.

To walk in His ways includes everything that makes for uprightness and for the improvement of character. This is what our Sages meant when they said, "As He is merciful and gracious, so be thou merciful and gracious." What they wish to point out is that all of a man's habits and actions should be regulated in accordance with the standard of uprightness and morality.

To love God is to be so imbued with the love of God that we are impelled, of our own accord, to give Him pleasure in the same way as a child sometimes feels moved to give pleasure to his father and mother. On the other hand, we should feel distressed whenever we, or others, are the cause of His being deprived of such pleasure.

To be whole-hearted is to serve God with pure motive, that is, for the sake of the worship itself, and without any ulterior aim. That excludes both hesitancy and mechanical observance.

Moses Mendelssohn (1729–1786)

Moses Mendelssohn is not only a "Jewish" writer; he occupies considerable space in the formidable hierarchy of German philosophers and estheticians. While he was still a young man, his brilliance won him the status of a "protected" Jew, meaning one exempt from laws regulating Jews, and from all special taxes. He gained early fame as a supporter of Leibnitz's controversial teachings and then produced a series of works on esthetic criticism which became classics in their own day. A rationalist, liberal-minded, a hater of tyranny, he was one. of the first German partisans of Rousseau and translated the young Frenchman's work into German.

The great work of his middle period was Phädon, *an examination of the ideas of immortality in the style of Plato, which won him the nickname of the "German Socrates." An analysis of Ecclesiastes and a commentary on Maimonides followed; then an enormous work: he translated the Pentateuch into German, complete with a Hebrew commentary by himself and other scholars. The great work of his last period,* Jerusalem, *was a product of his political activism, rare among scholars of that day; but Mendelssohn had identified himself with the victims of persecution and drew heavily upon his strength and finances to help fight anti-Semitism. His personal efforts were instrumental in defending Swiss Jews against persecution, and his followers began to turn out tracts in defense of the Jewish community, to which he added notes and prefaces. One of these works, a translation of Manasseh ben Israel's "Vindication of the Jews," provoked such a storm of reaction from anti-Semitic circles that Mendelssohn was inspired to write his* Jerusalem—*a close analysis of the Judaic ethic and a brilliantly argued case for minority rights.*

Mendelssohn's style is not easy. He was a complex thinker and he never strove to vulgarize his material. In this section from Jerusalem, *however, his argument attains eloquent clarity. He is discussing the development of the major currents in classic Jewish theology.*

On Superstition

To the disgrace of human reason and feelings, superstition understood well how to combine together the most incongruous notions, and to cause to prevail, side by side, human sacrifices and animal worship. In the most magnificent temples, built and ornamented according to all the rules of art, one would look about, as Plutarch expresses himself, to the disgrace of reason, for the deity which was to be worshipped there, and find upon the altar a disgusting baboon; and to this beast were sacrificed blooming youths and maidens. Thus low had idolatry degraded human nature! "They sacrificed men," as the Prophet expresses himself in an emphatic antithesis, "they sacrificed men, to offer them to the cattle they worshipped."

The lovers of wisdom (philosophers) occasionally ventured here and there to oppose this universal corruption, and to purify and enlighten openly, or through means of secret institutions, the prevailing notions. They endeavoured to restore to the images their ancient significations, or to substitute new ones, and thereby to breathe again, as it were, its own spirit into the dead carcass. But it was in vain! for upon the religion of the people their rational explanations had no influence. Eager as the uncultivated individual appears for information, so dissatisfied is he if it is given him in its real simplicity, he soon becomes cloyed with, and despises what is intelligible to him, and he will always seek after new, mysterious, and inexplicable things, and embrace them with redoubled gratification. His curiosity must be ever on the stretch, but never satisfied. The just named public instruction, therefore, met from the greatest mass with no attention, or rather it met, on the part of superstition and hypocrisy, with the most obstinate resistance, and received its customary reward, contempt, or hatred and persecution. The secret institutions and contrivances, in which the rights of truth should have been, in some degree, supported and preserved, went in part themselves the way of corruption, and became nurseries of every species of superstition, of all vices, and all abominations. A certain school of philosophers conceived the bold thought to remove the abstract ideas of man from everything pictorial or imaginable, and to bind them to such written characters as could, from their very nature, be taken for nothing else than they are; these were "the numbers." As numbers in themselves represent nothing, and stand in no natural connexion with any sensible impression, one would have believed that they were subject to no misapprehension; that they would necessarily be taken for arbitrary written tokens of our ideas, or be regarded as unintelligible. Here, one might have judged, that the rudest mind would not be able to confound the sign with the thing, and that through this wise artifice all abuse must necessarily be guarded against; for to him, who does not understand the numbers, they are unmeaning figures, and they can, at least, not mislead the man whom they do not enlighten.

In this manner the great founder of this school might have persuaded himself of the safety of his system. But very soon unreason went on its old course, even in this very school. Not content with that, which was found so intelligible and easy of comprehension, men sought in the numbers themselves for a secret power, in the signs again an inexplicable reality, through which means their

143

value as mere signs was again lost. Men believed, or, at all events, induced others to believe, that in these numbers all the mysteries of nature and the Deity lay concealed; they ascribed to them wonder-working power, and sought through, and by means of the same, to satisfy, not alone the curiosity and desire for knowledge of mankind, but their entire vanity, their striving after high and unattainable things, their impertinence, their covetousness, their avarice, and their frenzy. In one word, folly had once more rendered nugatory the calculations of wisdom, and annihilated again, or appropriated even to its own use, what the latter had provided for a better purpose.

Why the Jews Do Not Proselytise

In 1770, Mendelssohn clarified, for a non-Jewish correspondent, a point of Jewish dogma too infrequently spelled out.

Your question, why I do not try to make converts, has, I must say, somewhat surprised me. The duty to proselytise springs clearly from the idea that outside a certain belief there is no salvation. I, as a Jew, am not bound to accept that dogma, because, according to the teachings of the Rabbis, *the righteous of all nations shall have part in the rewards of the future world.* Your motive, therefore, is foreign to me; nay, as a Jew, I am not allowed publicly to attack any religion which is sound in its moral teachings.

Isaac D'Israeli (1766–1848)

Isaac D'Israeli, though less famous than his son Benjamin, the great Prime Minister of Victorian Great Britain, was a considerable figure in his own right, with a mind more interesting in many ways than his son's. Although he has fallen into disrepute among Jews because he had his children baptized, any fair appraisal of his work must recognize his unusual talent. His best-known work is a collection of essays called Curiosities of Literature, *but the most provocative of his thought is contained in a work called* The Genius of Judaism, *published anonymously. This was a critical examination of the Talmudic tradition, which he attacked as a dehydrating influence on the mystical fountains of Jewish thought. Although the senior D'Israeli's insights exceed his scholarship,* The Genius of Judaism *is a highly original work and should be rescued from the obscurity into which it has fallen.*

The Genius of Judaism:

NATURE

All Nature was consecrated to Religion; for the first fruits, a portion of the harvests, and certain animals were dedicated to its service. "The land is my own!" was the decree of the Lord. Judaism was in their fields. Their great festivals were connected with the production of every season. The Passover could not be kept till their flocks furnished the paschal lamb; the Pentecost till the wheat had ripened the fresh loaves of propitiation; and the thick boughs and branches could not cover their tabernacles till they had gathered in their vineyards and their olive grounds. The Israelites were reminded of their religious festivals by the living commemorations of Nature. The whole earth became a vast synagogue.

Such they were in their Holy Land and such they remain. The Hebrews are still accustomed to mark the seasons of the year and the dates of events by religious feasts and fasts. Still they are watching the sunset which brings their sabbath to all their habitations; the new moon to hold its solemn celebration, and the earliest star that calls them back to life, to break their penitential fast. The thunder and the rainbow receive the grace they equally give to their bread and wine. The God of Israel is the God of Nature, and they adore the Creator and his creation.

PROPERTY

The unequal distribution of property, that unavoidable evil among other people, was prevented in the Mosaic code by an agrarian law. "The land was the Lord's," and in Israel the prodigal could not alienate for ever the patrimony of his descendants, since, though he might deprive himself of his possessions, the land reverted to his indigent race, in the great sabbatic years.

IDOLATRY

As the Hebrew cast his eyes frequently towards heaven in the fervour of prayer, the Pagan, even as late as the Roman period, imagined that the Jew worshipped the material sky. The ancients conceived nothing but what was visible and palpable; even the mysteries of polytheism were scenical, and every divinity was an actor in a romance. Painters and sculptors have been the great corrupters of all divine conceptions, and are so to this day; the Deity is still represented in the imbecility of old age, and the Virgin and the Child are oftener worshipped than the God of nature. The frequent lapses into idolatry of the Israelite evinced his susceptibility of sensual impressions—the stealth into dark and voluptuous rites; nor had these criminal lapses been quelled but by the terrors of "the jealous God-ruler," when the celestial Sovereign manifested his dominion by his miracles.

To fix their vacillating faith, and to approach to their material conceptions, the Deity gratified his people by the appearance of a human sovereignty, and issued his edicts as a legislative and a military sovereign. Moses was even permitted to adopt into the exterior of his religion many of the rites, the ceremonies, and the customs of the Egyptians, and of the neighbouring nations. But the gross idolatry was abolished when the Legislator directed their practise to the worship of "the God of Israel," and the revealed doctrine of his solitary omnipotence.

THE ARK

The Jews had early become a military, as well as a sacerdotal people, and their conquests

146

were proclaimed in the name of the Lord of Hosts. *Jehovah Sebuot,* their god and their chief, was borne amid the four great standards of Israel; and in their military march the Ark of Alliance, covered by a veil of celestial blue, was guarded by an escort of Levites. To lay the hand on the Ark was incurring the penalty of death. (Once when the Ark appeared to be leaning on one side, a Levite was condemned to die, only for attempting to hold it up.) That "glory of Israel" was the visible sign of the presence of the Deity. The army of Israel was "the camp of the Eternal," and, what occurred to no other people but this sacerdotal race, the Levite alone was privileged to blow the silver trumpet which sounded to the charge. Even to this day the solemn response of a Jewish congregation on the Sabbath is the loud cry of "Holy! holy! holy! is the Lord of Hosts."

TRADITIONS AND CUSTOMS

The religious Judaism of the Theocracy degenerated into Rabbinical Judaism, by fabulous *traditions* and enslaving *customs.* Dictators of the human intellect, the Rabbins, like their successors, the papal Christians, attempted to raise a spurious theocracy of their own. A race of dreaming schoolmen contrived to place an avowed collection of mere human decisions among the hallowed verities and the duties of devotion; to graft opinions of men on the scion of divine institution; nay, even to prefer the gloss in direct opposition to the divine precept. Then oral traditions have become an integral part of their written law, and their customs have been converted into rites. We may ask by what perverse ingenuity, by what enthralling witchcraft, has such a revolution been brought about?

An artifice, or rather the marvellous imposture of a bold and obscure fiction, one which admitted of no evidence and which allowed of no denial, whose airy nature eluded the grasp while it charmed the eye, was the legend of the Rabbins, by which they assumed that their supplement to the Law of Moses was co-existent with the Law itself. They maintained the existence of "a chain of traditions," which had never been broken from the foundation of Judaism. Whenever they refer to a Talmudical authority, they exultingly exclaim, "This comes from Moses and Mount Sinai!"

The Jews had incurred the solemn reproach in the days of Jesus, of having annihilated the word of God by the load of their *Traditions.* The calamity became more fearful when, two centuries after, they received the fatal gift of their collected traditions called *Mishna,* and still more fatal, when in the lapse of the three subsequent centuries was produced the commentary graced with the title of the *Gemara,* Completeness, or Perfection! It was imagined that the human intellect had here touched its meridian. The national mind was completely Rabbinised. It became uniform, stable, and "peculiar." The Talmud, or the Doctrinal, as the whole is called, was the labour of nearly five hundred years.

Here, then, we find a prodigious mass of contradictory opinions, an infinite number of casuistical cases, a logic of scholastic theology, some recondite wisdom, and much rambling dotage; many puerile tales and oriental fancies; ethics and sophisms, reasonings and unreasonings, subtle solutions, and maxims and riddles; nothing in human life seems to have happened which these doctors have not perplexed or provided against, for their observations are as minute as Swift exhausted in his "Directions to Servants." The children of Israel, always children, were delighted as their Talmud increased its volume and their hardships. The *Gemara* was a third law to elucidate the *Mishna,* which was a second law, and which had thrown the first law, the law of Moses, into obscurity.

With the Israelites, everything is ancient, but nothing is obsolete.

Heinrich Heine (1797–1856)

There are few literary figures more fascinating than Heinrich Heine. A German Jew who submitted to baptism so that he would be permitted to practice law; a lawyer who abandoned his profession in order to write lyric verse; a philosophic Hellenist who, in his later years, found himself drawn to the stern religion of his fathers; a poet who turned to prose and was hailed as the wittiest writer since Voltaire—Heinrich Heine is a study in contradictions and a testimony to the vitality of genius in a most hostile environment.

His father was a prosperous merchant, his mother the daughter of a prominent physician. Their Jewish ties were very fragile. They educated their son in a Jesuit monastery, then in the universities of Bonn and Göttingen. His father intended him to take over the family business, but the young Heinrich abhorred commerce. To escape the pressure of his father's insistence, he consented to study law. This meant that he had to become a Christian, for at that time no Jew could follow a learned profession in Germany. After graduating from law school he was baptized, but he never professed Christianity nor practiced law. Instead, he became a free-lance journalist in Munich and, bedeviled by a series of unsatisfactory love affairs, wrote some of the most delicate love lyrics in the language.

Finally, he was forced to flee Germany because he drew the hostile attention of the authorities when he published a satiric pamphlet anatomizing the structure of the nobility with a scathing precision unmatched in German polemics.

Heine went to France and there found an atmosphere much more hospitable to his radiant talent. He continued to write exquisite poetry and to turn out a body of political satire that ranks with those of Swift. He was extremely happy in Paris. In piece after piece he celebrated the freedom of the human spirit unleashed by the French Revolution. He married a grisette and they lived a stormy joyous life together.

Then, in the flower of his career, he was struck down by a disease of the spine that slowly paralyzed and blinded him. He spent the last ten years of his life on a mattress in a garret, but his bitter humor was indomitable.

"I am no longer a joyous, somewhat corpulent, Hellenist," he wrote. "I am now a poor, fatally ill Jew, an emaciated picture of woe, an unhappy man." And then, just before he died, he delivered himself of his classic mot: "God will forgive me: c'est son métier [it is his business]."

From his work we have selected some fragments from his diaries and his "confessions," including samples of his powerful writings about Judaism.

Fragments

ON GOD

When I was a child, the beginning and the end of all my thoughts were concerned with God. What is God? what is His nature? even as a small child I asked: What is God like? what does he look like? At that time I could spend whole days looking up at the sky and in the evening I was quite disconsolate, that I had not sighted the most holy countenance of God, but had seen only the silly grimaces of the grey clouds. I grew entirely bemused by all the information learned from astronomy, which subject even the smallest child was not spared in that period of enlightenment. I could not get over the wonder of it, that all these thousands of millions of stars were great and beautiful globes, like our own, and that one simple God ruled over all these gleaming myriads of worlds. Once in a dream, I remember, I saw God, in the farthest distance of the high heavens. He was gazing contentedly out of a little window of heaven, a pious old face with a little Jewish beard; He was scattering handfuls of seeds, which as they fell from heaven opened out, as it were, in the immeasurable space, and grew to tremendous size, until they finally became bright, flourishing, inhabited worlds, each one as large as our own. I have never been able to forget this face; I often saw this cheerful old man in my dreams again, scattering the seeds of worlds out of His tiny window: I once even saw Him cluck with His lips, just as our maid used to do when she gave the hens their barley. I could only see the falling seeds, always expanding to vast shining globes: but the great hens, which were possibly lying in wait somewhere with wide-open beaks, to be fed with these world-spheres, those I could never see.

ON LIVING AND DYING

It is not merely what we have done, not merely the posthumous fruit of our activity, that entitles us to honourable recognition after death, but also our striving itself, and especially our unsuccessful striving—the shipwrecked, fruitless, but great-souled *Will* to do.

I was young and proud, and it still further raised my vanity to learn from Hegel that, not as my grandmother supposed, God who lived in heaven, but I myself here on earth, was the real God.

I have the most peaceable disposition. My desires are a modest cottage with a thatched roof, but a good bed, good fare, fresh milk and butter, flowers by my window and a few fine trees before the door. And if the Lord wished to fill my cup of happiness, he would grant me the pleasure of seeing some six or seven of my enemies hanged on those trees. With a heart moved to pity, I would, before their death, forgive the injuries they had done me during their lives. Yes, we ought to forgive our enemies, but not until they are hanged.

You know the decree of the German Diet of December, 1835, which completely interdicted me from literary activity. I wept like a child! I had taken so much trouble with the German language, with the accusative and dative cases; I had learned to string the words together so beautifully, like pearls; I was beginning to find pleasure in this occupation, which shortened the long winter evenings of my exile. Yea, when I wrote in German, I almost fancied myself at home again, beside my mother. And now all writing is positively forbidden me!

ON HISTORY AND LETTERS

Literary history is a great morgue where all seek the dead ones whom they love, or to whom they are related.

The bottles became emptier and the heads of the company fuller. One bellowed like an ox, a second piped, a third declaimed "The Crime," a fourth spoke Latin, a fifth preached temperance, and a sixth . . . lectured: "Gentlemen, the world is a round cylinder upon which human beings, as individual pieces, are scattered, apparently at random. But the cylinder revolves, the pieces knock together and give out tones, some very frequently and others but seldom; all of which causes a remarkably complicated sound which is generally known as universal history."

ON THE JEWS

How small Sinai appears when Moses stands upon it! This mountain is only the pedestal for the feet of the man whose head reaches up to the heavens, where he speaks with God. Formerly I could not pardon the legislator of the Jews his hatred against the plastic arts. I did not see that, notwithstanding his hostility to art, Moses was a great artist, and possessed the true artistic spirit. But this spirit was directed by him, as by his Egyptian compatriots, to colossal and indestructible undertakings. He built human pyramids, carved human obelisks; he took a poor shepherd family and created a nation from it—a great, eternal, holy people; a people of God, destined to outlive the centuries, and to serve as a pattern to all other nations, even as a prototype to the whole of mankind. He created Israel.

As of the master-builder, so of his work —the Hebrew people—I did not speak with sufficient reverence. I see now that the Greeks were only handsome youths, whilst the Jews were always men—powerful, indomitable men—who have fought and suffered on every battlefield of human thought.

152

ON THE BIBLE

It is strange! during my whole life I have been strolling through the various festive halls of philosophy, I have participated in all the orgies of the intellect, I have coquetted with every possible system, without being satisfied, like Messalina after a riotous night; and now, after all this, I suddenly find myself on the same platform whereon stands Uncle Tom. That platform is the Bible, and I kneel by the side of my dusky brother in faith with the same devotion.

What humiliation! With all my learning, I have got no farther than the poor ignorant negro who can hardly spell! It is even true that poor Uncle Tom appears to see in the holy book more profound things than I, who am not yet quite clear, especially in regard to the second part.

At an earlier period, when philosophy possessed for me a paramount interest, I prized Protestantism only for its services in winning freedom of thought. Now I chiefly honour Protestantism for its services in the discovery and propagation of the Bible. I say 'discovery,' for the Jews, who had preserved the Bible from the great conflagration of the sacred temple, and all through the Middle Ages carried it about with them like a portable fatherland, kept their treasure carefully concealed in their ghettos. Here came by stealth German scholars, the predecessors and originators of the Reformation, to study the Hebrew language and thus acquire the key to the casket wherein the precious treasure was enclosed.

Such a scholar was the worthy Reuchlin; and his enemies, the Hochstratens, in Cologne, who are represented as the party of darkness, and ignorance, were by no means such simpletons. On the contrary, they were far-sighted inquisitors, who foresaw clearly the disasters which a familiar acquaintance with the Holy Scriptures would bring on the Church. Hence the persecuting zeal with which they sought to destroy the Hebrew writings, at the same time inciting the rabble to exterminate the Jews, the interpreters of these writings. Now that the motives of their actions are known, we see that, properly considered, each was in the right. This reactionary party believed that the spiritual salvation of the world was endangered, and that all means, falsehood as well as murder, were justifiable, especially against the Jews. The lower classes, pinched by poverty, and heirs of the primeval curse, were embittered against the Jews because of the wealth they had amassed; and what to-day is called the hate of the proletariat against the rich, was then called hate against the Jews. In fact, as the latter were excluded from all ownership of land and from every trade, and relegated to dealing in money and merchandise, they were condemned by law to be rich, hated, and murdered. Such murders, it is true, were in those days committed under the mantle of religion, and the cry was: 'We must kill those who once killed our God.'

To the observant thinker it is a wonderful spectacle to view the countries where the Bible, since the Reformation, has been exerting its elevating influence on the inhabitants, and has impressed on them the customs, modes of thought, and temperaments which formerly prevailed in Palestine, as portrayed both in the Old and in the New Testament. In the Scandinavian and Anglo-Saxon sections of Europe and America, especially among the Germanic races, and also to a certain extent in Celtic countries, the customs of Palestine have been reproduced in so marked a degree that we seem to be in the midst of the ancient Judean life. Take, for example, the Scotch Protestants: are not they Hebrews, whose names even are biblical, whose very cant smacks of the Phariseeism of ancient Jerusalem, and whose religion is naught else than a pork-eating Judaism? It is the same in Denmark and in certain provinces of North Germany, not to mention the majority of the new sects of the United States, among whom the life depicted in the Old Testament is pedantically aped.

The readiness with which these races have adopted the Judaic life, customs, and modes of thought is, perhaps, not entirely attributable to their susceptibility of culture. The cause of this phenomenon is, perhaps, to be sought in the character of the Jewish people, which always had a marked elective affinity with the character of the Germanic, and also to a certain extent with that of the Celtic races. Judea has always seemed to me like a fragment of the Occident misplaced in the Orient. In fact, with its spiritual faith, its severe, chaste, even ascetic customs—in short, with its abstract inner life—this land and its people always offered the most marked contrasts to the population of neighbouring countries, who, with their luxuriantly varied and fervent nature of worship, passed their existence in a Bacchantic dance of the senses.

At a time when, in the temples of Babylon, Ninevah, Sidon, and Tyre, bloody and unchaste rites were celebrated, the description of which, even now, makes our hair stand on end, Israel sat under its fig-trees, piously chanting the praises of the invisible God, and exercised virtue and righteousness. When we think of these surroundings we cannot sufficiently admire the early greatness of Israel.

No Socialist was more of a terrorist than our Lord and Saviour. Even Moses was such a Socialist; although, like a practical man, he attempted only to reform existing usages concerning property.

Moses did not seek to abolish the right of property; on the contrary, it was his wish that every one should possess property, so that no one might be tempted by poverty to become a bondsman and thus acquire slavish propensities. Slavery itself, he bitterly, almost fiercely, hated; but even this barbarous institution he could not entirely destroy. It was rooted so deeply in the customs of that ancient time that he was compelled to confine his efforts to ameliorating by law the condition of the slaves.

But if a slave thus eventually freed by process of law declined to depart from the house of bondage, then, according to the command of

Moses, the incorrigibly servile, worthless scamp was to be nailed by the ear to the gate of his master's house, and after being thus publicly exposed in this disgraceful manner, he was condemned to lifelong slavery. Oh, Moses! our teacher, Rabbi Moses! exalted foe of all slavishness! give me hammer and nails that I may nail to the gate of Brandenburg our complacent, long-eared slaves in liveries of black, red, and gold.

HEINE IN PARIS

How many amusing things did I behold on my arrival in Paris! I visited all the chief resorts of public pleasure, and saw all the notable caricatures of the Capital. The serious and grave Frenchmen were the most amusing. I saw Arnal, Bouffé, Déjazet, Debureau, Odry, Mademoiselle Georges, the big pot on the Palace of the Invalides, the exhibition of the dead in the Morgue, and the French Academy. The latter, that is, the Academy, is a nursery for aged men of letters, in their second childhood—a truly philanthropic institution, the idea of which is taken from the Hindoos, who provide hospitals for aged and decrepit apes. The roof of the building, which protects the venerable heads of the members of the Institution—I speak of the French Academy and not of the Indian hospitals— consists of a great dome resembling an enormous marble periwig. I can never behold this poor old periwig without recalling the witticisms of the many men of genius who have made merry at the expense of the Academy, which, however, has not on that account ceased to exist. It is not correct therefore to say that in France ridicule kills. Of course I did not fail to visit the necropolis of the Luxembourg, where there is a complete collection of the mummies of perjury, so carefully embalmed that one may still read on their countenances the false oaths they swore to all the dynasties of French Pharaohs. In the Jardin des Plantes, I saw the palace of the real apes, the three-legged goat, and the giraffe, with which last I was specially entertained. I did not go to hear the grand opera, because I had come to Paris for amusement.

I must expressly contradict the rumour that the return to a personal God has brought me to the threshold of any Church, much less led me into its fold. No; my religious convictions and opinions have remained free from all sectarianism; I have been enticed by no church bell, I have been dazzled by no altar lights. I have coquetted with no symbolism, and I have not utterly renounced my reason. I have abjured nothing, not even my old heathen gods, from whom I have, it is true, turned aside, though parting from them in love and friendship. It was in May 1848, on the last occasion on which I went out-of-doors, that I bade farewell to the lovely idols that I had worshipped in the days of my prosperity. Painfully did I drag my limbs to the Louvre, and I almost fell into a swoon as I entered the splendid hall where the blessed goddess of beauty, our dear Lady of Milo, stands on her pedestal. Long time did I lie at her feet, weeping so bitterly that a stone must have had pity on me. And the goddess looked down on me with compassion, yet it was a compassion without comfort, as though she would say: "See'st thou not that I have no arms, and so cannot give thee help?"

Heinrich Graetz (1817–1891)

By common consent, Heinrich Graetz ranks with the world's greatest historians. He was undoubtedly the greatest Jewish historian since Flavius Josephus, some 1800 years before. Graetz's great work is the monumental History of the Jews, *the first of whose eleven volumes appeared in 1853 and the last in 1875.*

Although Graetz was German, he was not a "scientific" historian; he tended to dëemphasize economic and social factors. His approach is epic, poetic, his flow of language as eloquent as Michelet's. His History of the Jews *is a great saga whose themes are suffering, faith, learning and resurrection.*

The Secret of Israel's Immortality

Combine all the woes that temporal and ecclesiastical tyrannies have ever inflicted on men or nations, and you will not have reached the full measure of suffering which this martyr people was called upon to endure century upon century. It was as if all the powers of earth had conspired—and they did so conspire—to exterminate the Jewish people, or at least to transform it into a brutalised horde. History dare not pass over in silence these scenes of well-nigh unutterable misery. It is her duty to give a true and vivid account of them; to evoke due admiration for the superhuman endurance of this suffering people, and to testify that Israel, like his ancestor in the days of old, has striven with gods and with men, and has prevailed.

What has prevented this constantly migrating people, this veritable Wandering Jew, from degenerating into brutalised vagabonds, into vagrant hordes of gipsies? The answer is at hand. In its journey through the desert of life, for eighteen centuries, the Jewish people carried along the Ark of the Covenant, which breathed into its heart ideal aspirations, and even illumined the badge of disgrace affixed to its garment with an apostolic glory. The proscribed, outlawed, universally persecuted Jew felt a sublime, noble pride in being singled out to perpetuate and to suffer for a religion which reflects eternity, by which the nations of the earth were gradually educated to a knowledge of God and morality, and from which is to spring the salvation and redemption of the world.

Such a people, which disdains its present but has the eye steadily fixed on its future, which lives as it were on hope, is on that very account eternal, like hope.

The Babylonian Captivity

In the Babylonian captivity, Israel was obliged "to hold forth his body to be flogged, and his beard to be plucked." The haughty conqueror told him already at that time, "Kneel down that I may crush thee," and he acquired the endurance of seeing "his body exposed to the feet of his oppressors." The school of suffering, oppression, hatred, contempt, scorn, flogging, ill-usage and misapprehensions, which the Jewish race was to undergo at a later period, even through many centuries, and which impressed her history with tragical appearance, all this commenced during the Babylonian captivity.

But just amid these innumerable sufferings there rose a circle of ardent adherents to the God of Israel, whose hope in a brighter future never ceased. These were the "men of endurance," who suspended their harps on the willows and would not sing Zion's song in a foreign country. A few Judean servants of the court, and the eunuchs who kept the Sabbath and adhered to the Israelitish covenant, were likewise of this order. This then was the precious kernel of the "indestructible bone" from which the rejuvenescence proceeded.

But how was this wonderful fact, so rich in consequences, and showing its after-effect even unto this day, brought about? It proceeded from a single person, who certainly was a God-fearing man, and who understood the signs of the times in order to adopt the right plan, whose powerful and inspired voice was well calculated to transform depression into courage, despair into hope, timidity into confidence, indifference into participation, and even lethargy into sensibility. The pencil of history has not preserved the name of this prophet, and, therefore, he is commonly called the Babylonian or exiled Isaiah.

As soon as the historical work was undergoing a fresh change by the hand of the daring but mild conqueror, Cyrus, who led his strength of Media and Persia against the all-governing Chaldaic Babylonian kingdom, the exiled Isaiah sounded the word Zion! giving it an inimitable magic, so as to make it vibrate in the innermost recesses of the people's hearts. He represented Jerusalem as a widow shrouded in mourning, who had drained the cup of sorrow to the dregs. "She is the unhappy, distracted, disconsolate widow, who has borne so long the shame of being childless." He foretold a speedy redemption

through "Koresh" (Cyrus), whom God has called and chosen, and to whom He will impart strength in his conquests.

Israel, however, should not enter upon the approaching redemption in a state of contamination, but should merit the same through self-excellence and nobleness of mind. He should undo the knots of malice, loosen the fetters of slavery, discharge the oppressed from servitude, bestow bread on the hungry, give shelter to the suffering poor, clothe the naked, and not to turn away from the afflicted kinsmen of his own race. Then shall the light of Israel rise Aurora-like, and his cure will speedily be brought about. Israel's heavy afflictions were conceived by the great prophet of the exile in a very high point of view. The painful martyrdom was requisite for his cure. Not only Israel himself, but also the sinful world of heathenism, shall be expiated thereby.

No one better conceived and represented Israel's ideal vocation than did Isaiah. The Jewish nation is the apostle whom God sends to the idolatrous, wicked, morally corrupted world. The sorrowful, despised, crushed and servile form is called for a higher purpose, just on account of its suffering condition. The crown of thorns which this Messianic race bears so patiently makes her worthy of a kingly diadem.

The exiled prophet quickened the minds of his contemporaries in regard to another matter. "The neighbours, the strangers, the sons of heathenism shall not say the Lord will separate us from His people. But the strangers who will join Him, to serve Him, to love Him and to be His servants, He will rather lead them to His holy mountain, for His Temple will be a house of prayer for all nations." Under this inspiration the people consented to be aroused unto a resurrection.

The apparently dry bones moved one unto the other, became covered with flesh and skin, and took within them the breath of life. The circle of the "ardent men of the word of God" became larger day by day. The more Cyrus approached the Chaldean capital, the more did the hope revive of the recovery of the lost independence and nationality. The "Eunuchs" of the tribe of Judea, the descendants of the house of David, Zerubabel, "the strangers," who joined Judea from pure love of God, became all very active to realise the words of the prophet. Self-examination soon began; and the idolatry, with which many exiles were still affected, was thoroughly and forever abolished. As soon as Cyrus made an end to the Babylonian kingdom, he in a wonderful manner fulfilled the hopes of the exiles by proclaiming: "Whoever is willing to return to Jerusalem is permitted to do so." There were above 40,000 families who resolved upon returning home, at the head of whom moved a king's son of the family of David, and a high-priest of the house of Aaron. This small number formed a state once more, producing again its heroes—heroes of the sword and intellect—who became noted in name and in deed even unto the whole world. This small number has poured its healthy and nourishing sap into the veins of mankind.

Kaufmann Kohler (1843–1926)

In 1875, a debate was raging between those, who believed in the metaphysical reality of God, and the adherents of the new doctrine of Darwinism. When we read some of the arguments by professional religionists of the time they seem impoverished of ideas; in that debate, the evolutionists massacred the clergy. However, there was a rabbi named Kaufmann Kohler who devoted a sermon to that topic which still stands today as a remarkable piece of reasoning. He accepted the process of evolution, declaring that religious ideas themselves were constantly evolving, but rejected the concept that blind determinism is the source of human identity.

Rabbi Kohler was particularly equipped to confront the scientific spirit. He, himself, was a religious rationalist. The dominant figure in Reform Judaism in America in the late nineteenth and early twentieth centuries, he took the classic liberal position on theology, affirming the ethics of Judaism, its meliorism, its optimism and its activist habit. This sermon pivots upon the brilliant theme that evolution is compatible with religion because God reveals himself in endless forms of matter and in species of consciousness. It is recognized as a masterpiece of eloquence and precision.

Evolution and Religion

What is Evolution? To put it in fewest and plainest words: The things around about us and the ideas within us have not, as was the belief hitherto, been created and fixed by single creative acts of God, but have all along been and are still growing and developing from lower to ever higher and more complicated forms. Not only suns and stars, plant and animal life of all shape and size, but the speech, the conscience and reason we possess, and the religion we own, have been and are in constant process of growth, ever changing, moving, shifting. Of course, it is asked: What becomes of the divine sanctity of religion, of the authority and influence of morality, if the conscience is, as our evolutionists say, the product of society rather than the voice of the heavenly judge?

Let me, in answer to this, state that in these evolution doctrines there is a great deal of philosophical error mixed with the scientific truth. When Darwin first struck upon that grand idea of evolution, he staunchly held and asserted the belief in a divine creator. Only when, in search of the mechanical forces operating in response to the creative fiat, he after long scientific observation arrived at the conception of the "survival of the fittest in the great struggle for existence," the spectacle of that great fierce warfare carried on throughout the universe so bewildered him that he lost sight of the sublime Leader of Hosts marshalling all these forces from behind the scene. Yet does not each victory tell of a triumphant idea? Does the interacting of all these wheels within wheels in the great fabric of life not sufficiently betray the all-surveying Master-Mind? Chance will never drive your vessel into the safe harbor when left to the sway of wave and wind. There must be a captain at the helm somewhere to move and guide it. And whether you trace the oak tree to the acorn, and the hen to the egg, or not, time alone produces nothing unless there is a sperm that promises the future growth. Evolution accounts only for the *How*, not for the *What*. Far from excluding, it includes and necessitates a designing intellect at the start, and a great and holy moral purpose at the end. Instead of alienating us from God, it brings us right face to face with God; for we see Him steadily at work fashioning worlds and lives without number here and carving out new destinies for all beings there. In fact, evolution, as I conceive it, is the unfolding of divine life, the unbroken revelation of God first in endless varieties of *matter*, then in marvellous productions of the conscious *mind*.

And since matter and mind emanate from the same God, why should the lines not merge? If man forms the pinnacle of evolution, the blossom and fruit of earth-life, the sanctuary of the mind, why should there be no root, no threshold, no court-yard leading to the holy?

There is one little word in the human vocabulary which eludes the scientist's crucible. He cannot reduce it to mere chemical affinity or to animal sensation of pleasure or pain. It is the word *Ought*. Whether high up among the most civilized, or far down among the lower types of life, you find man always measuring his steps by duty's rule, by a voice heard calling: Thou oughtst and thou oughtst not! The voice of conscience may err, the judgment may mislead; but the judging and dictating power is there, not as the power of human society, but as its original and everlasting shaping power. Morality made man, not man morality. I am sure no evolutionist dares say: Truth is the invention of man. It is there from eternity, waiting for the human mind to grasp it, just as the flower waits for the light to give it life and beauty. Not all the people of the world can change the simple arithmetical fact and make twice two five instead of four. Neither can they declare theft and murder to be right, and honesty wrong. They may, as savage tribes do, misapply the rules, and for instance, allow theft or murder under certain conditions to be committed where we from a higher standpoint cannot: but they cannot change them. Morality, as a principle, is eternal like truth.

Need I then ask you which of the two is the higher conception of God: the one which has man fashioned by God of a piece of clay as by a potter and equipped with all the faculties of heart and mind befitting the Divine Mold, and then allowing him from his high station in Paradise to fall so low in intellect and manners as to become next-door neighbor to the orang-outang? Or the one which makes star and flower, worm and ape sigh for the moment when, as the highest and the most fitted in the scale of beings, man at last emerges with the conscious longing after a better state of things, which enables him to grope and work his way up into an ever nobler and finer stature until the Divine Life, unfolded all along, is mirrored in his world-encompassing mind and

heart? Yes, man *is* in the image of God; only that
is dimly felt or seen at the base, and grows ever
brighter and grander the nearer it reaches the top.

I think evolution offers a religion of
hope, of life grander than any other system. It accounts better for all our errors and failings, for
the shortcomings of our moral and religious life,
for the very evils that surround us within or from
without. As it took all the notes on the key-board
to discover the law of harmony and arrive at the
true secret of music, so man had first to learn the
letters of the alphabet of morals before the true
name of God could be spelled out. Neither the

Decalogue nor the Bible presents a complete code of ethics. They only drew the outline, they laid the foundation to the world's morality. Justice begins with: Thou shalt not! Love whispers: Thou shalt! The warning against sin and vice in one age leads to the practice of virtue in the next. Conditional toleration of polygamy, slavery and retaliation by the Mosaic law points to the recognition of the higher dignity of man and woman, of the sanctity of human life arrived at by later Judaism and Christianity. And what are all the conceptions of reward and punishment, what the notions of heaven and hell but symbols and suggestions of a celestial justice, leading to the realization of a higher righteousness? Judaism, the Bible, all the given religions are but evolutions of morality.

The Soul Thou Hast Given Me Is Pure

Here, from another sermon, is a characteristically lucid and enlightening statement of the Judaic conception of God's relation to man.

Next to God's unity, the most essential and characteristic doctrine of Judaism is that concerning God's relation to man. Heathenism degraded man by making him kneel before brutes and the works of his hand: Judaism declared man to be made in the image of God, the crown and culmination of God's creation, the appointed ruler of the earth. In him, as the end of Creation, the earthly and the divine are singularly blended.

Judaism rejects the idea of an inherent impurity in the flesh or in matter as opposed to the spirit. Nor does Judaism accept the doctrine of Original Sin. In the words of the daily morning prayer, "The soul that Thou hast given me is pure, Thou hast created it, Thou hast fashioned it, and Thou hast breathed it into me, and Thou preservest it within me, and at the appointed time Thou wilt take it from me to return it within me in the future."

V
VISION
AND ACTION

The pursuit of knowledge for its own sake, an almost
fanatical love of justice, and the desire for personal
independence—these are the features of the Jewish
tradition which make me thank my stars
that I belong to it.

Albert Einstein

Introduction

In classic Jewish thinking an idea is a program. The Mosaic Law, for instance, does not expound upon the sanctity of human life; it states simply, "Thou shalt not kill." The raging of the Prophets was directed against evil conduct. The great Talmudic teachers always capped their speculations with edicts. Thought was a plan for behavior, action a reflex of vision. It is strange that this enormous talent for metaphysics expressed itself so practically—or, perhaps, it is a comment on ourselves that we think it strange.

In any case, the habit of programmatic thinking never ceased. The 19th century produced Jewish thinkers who changed the map of the 20th century and, perhaps more significantly, redrew man's inner frontiers. The 19th century produced Marx, Herzl, Freud. These explosive theorists, working at first in complete obscurity and in desperate alienation from their fellow men, made marks on little pieces of paper that, after a season of dark gestation, moved men to incredible efforts —and changed the world forever.

Theodor Herzl (1860–1904)

Without challenge, Theodor Herzl is the most important political figure in modern Jewish history. And as events unfold, he emerges as one of the most important figures in all modern history. His was the first viable vision of a Jewish state—one that would be founded in Palestine, would organize itself as a political entity and would draw within its borders Jews from all over the world.

His pamphlet Der Judenstaat *(The Jewish State) hit the international Jewish community like a nuclear bomb. We are still feeling its fallout today. He was no mere ideologue; he was a political genius. For him vision was action. Around his burning dream of a Jewish state that would end the age-old degradation of his people he organized a political movement. He raised funds and badgered any power that could help—rich Jews, the German Kaiser, the British Prime Minister and the Turkish Sultan. He was indefatigable. He cared nothing for rank. He judged people only by what they could do to help form the Jewish State. One week he would be in Rome arguing with the Pope; the next week in some miserable little corner of Whitechapel in London, he was trying to persuade an Orthodox rabbi that the Jews could do something to help themselves before the actual arrival of the Messiah. Then he was off to Paris to dun a doubting Rothschild.*

Like Moses, Herzl was to see the great work begun, but not finished. Worn out by his labors and by opposition from much of the world, including a large segment of his fellow Jews, he died of a heart attack in Austria in 1904 at the age of 44. Thirty-five years later his coffin was reburied on a mountain west of Jerusalem, renamed Mt. Herzl.

The following selections have been culled from a number of Herzl's works. In the first section, we see the progression of his ideas as they develop from the first concept of Zionism until his pamphlet The Jewish State *appeared. Combined with these selections are entries from his diary—fascinating glimpses into the man's soul as he struggled to arm his vision. The second section is from his book* Altneuland, *a remarkable document in which he*

visualized the Jewish State as already having been estab-
lished, and wrote of it as if he were actually living there,
describing places, people and institutions. When we read
it now and consider the established state of Israel, we see
that he was writing prophecy—and incredibly accurate
prophecy.

The Struggle and the Dream

I have been pounding away for some time at a work of tremendous magnitude. It bears the aspect of a mighty dream. For days and weeks it has saturated me; it goes with me everywhere, hovers behind my ordinary talk, overwhelms and intoxicates me. What will come of it is still too early to say. However, I have had experience enough to tell me that even as a dream it is remarkable and should be written down—if not as a memorial for mankind, then for my own pleasure and meditation in years to come. If no action comes out of this romancing, a Romance at least will come out of this activity.

What dreams, thoughts, correspondence, meetings, activities I shall have to encompass—what disappointments if I fail, what grim struggles if I succeed. They must be seized and committed to paper.

In these times, so progressive in most respects, we know ourselves to be surrounded by the old, old hatred. Anti-Semitism is the up-to-date designation of the movement. The first impression which it made on modern Jews was one of astonishment, then it gave way to pain and resentment. Perhaps our enemies are quite unaware how deeply they wounded the sensibilities of just those of us who were possibly not the primary object of their attack. That very part of Jewry that had outgrown the ghetto and lost the habit of petty trading was pierced to the heart.

Far and near Jew hatred springs up. No civilised country lies so far to the West that it has not echoed to this ancient hue and cry; no semi-civilisation is so backward that it has not acquired the newest forms and catchwords. Suddenly a mob will rush through the streets and flames will consume Jewish property, and sometimes its owners as well.

We must roam the whole of the earth's surface to find a spot where God's ancient people is not cursed and persecuted.

Misery has swept over Jewry like a tidal wave. Those who have lived in the depths have been submerged. If the inhabitants of higher, more protected spots deny the truth of this shocking fact they are not doing credit to their insight or to their hearts.

We are probably as much hated for our gifts as for our faults.

We are what we were made in the ghetto.

We have honestly tried to submerge ourselves everywhere in the surrounding communities and to preserve only the faith of our fathers. We are not permitted to do so. In countries where we have already lived for centuries, we are still proclaimed strangers: often by those whose ancestors were not yet in the land when our forefathers were already sighing there.

Oppression and persecution cannot exterminate us. Jew-baiting has caused only our weaklings to fall away. Strong Jews stubbornly return to their stem when persecution breaks out.

The national personality of the Jews neither can, will, nor need be destroyed. It cannot be because external foes hold it together. It will not be; this it has shown during 2000 years of appalling suffering. It need not be; and this I am trying to prove once more in this pamphlet.

There is the proposal of assimilation as a solution of the Jewish question. Assimilation by intermarriage, so that the small stream of our race may be merged and lost in the broad stream of peoples among whom they live. Suppose the Jews were willing—a very large supposition—how is it to be imagined that people who will not

174

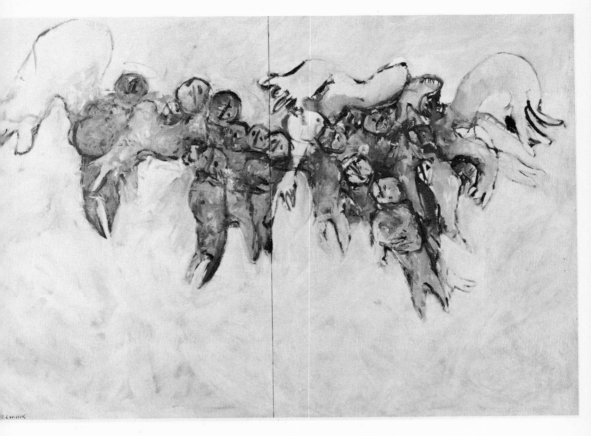

put up with us as neighbours will become allied to us as members of our families?

I am arguing this matter on the presumption that our people were willing to intermarry. But there is nothing the great body and bulk of our people hold to more strongly than the sentiment as to marriage. Intermarriage is not regarded with aversion even by the most Orthodox, so long as the person contracting a marriage with a Jew or Jewess becomes also a Jew or a Jewess.

I myself was an assimilated Jew, and I speak from experience. I think the Jews have rather a natural tendency to assimilate. There arrives a moment when they are well on the way. And then just at that moment comes anti-Semitism.

The Jews of Eastern Europe cannot stay where they are. Where are they to go? If you find that they are not wanted here, then some place must be found to which they can migrate

175

without by that migration raising the problems that confront them here. These problems will not arise if a home be found which will be legally recognised as Jewish.

One of the major battles I shall have to wage will be against the Jewish spirit of scoffing. The spirit represents at bottom the impotent attempt of prisoners to give themselves the air of being free men. That is why their mockery touches me so closely. For the present there is no helping the Jews. If someone showed them the Promised Land they would scoff at him. For they are demoralised.

We shall have to sink still lower, we shall have to be more widely insulted, spat upon, mocked, beaten, robbed and slain before we are ripe for the idea.

At present we shall have to swallow the affronts; in high society, where we try to push our way; among the middle classes, the economic squeeze, and at the bottom layer, the most horrible misery.

We are not yet desperate enough. So a rescuer is greeted with laughter. Laughter?—no, smiles. We no longer have the strength to laugh.

I think the Jewish Question is neither a social nor a religious one, although it may likewise take these and other forms. It is a national question, which can be solved only by making it a political world-question to be dealt with by the civilised nations of the world in council.

I will give you my definition of a nation, and you can add the adjective "Jewish." A nation is a historical group of men of a recognisable cohesion held together by a common enemy. That is in my view a nation. Then if you add to that the word "Jewish" you have what I understand to be the Jewish nation. And the common enemy is the anti-Semite.

I believe that a generation of wondrous Jews will grow forth from the earth. The Maccabeans will rise again. The Jews who so de-

sire will have their State. Let us live as free men on our own soil, and die peacefully in our own Homeland. The world will be freed by our liberty, enriched by our wealth, magnified by our greatness.

Those of us who are today prepared to hazard our lives for the cause would regret having raised a finger, if we were able to organise only a new social system and not a more righteous one.

It is true that we aspire to our ancient land. But what we want in that ancient land is a new blossoming of the Jewish spirit.

Jewry is a tremendous tenement of misery, with branches all over the world. These are the things which we want to change for the better. We believe that salvation is to be found in wholesome work in a beloved land.

It is more and more to the interest of the civilised nations and of civilisation in general that a cultural station be established on the shortest road to Asia. Palestine is this station, and we

Jews are the bearers of culture who are ready to give our property and our lives to bring about its creation.

The site which is suited for our use is of a peculiar nature. No spot on earth has been so coveted as this, and many nations desired it so intensely that the ardour of their longing dried it up. We, however, believe that this desolate corner of the Orient has, like us, not only a past but a future. On that soil, where so little grows at present, there grew ideas for all mankind. And for that very reason nobody can deny that there is a deathless relation between our people and that land.

We have everything in abundance—people, material, plans. We need nothing more than a site!

But I am convinced that those Jews who stand aside today with a malicious smile and with their hands in their trousers' pockets will also want to dwell in our beautiful home.

We are organising Jewry for its coming destiny.

Although I now appeal to reason, I am fully aware that reason alone will not suffice. Old prisoners do not willingly leave their cells. We shall see whether the youth we require are at our command; the youth who sweep the old along, carry them forward on powerful arms and transform rational considerations into enthusiasm.

Great things need no solid foundation. An apple must be put on a table so that it will not fall. The earth floats in mid-air. Similarly, I may be able to found and stabilise the Jewish State without any firm support.

My five hundred copies [Jewish State] came this evening. When I had the bundle carted to my room I trembled violently. The great decision stands wrapped up in this bundle. From here on, my life will perhaps take a new turn. The most remarkable of all things is when a man never gives up.

When the Future Arrives:
A Vision

Only we Jews could have done it. We only were in a position to create this New Society, this new center of civilisation here. One thing dove-tailed into another. It could have come only through us, through our destiny. Our moral sufferings were as much a necessary element as our commercial experience and our cosmopolitanism.

Great ships lay anchored in the roadstead between Acco and the foot of the Carmel. Behind this fleet the noble curve of the Bay. At its northern end, the gray fortress walls, heavy cupolas and slender minarets of Acco. To the south, below the ancient city of Haifa, splendid things had grown up. Thousands of white villas gleamed out of luxuriant green gardens. All the way from Acco to Mount Carmel stretched what seemed to be one great port. The mountain itself, also, was crowned with beautiful structures.

A magnificent city had been built beside the sapphire-blue Mediterranean. The magnificent stone dams showed the harbour for what it was: the safest and most convenient port in the eastern Mediterranean. Craft of every shape and size, flying the flags of all the nations, lay sheltered there.

The hillsides everywhere were cultivated up to the very summits; every bit of soil was exploited. The steep slopes were terraced with vines, pomegranates and fig trees as in the ancient days of Solomon. Numerous tree nurseries bore witness to the intelligent efforts at a forestation of the once barren tracts. Pines and cypresses on the ridges of the hills towered against the blue sky.

The Old City within the walls had altered least. The Holy Sepulcher, the Mosque of Omar, and other domes and towers had remained the same; but many splendid new structures had been added. That magnificent new edifice was the Peace Palace. A vast calm brooded over the Old City.

Outside the walls the picture was altogether different. Jerusalem was not a twentieth century metropolis. What was that wonderful structure of white and gold, whose roof rested on a whole forest of marble columns with gilt capitals? That is the Temple!

Those [Arabs] who had nothing stood to lose nothing and could only gain. And they did gain: Opportunities to work, means of livelihood, prosperity. Nothing could have been more wretched than an Arab village at the end of the nineteenth century. The peasants' clay hovels were unfit for stables. Now everything is different.

The Promised Land. Where at last we can live as free men on our own soil, and where we can die tranquilly in our own homeland. Where we can expect the reward of honour for great deeds; where we shall live at peace with all the world, which we have freed through our own freedom, enriched by our wealth, and made greater by our greatness.

When I remember thee in days to come, O Jerusalem, it will not be with delight. The musty deposits of 2000 years of inhumanity, intolerance, and foulness lie in your reeking alleys. The one man who has been present here all the while, the lovable dreamer of Nazareth, has done nothing but increase the hate.

The New Society did not care whether a man sought the eternal verities in a temple, church or a mosque, in an art museum or at a philharmonic concert.

We are a commonwealth. In form it is new, but in purpose very ancient. Our aim is mentioned in the First Book of Kings: "Judah and Israel shall dwell securely, each man under his own vine and fig tree, from Dan to Beersheba."

The New Society is not a state, but a large cooperative association. The cooperative association with an infinite ideal.

We see a new and happy form of human society here. What created it?

Necessity!
The reunited people.
Knowledge!
Will Power!
The Forces of Nature!
Mutual Tolerance!
Self-Confidence!
Love and Pain!
God!

Sigmund Freud (1856–1939)

This Viennese doctor—loathed by the local medical association, abhorred by the Christian community and profoundly regretted by the rabbinate—is now recognized as one of the four key thinkers of modern times, one of the creators of the contemporary consciousness. (The other three are Darwin, Marx and Einstein; Darwin's inclusion, of course, being testimony to the nonexclusion policy of the Jews.) Freud is the father of psychoanalysis. Those alienated by the lifeless jargon which has grown like a fungus about his concepts, and by the mechanical outlook and methodology of those who have sought in psychoanalysis not a healing technique but a life style, should go to the original works of the master. There they would encounter one of the great minds in the history of the human intellect. He is a bold, original thinker who has gone deeper into the structure of dreams and of man's hidden selves than anyone else who has been preoccupied with the nature of man. It can be argued that he is not really a scientist, but a poet who has constructed incredibly persuasive metaphors for the human condition. Whether scientist or poet, he is unique.

His work has always offended religionists of every breed, since he views religion as a kind of mass neurosis. However, the Jews were especially offended by his book Moses and Monotheism, *in which he advances three key theories: that monotheism was not a Jewish conception but that of the great Pharaoh Ikhnaton; that Moses was not a Jew but an Egyptian prince, a follower of Ikhnaton, who, having fallen out of favor with the ruling*

clique, adopted the Israelites as his people so that he would
have someone to lead; and finally, that the Israelites, having
murdered Moses in the desert and perhaps having eaten
him, were afflicted by a slow remorse that made them
accessible to the word of God.

It is impossible to conceive any set of proposi-
tions more calculated to infuriate religious Jews.

In this same Moses and Monotheism, *there is a*
sharply probing analysis of the psychological roots of anti-
Semitism, conceived in startlingly original terms, which for
all its brevity stands as one of the most enlightening of
such analyses. It is this discussion that we have selected.

Jew-Hatred

The poor Jewish people, who with its usual stiff-necked obduracy continued to deny the murder of their "father," has dearly expiated this in the course of centuries. Over and over again they heard the reproach: "You killed our God." And this reproach is true, if rightly interpreted. It says, in reference to the history of religion: "You won't *admit* that you murdered God" (the archetype of God, the primeval Father, and his reincarnations). Something should be added—namely: "It is true, we did the same thing, but we *admitted* it, and since then we have been purified." Not all accusations with which antisemitism pursues the descendants of the Jewish people are based on such good foundations.

There must, of course, be more than one reason for a phenomenon of such intensity and lasting strength as the popular hatred of Jews. A whole series of reasons can be divined; some of them, which need no interpretation, arise from obvious considerations; others lie deeper and spring from secret sources, which one would regard as the specific motives.

In the first group the most fallacious is the reproach of their being foreigners, since in many places nowadays under the sway of antisemitism the Jews were the oldest constituents of the population or arrived even before the present inhabitants. This is so, for example, in the town of

Cologne, where Jews came with the Romans, before it was colonised by Germanic tribes.

Other grounds for antisemitism are
stronger, as, for example, the circumstance that
Jews mostly live as a minority among other peoples, since the feeling of solidarity of the masses,
in order to be complete, has need of an animosity
against an outside minority, and the numerical
weakness of the minority invites suppression.

Two other peculiarities that the Jews
possess, however, are quite unpardonable. The first
is that in many respects they are different from
their "hosts." Not fundamentally so, since they are
not a foreign Asiatic race, as their enemies maintain, but mostly consist of the remnants of Mediterranean peoples and inherit their culture. Yet
they are different—although sometimes it is hard
to define in what respects—especially from the Nordic peoples, and racial intolerance finds stronger
expression, strange to say, in regard to small differences than to fundamental ones.

The second peculiarity has an even
more pronounced effect. It is that they defy oppression, that even the most cruel persecutions
have not succeeded in exterminating them. On the
contrary, they show a capacity for holding their
own in practical life and, where they are admitted,
they make valuable contributions to the surrounding civilisation.

The deeper motives of antisemitism
have their roots in times long past; they come from
the unconscious, and I am quite prepared to hear
that what I am going to say will at first appear
incredible. I venture to assert that the jealousy
which the Jews evoked in other peoples by maintaining that they were the first-born, favourite
child of God the Father has not yet been overcome
by those others, just as if the latter had given
credence to the assumption.

Furthermore, among the customs
through which the Jews marked off their aloof
position, that of circumcision made a disagreeable,
uncanny impression on others. The explanation
probably is that it reminds them of the dreaded

castration idea and of things in their primeval past which they would fain forget.

Then there is lastly the most recent motive of the series. We must not forget that all the peoples who now excel in the practise of anti-semitism became Christians only in relatively recent times, sometimes forced to it by bloody compulsion. One might say they all are "badly christened"; under the thin veneer of Christianity they have remained what their ancestors were, barbarically polytheistic. They have not yet overcome their grudge against the new religion which was forced on them, and they have projected it on to the source from which Christianity came to them. The fact that the Gospels tell a story which is enacted among Jews, and in truth treats only of Jews, has facilitated such a projection.

The hatred for Judaism is at bottom hatred for Christianity, and it is not surprising that in the German National Socialist revolution this close connection of the two monotheistic religions finds such clear expression in the hostile treatment of both.

Franz Kafka (1883–1924)

Franz Kafka was born in 1883 in Prague—then a part of the Austro-Hungarian Empire. His father was a successful merchant, a burly aggressive man, full of vitality. His mother was gentle and imaginative. There were three younger sisters. Franz was a disappointment to his father; he was puny, withdrawn, full of secret thoughts. He went through school without distinction, then studied for the law, choosing it because all careers were equally uninteresting to him. He knew he would never practice law, and used his education to get a civil service job—something without competitive pressure that he could do with minimum thought. He was a failure even at such jobs and lost two of them before he settled in as a lowly clerk in the State Insurance office. Everything else he did the world could see was a failure, too. He had practically no social life, traveled very little, and when he finally fell in love and became engaged, he was so torn by doubt and misgivings that the engagement was broken off. A few years later he found another girl very much like the first. The outcome was the same. He loved the girl, wanted to marry her—and it came to nothing. They parted.

But all this time, in the secret hours, he had been writing. Very little of this work was published during his lifetime . . . a few stories, a small book of aphorisms called Meditations. *And none of it attracted any attention whatsoever. He had weak lungs. He became tubercular. In 1924, at the age of forty-one, he died, leaving a pile of manuscripts which he had asked his friend, Max Brod, to burn.*

So Kafka's friend was left in a cold little room with a pile of unpublished manuscripts. Among them were three novels, The Trial, The Castle, Amerika, *about twenty short stories and pages full of fragments, any one of which is packed with more originality than most writers can produce in a full lifetime.*

There are writers and writers. Without considering the poor ones, there are the great, the near-great, the excellent. Then there is the kind of writer who is simply a different order of event. When you touch him you touch a radiance. You read him and you are not only entertained, you are possessed. Your life is changed in some way. Kafka is one of these rare artists. For him, writing was not a profession, a trade, a hobby or an esthetic exercise. It was prayer. In his stories and novels, we are confronted with dreams from which we cannot awake. They are a unique reading experience.

Franz Kafka died about ten years before the Nazis came to power in Germany, but he did not have to experience the holocaust to predict it. By the logic of the evil he saw so clearly, from the momentum of that massive indifference which he depicted as the deadliest sin, the Evil Ones had to come. He knew they had to come. He had seen them in his dreams—without costume, without fanfare— tracking him down the endless corridors of an office building, as in The Trial. *He had dreamed of them as little bureaucrats who guarded the throne room in* The Castle *and barred his entrance simply because he wanted very much to go in and their function in life was to deny. He had seen them in his dreams and had written down those dreams, and they became books.* Amerika *is a very strange book written about a land the author had never seen. And yet enormous landscapes, eerily towering buildings, and*

the innocence of the new immigrant who goes looking for a new relationship between man and man and finds only a more brutal violence, a lonelier loneliness, convey the immigrant experience in a way no one else ever has conveyed it. The Castle and The Trial are the most magnificent confrontation of God by man since the Book of Job. Of his three major works, the one Kafka never finished is Amerika. Yet we read it, too, with no sense of incompletion . . . only a dream sense of streets spiraling off into infinity.

Max Brod had to make a decision—and he fortunately chose to deny Kafka's last request. He kept the manuscripts. After many years, they became books—too late for any of Kafka's family to read them. His three sisters and the women he had loved had all been killed. As in his books, they were accused of a nameless crime, were found guilty by invisible judges and were executed by people they did not know. All of them died in a small concentration camp established by the Nazis for the Jews of Prague.

From Kafka's work, we have selected self-sufficient excerpts. The first is from a letter to his father—one of those bundles of papers he had wanted to burn; a letter enormously long, unmailed. It is a remarkable document. It analyzes a father-son relationship in a way that has never been done before or since, and includes what amounts to an indictment of the deadening imposition of superficial religious habits. It is fascinating also because in it are the seeds of those obsessions that entered Kafka's novels and helped to make them immortal.

Letter to My Father

I'm not going to say, of course, that I have become what I am only as a result of your influence. That would be very much exaggerated (and I am indeed inclined to this exaggeration). It is indeed quite possible that even if I had grown up entirely free from your influence I still could not have become a person after your own heart. I should probably have still become a weakly, timid, hesitant, restless person, neither Robert Kafka nor Karl Hermann, but yet quite different from what I really am, and we might have got on with each other excellently. I should have been happy to have you as a friend, as a chief, an uncle, a grandfather, even indeed (though this rather more hesitantly) as a father-in-law. Only as what you are, a father, you have been too strong for me, particularly since my brothers died when they were small and my sisters only came along much later, so that I had to bear the whole brunt of it all alone, something I was much too weak for. . . .

I was a timid child. For all that I am sure I was also obstinate, as children are. I am sure that Mother spoilt me too, but I cannot believe I was particularly difficult to manage. I cannot believe that a kindly word, a quiet taking of me by the hand, a friendly look, could not have got me to do anything that was wanted of me. Now you are after all at bottom a kindly and a softhearted person (what follows will not be in contradiction to this, I am speaking only of the impression you made on the child), but not every child has the endurance and fearlessness to go on searching until it comes to the kindliness that lies beneath the surface. You can only treat a child in the way you yourself are constituted, with vigor, noise, and hot temper, and in this case this seemed to you, into the bargain, extremely suitable, because you wanted to bring me up to be a strong brave boy.

There is only one episode in the early years of which I have a direct memory. You may remember it, too. Once in the night I kept whimpering for water, not, I am certain, because I was thirsty, but probably partly to be annoying, partly to amuse myself. After several vigorous threats had failed to have any effect, you took me out of bed, carried me out onto the *pavlatche* and left me there alone for a while in my nightshirt, outside the shut door. I am not going to say that this was wrong—perhaps at that time there was really no

other way of getting peace and quiet that night—
but I mention it as typical of your methods of
bringing up a child and their effect on me. I dare
say I was quite obedient afterwards at that period,
but it did me inner harm. What was for me a
matter of course, the senseless asking for water,
and the extraordinary terror of being carried outside were two things that I, my nature being what
it was, could never properly connect with each
other. Even years afterwards I suffered from the
tormenting fancy that the huge man, my father,
the ultimate authority, would come almost for no
reason at all and take me out of bed in the night
and carry me out onto the *pavlatche,* and that
therefore I was such a mere nothing for him.

At that time, and at that time everywhere, I would have needed encouragement. I was,
after all, depressed even by your mere physical
presence. I remember, for instance, how we often
undressed together in the same bathing hut. There
was I, skinny, weakly, slight; you strong, tall,
broad. Even inside the hut I felt myself a miserable
specimen, and what's more, not only in your eyes
but in the eyes of the whole world, for you were
for me the measure of all things. But then when
we went out of the bathing hut before the people,
I with you holding my hand, a little skeleton, un-
steady, barefoot on the boards, frightened of the
water, incapable of copying your swimming
strokes, which you, with the best of intentions, but
actually to my profound humiliation, always kept
on showing me, then I was frantic with desperation
and all my bad experiences in all spheres at such
moments fitted magnificently together. What made
me feel best was when you sometimes undressed
first and I was able to stay behind in the hut alone
and put off the disgrace of showing myself in public until at length you came to see what I was
doing and drove me out of the hut. I was grateful
to you for not seeming to notice my extremity, and
besides, I was proud of my father's body. For the
rest, this difference between us remains much the
same to this very day.

But that was what your whole method
of upbringing was like. You have, I think, a gift

for bringing up children; you could, I am sure, have been of use to a human being of your own kind with your methods; such a person would have seen the reasonableness of what you told him, would not have troubled about anything else, and would quietly have done things the way he was told. But for me as a child everything you shouted at me was positively a heavenly commandment, I never forgot it, it remained for me the most important means of forming a judgment of you yourself, and there you failed entirely. Since as a child I was together with you chiefly at meals, your teaching was to a large extent teaching about proper behavior at table. What was brought to the table had to be eaten up, there could be no discussion of the goodness of the food—but you yourself often found the food uneatable, called it "this swill," said "that brute" (the cook) had ruined it. Because in accordance with your strong appetite and your particular habit you ate everything fast, hot and in big mouthfuls, the child had to hurry, there was a somber silence at table, interrupted by admonitions: "Eat first, talk afterwards," or "faster, faster, faster," or "there you are, you see, I finished ages ago." Bones mustn't be cracked with the teeth, but you could. Vinegar must not be sipped noisily, but you could. The main thing was that the bread should be cut straight. But it didn't matter that you did it with a knife dripping with gravy. One had to take care that no scraps fell on

the floor. In the end it was under your chair that there were most scraps. At table one wasn't allowed to do anything but eat, but you cleaned and cut your fingernails, sharpened pencils, cleaned your ears with the toothpick. Please, Father, understand me rightly: these would in themselves have been utterly insignificant details, they only became depressing for me because you, the man who was so tremendously the measure of all things for me, yourself did not keep the commandments you imposed on me. Hence the world was for me divided into three parts: into one in which I, the slave, lived under laws that had been invented only for me and which I could, I did not know why, never completely comply with; then into a second world, which was infinitely remote from mine, in which you lived, concerned with government, with the issuing of orders and with annoyance about their not being obeyed, and finally into a third world where everybody else lived happily and free from orders and from having to obey. I was continually in disgrace, either I obeyed your orders, and that was a disgrace, for they applied, after all, only to me, or I was defiant and that was a disgrace too, for how could I presume to defy you, or I could not obey because, for instance, I had not your strength, your appetite, your skill, in spite of which you expected it of me as a matter of course; this was the greatest disgrace of all. What moved in this way was not the child's reflections, but his feelings.

Fortunately there were, I admit, exceptions to all these things, mostly when you suffered in silence, and affection and kindliness by their own strength overcame all obstacles, and moved me immediately. Admittedly this was rare, but it was wonderful. For instance, when in earlier times, in hot summers, when you were tired after lunch, I saw you having a nap at the office, your elbow on the desk, or when you joined us in the country, in the summer holidays, on Sundays, worn out from work at the office, or the time when Mother was gravely ill and you stood holding on to the bookcase, shaking with sobs; or when, during my last illness, you came tiptoeing to Ottla's room to see me, stopping in the doorway, craning your neck to see me and out of consideration for me only waved your hand to me. At such times one would lie back and weep for happiness, and one weeps again now, writing it down. . . .

I found equally little means of escape from you in Judaism. Here some escape would, in principle, have been thinkable that we might both have found each other in Judaism or even that we might have begun from there in harmony. But what sort of Judaism was it I got from you? In the course of the years I have taken roughly three different attitudes to it.

As a child I reproached myself, in accord with you, for not going to the synagogue enough, for not fasting, and so on. I thought that in this way I was doing a wrong not to myself but to you, and I was penetrated by a sense of guilt, which was, of course, always ready to hand. Later, as a boy, I could not understand how, with the insignificant scrap of Judaism you yourself possessed, you could reproach me for not (if for no more than the sake of piety, as you put it) making an effort to cling to a similar insignificant scrap. It was indeed really, so far as I could see, a mere scrap, a joke, not even a joke. On four days in the year you went to the synagogue, where you were, to say the least of it, closer to the indifferent than to those who took it seriously, patiently went through the prayers by way of formality, sometimes amazed me by being able to show me in the prayer book the passage that was being said at the moment, and for the rest, so long (and this was the main thing) as I was there in the synagogue I was allowed to hang about wherever I liked. And so I yawned and dozed through the many hours (I don't think I was ever again so bored, except later at dancing lessons) and did my best to enjoy the few little bits of variety there were, as, for instance, when the Ark of the Covenant was opened, which always reminded me of the shooting galleries where a cupboard door would open in the same way whenever one got a bull's-eye, only with the difference that there something interesting always came out and here it was always just the same old dolls with no heads. Incidentally, it was also very frightening for me there, not only, as goes without saying, because of all the people one came into close contact with, but also because you once mentioned, by the way, that I too might be called up to read the Torah. That was something I went in dread of for years. But otherwise I was not fundamentally disturbed in my state of boredom, unless it was by the *bar mizvah,* but that meant no more than some ridiculous learning by heart, in other words, led to nothing but something like the ridiculous passing of an examination and then, so far as you were concerned, by little, not very significant incidents, as when you were called up to read the Torah and came well out of the affair, which to my way of feeling was purely social, or when you stayed on in the synagogue for the prayers for the dead, and I was sent away, which for a long time obviously because of being sent away and lacking, as I did, any deeper interest, aroused in me the more or less unconscious feeling that what was about to take place was something indecent. That was how it was in the synagogue, and at home it was, if possible, even more poverty-stricken, being confined to the first evening of Passover, which more and more developed into a farce, with fits of hysterical laughter, admittedly under the influence of the growing children. (Why did you have to give way to that influence? Because you brought it about in the first place.) And so there was the religious material that was handed on to me, to which may be added at most the outstretched hand pointing to "the sons of the millionaire Fuchs," who were in the synagogue with their father at the high holidays. How one could do anything better with this material than get rid of it as fast as possible was something I could not understand; precisely getting rid of it seemed to me the most effective act of "piety" one could perform. . . .

You struck nearer home with your dislike of my writing and all that, unknown to you, was connected with it. Here I had, in fact, got some distance away from you by my own efforts, even if it was slightly reminiscent of the worm that, as a foot tramples on the tail end of it, breaks loose with its top end and drags itself aside. To a certain extent I was in safety; there was a chance to breathe freely. The dislike that you naturally and immediately had of my writing too was, by the way of exception, welcome to me. My vanity and my ambition did suffer, it is true, under your soon proverbial way of hailing the arrival of my books: "Put it on my bedside table!" (as it happened, you were usually playing cards when a book came), but fundamentally I was thoroughly glad of it, not only out of rebellious malice, not only out of delight at a new confirmation of my view of our relationship, but quite spontaneously, because to me that formula sounded something like: "Now you are free!" Of course it was a delusion; I was not, or, to put it most optimistically, was not yet, free. My writing was all about you; all I did there, after all, was to bemoan what I could not bemoan upon your breast. It was an intentionally long-drawn-out leave-taking from you, only although it was brought about by force on your part, it did not take its course in the direction determined by me. But how little all this amounted to! It is all only worth talking about at all because it has happened in my life, otherwise it would not be worthy of remark at all; and then too for the reason that in my childhood it ruled my life as a premonition, later as a hope, and still later often as despair, dictating—it may be said, yet again in your shape—my few little decisions to me.

That is what my life with you has been like up to now, and these are the prospects inherent in it for the future.

Aphorisms

Kafka was a master of the aphorism. Time and time again, in one or two sentences, he would pierce the essence of the human condition—as in these selections from Reflections on Sin, Suffering, Hope, and the True Way.

There are two main human sins from which all the others derive: impatience and indolence. It was because of impatience that they were expelled from Paradise; it is because of indolence that they do not return. Yet perhaps there is only one major sin: impatience. Because of impatience they were expelled, because of impatience they do not return.

One of the first signs of the beginnings of understanding is the wish to die. This life appears unbearable, another unattainable. One is no longer ashamed of wanting to die; one asks to be moved from the old cell, which one hates, to a new one, which one will only in time come to hate. In this there is also a residue of belief that during the move the master will chance to come along the corridor, look at the prisoner and say: "This man is not to be locked up again. He is to come to me."

The crows maintain that a single crow could destroy the heavens. There is no doubt of that, but it proves nothing against the heavens, for heaven simply means: the impossibility of crows.

One cannot pay Evil in instalments—one always keeps on trying to.

It is only our conception of time that makes us call the Last Judgment by this name. It is, in fact, a kind of martial law.

There is nothing besides a spiritual world; what we call the world of the senses is the Evil in the spiritual world, and what we call Evil is only the necessity of a moment in our eternal evolution.

One can disintegrate the world by means of very strong light. For weak eyes the world becomes solid, for still weaker eyes it seems to develop fists, for eyes weaker still it becomes shame-faced and smashes anyone who dares to gaze upon it.

We are sinful not only because we have eaten of the Tree of Knowledge, but also because we have not yet eaten of the Tree of Life. The state in which we are is sinful, irrespective of guilt.

We too must suffer all the suffering around us. We all have not *one* body, but we have *one* way of growing, and this leads us through all anguish, whether in this or in that form. Just as the child develops through all the stages of life right into old age and to death (and fundamentally to the earlier stage the later one seems out of reach, in relation both to desire and to fear), so also do we develop (no less deeply bound up with mankind than with ourselves) through all the sufferings of this world. There is no room for justice in this context, but neither is there any room for fear of suffering or for the interpretation of suffering as a merit.

You can hold yourself back from the sufferings of the world: this is something you are free to do and is in accord with your nature, but perhaps precisely this holding back is the only suffering that you might be able to avoid.

There is no need for you to leave the house. Stay at your table and listen. Don't even listen, just wait. Don't even wait, be completely quiet and alone. The world will offer itself to you to be unmasked; it can't do otherwise; in raptures it will writhe before you.

Abraham Isaac Kuk (1865–1951)

Abraham Isaac Kuk, an Orthodox theologian and passionate mystic, was the first chief rabbi of Palestine. He was born in 1865 in a Russian shtetl. Serving as rabbi in the town of Boisk, he threw his influence behind Zionism and urged his congregation to support the movement. In 1904, he moved to Palestine, served as rabbi in Jaffa, became chief rabbi of Jerusalem, then chief rabbi of Palestine. For an Orthodox theologian, his thinking was unique. He saw the Jewish nationalist movement as a final avatar of the holiness of the tradition; he accepted the role of the nonreligious pioneers and became one of the most beloved figures in all of Palestine.

In his writing, he transmits a sense of the mystical experience in passages that mount to ecstatic poetry. He was a religious optimist equating faith and God with a belief in the possibility of social betterment—all pivoting upon the ultimate worth of the human soul.

The Rebirth of Israel

The world and all that it contains is waiting for the Light of Israel. This people was fashioned by God to speak of His Glory; it was granted the heritage of the blessing of Abraham so that it might disseminate the knowledge of God, and it was commanded to live its life apart from the nations of the world. God chose it to cleanse the whole world of all impurity and darkness; this people is endowed with a hidden treasure, with the Torah, the means by which the Heaven and the Earth were created.

The Light of Israel is not a utopian dream, or some abstract morality, or merely a pious wish and a noble vision. It does not wash its hands of the material world and all its values.

The world of the gentiles is tattered and rent. In its view the body is divided from the soul, and there is no inner bond and identity between matter and spirit, no basic unity between action and idea. At present, before the Light of Israel becomes manifest, the doctrine of Communism represents the highest spiritual ascent of

gentile culture. But how poor is a world in which this black evil has raised its head and pretends to be its highest aspiration. What a treasure chest of wickedness is hidden in this most fearful lie, which has such a dangerous exterior sheen of purity! How pitiable are the spiritual streams out of the Jewish world of true holiness which are pouring into this swamp of wickedness! How much more incandescent the Light will have to become in order to redeem the rays which have fallen into darkness! But they will be redeemed, once and for all, with the redemption of the Holy People.

Redemption is continuous. The Redemption from Egypt and the Final Redemption are part of the same process, "of the mighty hand and outstretched arm," which began in Egypt and is evident in all of history. The spirit of Israel is attuned to the hum of the redemptive process, to the sound waves of its labors which will end only with the coming of the days of the Messiah.

It is a grave error to be insensitive to the distinctive unity of the Jewish spirit, to imagine that the Divine stuff which uniquely characterizes Israel is comparable to the spiritual content of all the other national civilizations. This error is the source of the attempt to sever the national from the religious element of Judaism. Such a division would falsify both our nationalism and our religion, for every element of thought, emotion, and idealism that is present in the Jewish people belongs to an indivisible entity, and all together make up its specific character.

But, mistaken as is the attempt to divide these indivisible components of the Jewish spirit, it is an even greater error to imagine that such a sundering could possibly succeed; it is, therefore, pointless to wage a bitter and ill-conceived war against those who are loyal to only one aspect of the Jewish character. No matter what they may think, the particular element of the Jewish spirit that they may make their own, being rooted in the total life of our people, must inevitably contain every aspect of its ethos.

Our quarrel with them must be directed only to the specific task of demonstrating their error and of proving to them that all their effort to fragmentize the higher unity of Israel is foredoomed to failure. We who represent the integrity of the Jewish will and spirit must react in a deeply natural way, by merely analyzing the opposing positions to show that any individual element of the Jewish spirit cannot help but include all the values that the "sunderers" hope to forget and destroy. Once this truth is established, our opponents will ultimately have to realize that they were wasting their effort. The values they attempted to banish were nonetheless present, if only in an attenuated and distorted form, in their theories, and the result of their labors could only be spiritual hunger, narrowed horizons, and the loss of any true sense of direction.

One path alone will then be open to our adversaries; to acknowledge the truth proved by experience and to cleave to the entire living and holy content of the fully manifest Light of Israel. Their souls will then no longer be tortured by nebulous and ghost-like ideas from which they could neither free themselves nor find in them clear illumination of the spirit. They will then realize that nationalism, or religion, or any other element of the spirit of Israel, can realize itself only in the context of a Jewish life that is full, stirring, and entirely true to every shade of its essence.

Leo Baeck (1873–1956)

Leo Baeck, who died in 1956 at the age of 83, is looked upon as a kind of saint. Historian, theologian, expert in Jewish literature, he was a pillar of Reform ideology in Germany and served as its official leader from 1922 until deep into the Nazi era. He was also head of the Jewish community in Germany.

Refusing to flee the country despite the pleas of his followers and friends, he continued to exercise leadership until the Jewish community was liquidated. Inevitably, he was taken by the Gestapo in 1943 and shipped to the concentration camp at Theresienstadt. But this spiritual fortitude created a physical vitality that kept him alive amid the ordeals of the camp. He never stopped writing during his entire imprisonment.

After Germany's defeat in 1945, Baeck went to London and became president of the World Union for Progressive Judaism, which he had founded. He was a frequent visitor to the United States and taught at the Hebrew Union College in Cincinnati.

His essays express the profundity of his spirit. For him, the genius of Judaism lay in its ethical system translated into moral acts. He also believed that the Jewish religion was tied to Jewish national entity—in other words, that the Jews were a nation.

The passages that follow are from his great essay, God and Man in Judaism, *and from* The Essence of Judaism.

God and Man

With the Hebrew religion an entirely new formative principle appeared among mankind. In the history of religions it stands for a revelation or, what is the same thing, a revolution, and as such it has been one of the most powerful forces of civilisation.

Revolution—of course we are using the word not in a political, but in its intellectual and spiritual meaning—is not the same thing as mere reform. Reform is new only in a qualified sense; it is a new expression of an old way of thinking.

In revolution, on the other hand, we hear the voice of something that is fundamentally new. It demands a breach with the entire past, with all that has been and with all, other than itself, that is. Even from a purely historical point of view, therefore, and apart from the supernatural, a religion that thus appears on the scene as a revolution bears the character of a revelation, a new beginning from which everything must proceed.

But also in a supernatural sense such a religion comes into the world as a revelation. It is able to stand up for the One Thing, and therefore to oppose everything else, only because it knows itself to be the working of the sole higher power that exists, the Word that comes forth from God. When the way is being prepared for something that is quite new and different, for the One and Absolute, there is a disclosure of the Beyond, a revelation. Into the heart of the man who experiences this comes that which is higher than he.

It was through men who had had this experience that the Hebrew religion came into existence. Its nature and its results are due not only to its contents, but to the fact that it was shaped and formulated by men of revelation, by prophets. These men were prophets in a quite special sense; they have no peers. The consciousness that they were touched by God overwhelmed them, body and soul. What made them the unique prophets they were was the commandment that came to them to carry out the work of God, the realisation that they had been appointed to stand up for the one, the essential thing, against their nation and their time.

This distinguishes the Hebrew prophet from the mystic. The mystic too has his moments of ecstasy; it is in such hours that he has his knowledge of God. But he lacks the impelling conviction that God has laid a task upon him. To him his experience is an end in itself. To the prophet, on the other hand, his experience is a summons, an equipment for his mission.

Here lies the explanation of what is often called the ethical character of Hebrew prophetism. The prophet is conscious of having been called by God to proclaim to men the one absolute message that comes from God. What sets him apart is that it is the *commandment of God* that he must preach to men. He is full of power by the spirit of the Lord, so that his theme is and can only be righteousness and wickedness. He cannot soften it down nor omit any part of it. He never bargains with the world nor concludes a compromise with it.

It is to men as such that the message of the Hebrew prophet is addressed, to every man whoever and wherever he may be.

Religious revolution aims at permeating the world with a new religious principle. It aims at a new world. This imperative that comes from the Beyond seeks the ear of the whole world. It is the power that resides in this idea, peculiar to the religion of Israel, that makes it a world religion. At an early stage it became conscious of it, and this consciousness found expression in the assurance that Israel was an elect nation and in the conviction that the goal of all history was contained in that election.

To Be A Jew

Judaism bears witness to the power of the idea as against the power of mere numbers and of outward success; it stands for the enduring protest of those who seek to be true in their own selves, of those who claim to be different, as against the crushing pressure of the victor and the leveller, who want all to think alike.

Judaism, by its mere existence, is a never silent protest against the assumption that the multitude can be greater than right, that force may be the ruler over truth, that in the battle between spirit and the utilities, profit may have the last word.

As long as Judaism continues, nobody will be able to say that the soul of man has allowed itself to be subjugated.

The mere fact of Judaism's existence shows that it is impossible to conquer the spirit, that the spirit can make men invincible, and that though spirit and mind may sometimes assume the appearance of an extinct volcano—Judaism has often been depicted thus—power yet dwells in them, power which quietly renews itself, and breaks out afresh, and causes movement.

Albert Einstein (1879–1955)

Shortly after the Nazis came to power, an event occurred that sealed the doom of the "thousand-year Reich" and its allies and guaranteed American military supremacy for years to come. These dooms and triumphs were set in motion when a German refugee disembarked in New York and applied for American citizenship: his name, Albert Einstein. Years later, at a time when German might was crushing all opposition and when the shadow of Hitler was cast over the whole civilized world, this physicist wrote a letter to President Roosevelt. This letter inspired a conference, a mobilization, a secret project and, finally, the atom bomb. Einstein's ideas about the nature of mass and energy and the structure of the atom are still the seminal concepts of nuclear physics. But Albert Einstein will not be remembered as the father of the atom bomb; his contribution is far larger than that. He is recognized as the greatest physicist since Isaac Newton. His theory of relativity revolutionized contemporary thinking. His genius is unchallenged.

But he was even more than this. He was a lover of music and a fine violinist. He was a humanist, a champion of liberal causes, an enthusiastic Zionist. Indeed, he was urged to run for the Presidency of Israel after Chaim Weizmann's death and would undoubtedly have won had he chosen to accept.

He wrote on many subjects besides physics. Among his books are The World as I See It *and* Out of My Later Years, *which contain some superb essays on the nature of Judaism and the Jewish ethic.*

The Meaning of Life

What is the meaning of human life, or of organic life altogether? To answer this question at all implies a religion. Is there any sense then, you ask, in putting it? I answer, the man who regards his own life and that of his fellow-creatures as meaningless is not merely unfortunate but almost disqualified for life.

What an extraordinary situation is that of us mortals! Each of us is here for a brief sojourn; for what purpose he knows not, though he sometimes thinks he feels it. But from the point of view of daily life, without going deeper, we exist for our fellow-men—in the first place for those on whose smiles and welfare all our happiness depends, and next for all those unknown to us personally with whose destinies we are bound up by the tie of sympathy. A hundred times every day I remind myself that my inner and outer life depends on the labours of other men, living and dead, and that I must exert myself in order to give in the same measure as I have received and am still receiving. I am strongly drawn to the simple life and am often oppressed by the feeling that I am engrossing an unnecessary amount of the labour of my fellow-men. I regard class differences as contrary to justice and, in the last resort, based on force. I also consider that plain living is good for everybody, physically and mentally.

In human freedom in the philosophical sense I am definitely a disbeliever. Everybody acts not only under external compulsion but also in accordance with inner necessity. Schopenhauer's saying, that "a man can do as he will, but not will as he will," has been an inspiration to me since my youth up, and a continual consolation and unfailing well-spring of patience in the face of the hardships of life, my own and others'. This feeling mercifully mitigates the sense of responsibility which so easily becomes paralysing, and it prevents us from taking ourselves and other people too seriously; it conduces to a view of life in which humour, after all, has its due place.

To inquire after the meaning or object of one's own existence or of creation generally has always seemed to me absurd from an objective point of view. And yet everybody has certain ideals which determine the direction of his endeavours and his judgments. In this sense I have never looked upon ease and happiness as ends in themselves—such an ethical basis I call more proper for a herd of swine. The ideals which have lighted me on my way and time after time given me new courage to face life cheerfully have been Truth, Goodness and Beauty. Without the sense of fellowship with men of like mind, of preoccupation with the objective, the eternally unattainable in the field of art and scientific research, life would have seemed to me empty. The ordinary objects of human endeavour—property, outward success, luxury—have always seemed to me contemptible.

My passionate sense of social justice and social responsibility has always contrasted oddly with my pronounced freedom from the need for direct contact with other human beings and human communities. I gang my own gait and have never belonged to my own country, my home, my friends, or even my immediate family, with my whole heart; in the face of all these ties I have never lost an obstinate sense of detachment, of the need for solitude—a feeling which increases with the years. One is sharply conscious, yet without regret, of the limits to the possibility of mutual understanding and sympathy with one's fellow-creatures. Such a person no doubt loses something in the way of geniality and light-heartedness; on the other hand, he is largely independent of the opinions, habits and judgments of his fellows and avoids the temptation to take his stand on such insecure foundations.

My political ideal is that of democracy. Let every man be respected as an individual and no man idolised. It is an irony of fate that I myself have been the recipient of excessive admiration and respect from my fellows through no fault, and no merit, of my own. The cause of this may well be the desire, unattainable for many, to understand the one or two ideas to which I have with my feeble powers attained through ceaseless struggle. I am quite aware that it is necessary for the success of any complex undertaking that one man should do the thinking and directing and in general bear the responsibility. But the led must not be compelled, they must be able to choose their leader. An autocratic system of coercion, in my opinion, soon degenerates. For force always attracts men of low morality, and I believe it to be an invariable rule that tyrants of genius are succeeded by scoundrels. For this reason I have always been passionately opposed to systems such as we see in Italy and Russia today. The thing that has brought discredit upon the prevailing form of democracy in Europe today is not to be laid to the door of the democratic idea as such, but to lack of stability on the part of the heads of governments and to the impersonal character of the electoral system. I believe that in this respect the United States of America have found the right way. They have a responsible President who is elected for a sufficiently long period and has sufficient powers to be really responsible. On the other hand, what I value in our political system is the more extensive provision that it makes for the individual in case of illness or need. The really valuable thing in the pageant of human life seems to me not the State but the creative, sentient individual, the personality; it alone creates the noble and the sublime, while the herd as such remains dull in thought and dull in feeling.

The fairest thing we can experience is the mysterious. It is the fundamental emotion which stands at the cradle of true art and true science. He who knows it not and can no longer wonder, no longer feel amazement, is as good as dead, a snuffed-out candle. It was the experience of mystery—even if mixed with fear—that engendered religion. A knowledge of the existence of something we cannot penetrate, of the manifestations of the profoundest reason and the most radiant beauty, which are only accessible to our reason in their most elementary forms—it is this knowledge and this emotion that constitute the truly religious attitude; in this sense, and in this alone, I am a deeply religious man. I cannot conceive of a God who rewards and punishes his creatures, or has a will of the type of which we are conscious in ourselves. An individual who should survive his physical death is also beyond my comprehension, nor do I wish it otherwise; such notions are for the fears or absurd egoism of feeble souls. Enough for me the mystery of the eternity of life, and the inkling of the marvellous structure of reality, together with the single-hearted endeavour to comprehend a portion, be it ever so tiny, of the reason that manifests itself in nature.

Jewish Ideals

The pursuit of knowledge for its own sake, an almost fanatical love of justice, and the desire for personal independence—these are the features of the Jewish tradition which make me thank my stars that I belong to it.

Those who are raging today against the ideals of reason and individual liberty and are trying to establish a spiritless State-slavery by brute force rightly see in us their irreconcilable foes. History has given us a difficult row to hoe; but so long as we remain devoted servants of truth, justice, and liberty, we shall continue not merely to survive as the oldest of living peoples, but by creative work to bring forth fruits which contribute to the ennoblement of the human race, as heretofore.

In the philosophical sense there is, in my opinion, no specifically Jewish outlook. Judaism seems to me to be concerned almost exclusively with the moral attitude in life and to life. I look upon it as the essence of an attitude to life which is incarnate in the Jewish people rather than the essence of the laws laid down in the Torah and interpreted in the Talmud. To me, the Torah and the Talmud are merely the most important evidence for the manner in which the Jewish conception of life held sway in earlier times.

The essence of that conception seems to me to lie in an affirmative attitude to the life of all creation. The life of the individual has meaning only so far as it aids in making the life of every living thing nobler and more beautiful. Life is sacred—that is to say, it is the supreme value, to which all other values are subordinate. The hallowing of the supra-individual life brings in its train a reverence for everything spiritual—a particularly characteristic feature of the Jewish tradition.

Judaism is not a creed: the Jewish God is simply a negation of superstition, an imaginary result of its elimination. It is also an attempt to base the moral law on fear, a regrettable and discreditable attempt. Yet it seems to me that the strong moral tradition of the Jewish nation has to a large extent shaken itself free from this fear. It is clear also that "serving God" was equated with "serving the living." The best of the Jewish people, especially the Prophets and Jesus, contended tirelessly for this.

Judaism is thus no transcendental religion; it is concerned with life as we live it and can up to a point grasp it, and nothing else. It seems to me, therefore, doubtful whether it can be called a religion in the accepted sense of the word, particularly as no "faith" but the sanctification of life in a supra-personal sense is demanded of the Jew.

But the Jewish tradition also contains something else, something which finds splendid expression in many of the Psalms—namely, a sort of intoxicated joy and amazement at the beauty and grandeur of this world, of which man can just form a faint notion. It is the feeling from which true scientific research draws its spiritual sustenance, but which also seems to find expression in the song of birds. To tack this on to the idea of God seems mere childish absurdity.

Is what I have described a distinguishing mark of Judaism? Is it to be found anywhere else under another name? In its pure form, nowhere, not even in Judaism, where the pure doctrine is obscured by much worship of the letter. Yet Judaism seems to me one of its purest and most vigorous manifestations. This applies particularly to the fundamental principle of the sanctification of life.

It is characteristic that the animals were expressly included in the command to keep holy the Sabbath day, so strong was the feeling that the ideal demands the solidarity of all living things. The insistence on the solidarity of all human beings finds still stronger expression, and it is no mere chance that the demands of Socialism were for the most part first raised by Jews.

How strongly developed this sense of the sanctity of life is in the Jewish people is admirably illustrated by a little remark which Walter Rathenau once made to me in conversation: "When a Jew says that he is going hunting to amuse himself, he lies." The Jewish sense of the sanctity of life could not be more simply expressed.

Hayim Greenberg (1889–1953)

The writer Hayim Greenberg defies pigeon-holing. He believed passionately in the Jewish state and hated the ideas of states. He was a pacifist who called for the physical destruction of the Nazis. He was a Socialist who accepted the validity of religious vision and successively repudiated Russian Communism as it crystallized into forms of tyranny. He worked as a journalist and was a rather powerful orator. But his greatest distinction was as an essayist. He wrote in Russian, in Hebrew and in Yiddish, but mostly in Yiddish, and his diction is a remarkable instrument, fusing a warm personal idiom with the clarity, precision and insight of the born ideologue.

His essays range over a whole world of Jewish interests. He writes about the Bible, about the characters of the Bible, about the crucifixion, about Martin Luther, Einstein, capital punishment, Zionism, Soviet Russia, Gandhi and the east side of New York. Only now, years after his death, are his essays, newly translated into English, finding a wide audience. But from the first his readers, al-

though few, were passionate. They insisted on the greatness of his spirit, the brilliance of his mind, on the depth of his originality—a verdict that will be upheld.

The Dybbuk is a hybrid, half essay, half story, and wholly charming.

The Dybbuk

Mr. X is a very busy man. I am familiar with his work and I know that his duties are burdensome and involve heavy responsibility. I also know that he thinks of himself as a "good Jew," even though he is somewhat remote from Jewish community life. This estrangement is not a result of snobbishness. The circumstances of his life have brought it about despite his sensitive appreciation of the average Jewish man. He knows Yiddish, since he was born in the Old Country, but he seldom uses the language because most of his friends and professional associates are estranged from it. Some time ago I was informed by one of our mutual friends that "something is the matter" with X.

For years X had been in the habit of taking an hour off after lunch. This hour, weather permitting, he would spend in Central Park. These solitary walks were his only recreation and also took the place of vacations. He frequently declared that they refreshed and stimulated him. But in recent months, I was told, he began to behave strangely during these strolls. He had been observed talking to himself, and was overheard simulating different voices, like an actor reciting a dialogue. At times he also sings. But what was strangest about these soliloquies was that they were in Yiddish and articulated in the specific dialect and intonation that used to characterize Podolia and Bessarabia. His urge to talk to himself was suspect enough in itself, but the additional puzzle was, why Yiddish? Why talk to himself in a language which he seldom read and which he had not used for years in his social contacts? This added mystery to the riddle of his behavior and his family was deeply concerned and wondered how he could be persuaded to consult a doctor—more correctly, a psychiatrist.

I find it difficult to analyze my motives in offering advice in the case, but I suggested to the family to avoid a professional "heart prober" for the moment. Let us cautiously try to examine the case ourselves, I said. Perhaps he will tell us himself what troubles him, if we "provoke" him delicately. We may yet find that his conduct is neither dangerous nor perplexing.

I will not describe here the strategy we used to inform him that his family and friends were aware of his new mode of spending his hours in the park. He paled noticeably and said nothing for a while. He paced about the room nervously, immersed in thought. Then he sat down and addressed us calmly.

"Please do not ask any more questions. Since I have been 'caught in the act,' I will explain to you. I am no less normal now than I have ever been. You can judge this yourselves. My new conduct has not affected my work or my ability to make decisions or my relations with other people. I need no therapy and I will not submit to any; nor should you press me to embark on a long series of seances with a neurologist or a psychoanalyst. I know their methods and their detection tricks and I do not require them. If what I am about to tell you should strike you as abnormal, I would not care. I believe that perfectly normal people display certain abnormalities—under unusual or abnormal conditions, naturally. But I would rather not continue along this phase of the subject. You might get the impression that you are confronting one who is a little 'touched in the head' and is becoming set in his madness to the point of considering it a special accomplishment. I know this type of madman, and I want to assure you that I don't belong in this category. But perhaps I'd better tell you what is happening within me.

"Lately I have been deriving great pleasure—a pleasure, true, that is not unmixed with anguish and even with physical pain—from becoming for one hour each day a small-town Jew, the type of small-town Jew of South Russia where, as you know, I hail from. Through some process unknown to me the small town, the *shtetl*, suddenly became resurrected within me. It is not I who am talking; it is the *shtetl* that talks through my mouth. Local Yiddish idioms and expressions that had lain dormant within me for many years suddenly reawakened. Images, gestures and scenes that are no longer to be found in the *shtetl* of my early childhood have risen to the surface of my memory. Indeed, how is one to find these scenes and images and gestures when the *shtetl* has been eradicated together with all its Jews? Now the *shtetl* lives in me, with all its wisdom and futility, its charms and vulgarities, except that I now feel tenderness even toward the latter. My grandmother would probably define this as a Dybbuk. Call it a Dybbuk if you wish, I don't care. But I do not want this Dybbuk to be exorcised. For, basically, what is a Dybbuk? It is someone or something that is no longer alive, according to our material concepts, but persists in wishing to live and seeks a 'vessel' in which to continue living. He or it lives in this medium and talks through it. I do not care what specialists say about this. I consider it as entirely normal, and no one should get panicky over it.

"I do not remember exactly when it began or how it suddenly commenced, but I began to talk Yiddish as the *shtetl* talked it and now tries to talk through me. Do you want to know what I say? Very well, I will try to restore for you, in part at least, the contents of one such Dybbuk hour.

"For instance, there appear in my mind Moishe Zolotucha and Yankel the tinsmith. I see them meeting in the street and I talk for both of them.

> *Yankel:* How are you, Reb Moishe?
> *Moishe:* Can't complain.
> *Yankel:* I heard your cow calved. . . .
> *Moishe:* Not one; both of them. But I had a loss this week, a colt was stolen.
> *Yankel:* An inside job, you think?
> *Moishe:* What are you saying? Jews don't steal.

Yankel: Easy to say "Jews don't steal." Reb Boruchl the *Dayan* doesn't steal; Chatzkel the *Melamed* doesn't steal; the pharmacist doesn't steal, but . . . well, I'd better say no more.

Moishe: Better not. I was thinking, maybe Andriusha, my neighbor's son.

Yankel: Did you question him?

Moishe: Yeh, casually kind of I asked if he hadn't an idea what could have become of the colt. You should have seen the thievish grin on him when he said, "The tzotzelists must have stolen it; they need money for new flocamations" (proclamations).

"These two disappear. For a couple of minutes they lived and talked through me. I was they.

"Then Zeidel the usurer, the one with the bushy, angry eyebrows and the little greasy eyes, appears. He stops Sender the *Melamed* and asks him casually.

Zeidel: When is your brother marrying off his daughter?

Sender: The Saturday after Shavuoth, God willing.

Zeidel: She is already, may no evil eye. . .

Sender: What is she, may no evil eye. . . ?

Zeidel: Never mind. Only I was thinking, she must be over thirty, high time. . .

"And here is Gitel the seamstress sitting dreamily on the porch on a moonlit evening. Softly she hums a plaintive tune (my voice imitating hers must sound weird). I remember only the first two lines of the song, and even these probably not correctly:

I will send you an allotment to the regiment,
While I wait for you in sorrow at my work.

"Then there goes by the *Melamed* from Lithuania, the one who teaches the older boys. He had been in the *shtetl* for seven years and never once went to see his family—not even for Passover —because of his stinginess. A gang of small fry

from other schools trail after him shouting a satir-
ical ditty they had themselves composed. I still remember the tune.

> Litvak, Litvak, where's your wife?
> Litvak, Litvak, where's your child?
> Litvak, you are getting grey.
> Seven years he is in town,
> Never wrote to his own.

"And here is another gang of small
fry singing what they call a 'Gypsy' song. I don't
know who composed it—it is not language at all
and they recite it as one would an incantation:

> Ana, Mana, chitra broch,
> Brako lomti, lomti doch.
> Mune lune moste neka,
> Vuka luste kante breka.

"Suddenly I find myself at Eli Zel-
niker's store. Rachel, the daughter-in-law of the
richest man in the *shtetl*, who hails from 'far away
Chernigoff' stops to examine some items. Her thin
lips are distorted with a sneer as she announces in
pampered disdain: 'These two ribbons don't pair.'

"I say these words and it occurs to me
that 'pairing' is a better term than 'matching,' and
then I laugh at myself: A new philologist, in Yiddish yet.

"Rachel from 'far away Chernigoff'
leaves the store empty handed and I exclaim in the
angry thin voice of Eli Zelniker's wife: 'It doesn't
pair; may her guts be pared.'

"Enough? No, that's not quite all. I
see Osher the bookkeeper standing near the post
office engaged in an argument with Boruch the
matchmaker concerning the curriculum of the new
girls' school. Boruch the matchmaker tries to demonstrate that Hebrew, not *Loshen Kodesh* (the
holy tongue) is taught in the school. Osher sneers
at him: 'Hebrew and Loshen Kodesh are the same
thing!' But Boruch will not be persuaded so easily.
'The same thing, you say? Just as a magpie and a
goat are the same thing. Loshen Kodesh is . . . well,
you know what Loshen Kodesh is, *kidush,* and
Shema Israel, and *havdalah,* this is Loshen Kodesh.

But what do they teach in the school? A bird, a dog, a horse. I went, you went, he went, go to hell —that's Hebrew.'

"And this still isn't all. An hour is a long time. It is Saturday afternoon and a group of maids are strolling down the paved street dressed in their best. Their hair is neatly combed and gives off the tell-tale aroma of kerosene. They walk mincingly, like rich men's daughters, their heads held higher than on week days—it's the Sabbath, after all. Their talk is 'dainty Yiddish' (their own expression) with more stress on intonation and with a sprinkling of Germanisms which they picked up from the Yiddish love stories they had been reading. Their conversation is part of an act and consists of borrowed or imagined situations, but not one of them will ever accuse the other of telling lies. Dream and fantasy are not falsehoods. The talk runs as follows:

Have you received a letter from your sweetheart?

Two letters, about a week ago.

Where is he now?

In Amsterdam.

When will he return?

He will never return here. Soon he will send someone to bring me to him. Mother will come later, after the house and garden are finished.

"You must be tired. I too am tired. I don't get tired when I am alone in the park, or rather when I am with them. Then it is genuine, alive. Here I am merely reporting. And now, what is your verdict? Am I insane? Senile? Cracked? Is it morbid nostalgia? Say what you will, but I will not consult a doctor. I know something that the doctor doesn't know; something that, perhaps, he doesn't have to know. I am not a mystic; at any rate, I am not a spiritualist. Nevertheless I know that my *shtetl* is suspended in limbo and that it wants to live. It knows that it can never again be restored, that it is past, one hundred percent finished history—still it wants to live in somebody and through somebody. The Jews of the *shtetl*? They have been gassed, burned, shot, hanged,

strangled, buried alive, yet being corpses they want to live in somebody and through somebody. They want to live in me and in thousands of others like me. You may say that others do not hear this appeal of the dead to live within us one hour a day, one hour a week, or even one hour a year. That only proves that the others are deaf. I am not deaf, neither am I blind. Therefore, I live in their stead, I speak in their stead, and when I do so I speak Yiddish. It is remarkable, they remember the Yiddish that I forgot, and remembering they also remind me."

X did not go to a doctor. His family became accustomed to his conduct and took it more calmly. He continues to do his work conscientiously and with as much efficiency as before. He is normal twenty-three hours of every day. He is "abnormal" during one hour only, when he takes his stroll in the park and talks to himself in Yiddish.

How did he succeed in disciplining his Dybbuk? How did he force the Dybbuk to restrict its functioning to one specific hour a day? This is X's secret. I doubt very much whether he could explain it himself. I will never ask him.

Martin Buber (1878–1965)

Martin Buber has influenced the thinking of modern theologians perhaps more profoundly than any other religious writer—and his impact has been greater upon Christian than upon Jew. This is not surprising. His thinking derives from the mystic and apocalyptic current in Jewish theology rather than from the rationalistic which is dominant today. He also drew some of his ideas from the writings of Søren Kierkegaard. More than forty years ago, a small book appeared, entitled I and Thou, *in which Buber expresses the node of his thought: that religious faith is a dialogue between man and God; that the ultimate human experience is to strip all commodity connotations from the ideas of another being, whether animal, human or divine, and to achieve an intimacy of communion that can rise to ecstasy. The Bible, he holds, is a stammering record of that dialogue between Israel as a people and their God, wherein certain of the more spiritually talented—the leaders—knew themselves to be addressed by God; they listen with all their faculties and then obey, this perfect listening and obedience being their response.* I and Thou *is a poem and must be read as such. Words are used in new ways. Their reverberations must be attended to. Their relationships are all-important. Taking it as a poem, the reader exposes himself, his ears, his eyes, his nerve ends to Buber's muted words—which, if properly absorbed, can color one's thinking forever.*

Thinking as he did, Buber became the chief reinterpreter of cabala to the modern world. He was an ardent Zionist in his youth and, indeed, influenced its ideology. When the Nazis began to emerge in Germany, he left his work as an editor, translator and professor of philosophy and went to Jerusalem to teach at the Hebrew University. There he remained until his death. He was not enormously esteemed in Israel, except by those fortunate enough to know him personally or to have been taught by him, for he had fallen away from political Zionism and held that the redemption of the Jewish people could not be achieved only by political means but must happen through a spiritual regeneration. He lived in a quiet house on a quiet street in Jerusalem, a short, stout, unassuming little man. But this little man in the little house was a giant of intellect. His thought had spread a radiance throughout the civilized world, and to that quiet house came people from all over the world to pass a few words with the master. He cannot be known through the events of his life, only through his books, and especially through I and Thou.

I Consider A Tree

I can look on it as a picture: stiff column in a shock of light, or splash of green shot with the delicate blue and silver of the background.

I can perceive it as movement: flowing veins on clinging, pressing pith, suck of the roots, breathing of the leaves, ceaseless commerce with earth and air—and the obscure growth itself.

I can classify it in a species and study it as a type in its structure and mode of life.

I can subdue its actual presence and form so sternly that I recognise it only as an expression of law—of the laws in accordance with which a constant opposition of forces is continually adjusted, or of those in accordance with which the component substances mingle and separate.

I can dissipate it and perpetuate it in number, in pure numerical relation.

In all this the tree remains my object, occupies space and time, and has its nature and constitution.

It can, however, also come about, if I have both will and grace, that in considering the tree I become bound up in relation to it. The tree is now no longer *It*. I have been seized by the power of exclusiveness.

To effect this it is not necessary for me to give up any of the ways in which I consider the tree. There is nothing from which I would have to turn my eyes away in order to see, and no knowledge that I would have to forget. Rather is everything, picture and movement, species and type, law and number, indivisibly united in this event.

Everything belonging to the tree is in this: its form and structure, its colours and chem-

ical composition, its intercourse with the elements and with the stars, are all present in a single whole.

The tree is no impression, no play of my imagination, no value depending on my mood; but it is bodied over against me and has to do with me, as I with it—only in a different way.

Let no attempt be made to sap the strength from the meaning of the relation; relation is mutual.

The tree will have a consciousness, then, similar to our own? Of that I have no experience. But do you wish, through seeming to succeed in it with yourself, once again to disintegrate that which cannot be disintegrated? I encounter no soul or dryad of the tree, but the tree itself.

All real living is meeting.

The Silent Question

From time to time, I seem to hear a question echoing out of the depths of stillness. But he who asks it does not know that he is asking it, and he to whom the question is addressed is not aware that he is being questioned. It is the question which the world of today, in utter unawareness, puts to religion. This is the question: "Art thou, perhaps, the power that can help me? Canst thou teach me to believe? Teach me to have faith in reality, in the verities of existence, so that life will afford some aim for me and existence will have some meaning. Who, indeed, can help me if thou canst not?"

Whosoever listens closely to the question of which I speak observes that Judaism is included in the foremost ranks of those religions to which the appeal is made. That the world expects something from Judaism is in itself a new phenomenon. For centuries, the deeper spiritual content of Judaism was either unknown or given scant attention, for the reason perhaps that, during the period of the ghetto, the underlying reality of Jewish life was hardly glimpsed by the outside world, while during the emancipation period, Jews only—not Judaism—appeared upon the open scene.

A change seems to be taking place. Why? Is it because of the massacre of millions of Jews? That does not explain it. Or is it because of the establishment of a Jewish State? That does not explain it either. And yet both of these events are basically part of the reason why the real content of Judaism is beginning to become more perceptible. Now the world has gradually begun to perceive that within Judaism there is something which has its special contribution to make, in a special way, to the spiritual needs of the present time.

Will Jewry itself perceive that its very existence depends upon the revival of its religious existence? The Jewish State may assure the future of a nation of Jews, even one with a culture of its own; Judaism will live only if it brings to life again the primeval Jewish relationship to God, the world, and mankind.

Hasidic Sayings

Why do we say: "Our God and the God of our fathers"?

There are two kinds of people who believe in God. One believes because he has taken over the faith of his fathers, and his faith is strong. The other has arrived at faith through thinking and studying. The difference between them is this: The advantage of the first is that, no matter what arguments may be brought against it, his faith cannot be shaken; his faith is firm because it was taken over from his fathers. But there is one flaw in it: he has faith only in response to the command of man, and he has acquired it without studying and thinking for himself. The advantage of the second is that, because he found God through much thinking, he has arrived at a faith of his own. But here too there is a flaw; it is easy to shake his faith by refuting it through evidence. But he who unites both kinds of faith is invincible. And so we say, "Our God" with reference to our studies, and "God of our fathers" with an eye to tradition.

The understanding of man is not great enough to grasp the fact that God is beyond time. But you must understand that time exists only because we do not grasp it, only because our understanding is small. For the greater our understanding, the more time is on the wane. In a dream we live seventy years and discover, on awakening, that it was a quarter of an hour. In our life, which passes like a dream, we live seventy years and then we waken to a greater understanding which shows us that it was a quarter of an hour. With our small understanding we can never grasp what we will know with the greater. Perfect understanding is beyond time.

Every movement you make is bound up with the will of the Creator. That is why it is written: "Noah walked with God." For every movement is made through the impulse given by God. Noah clung to God with such very great devotion that it seemed to him that, whenever he walked, God was moving his feet. At every step it seemed to him that God was facing him and guiding him as a father teaches his little son to walk, and when the father moves further away from him the child knows it is for his own good.

We do not even know how we are supposed to pray. All we do is call for help because of the need of the moment. But what the soul intends is spiritual need, only we are not able to express what the soul means. That is why we do not merely ask God to hear our call for help, but also beg him, who knows what is hidden, to hear the silent cry of the soul.

A prayer which is not spoken in the name of all Israel is no prayer at all.

If a man has fulfilled all the commandments, he is admitted to the Garden of Eden, even though he has not burned with fervour and has not experienced delight. But since he has felt no delight on earth, he feels none there either. Finally, he even grumbles: "And they make all that to-do about paradise!" And hardly have the words left his lips, when he is thrown out!

It is impossible to tell men what way they should take. For one way to serve God is by the teachings, another by prayer, another way by fasting, and still another by eating. Everyone should carefully observe which way his heart draws him, and then choose that way with all his strength.

Infinity shall be contained in every deed of man, in his speaking and seeing, listening and walking, standing still and lying down.

"You can learn from everything," the rabbi of Sadagora once said to his hasidim. "Everything can teach us something, and not only everything God has created. What man has made has also something to teach us."

"What can we learn from a train?" one hasid asked dubiously.

"That because of one second one can miss everything."

"And from the telegraph?"

"That every word is counted and charged."

"And the telephone?"

"That what we say here is heard there."

The world is a spinning die, and everything turns and changes: man is turned into angel, and angel into man, and the head into the foot, and the foot into the head. Thus all things turn and spin and change, this into that, and that into this, the topmost to the undermost, and the undermost to the topmost. For at the root all is one, and salvation inheres in the change and return of things.

Man is afraid of things that cannot harm him, and he knows it; and he craves things that cannot help him, and he knows it. But actually, it is something within man he is afraid of, and it is something within man that he craves.

If you want to raise a man from mud and filth, do not think it is enough to stay on top and reach a helping hand down to him. You must go all the way down yourself, down into mud and filth. Then take hold of him with strong hands and pull him and yourself out into the light.

The Evil Inclination is like one who runs about the world keeping his hand closed. Nobody knows what he has inside of it. He goes up to everyone and asks: "What do you suppose I have in my hand?" And every person thinks that just what he wants most of all is hidden there. And everyone runs after the Evil Inclination. Then he opens his hand, and it is empty.

Question: Why on the Day of Atonement is the confession of sins given in alphabetical order?

Answer: If it were otherwise we should not know when to stop beating our breast. For there is no end to sin, and no end to the awareness of sin, but there is an end to the alphabet.

There is no room for God in him who is full of himself.

It is written that Moses was meek above all men. How are we to interpret this? He with whom God spoke face to face and whose work was so mighty—how could he think himself less than all others? The reason is this: during those forty days which Moses spent on the heights, his body had become pure and luminous like that of the attendant angels. After that time, he said to himself: "Of what importance is it, if I, whose body has been purified, give service to God? But one of Israel, who is still clad in his dull and turbid flesh and yet serves God—how much greater he is than I!"

If a pregnant woman goes into labour in the eighth month, when her time is not yet come, doctors try to stop her labour. But not so in the ninth month. If the woman goes into labour then, doctors try to increase it, so that she may soon give birth. That is why, formerly, when people called to heaven, begging God to free the earth of some misery, their prayer was granted, for the time was not yet come. But now that redemption is near, no prayer which ascends in behalf of the sorrowful world is of avail, but sorrow is heaped upon sorrow, so that the birth may soon be accomplished.

VI
HOLOCAUST AND HOMECOMING

The most cherished ideals of our own history had been
sanctioned by the conscience of all mankind.

Chaim Weizmann

Introduction

The two most important Jewish thinkers of the 20th century were Einstein and Kafka. In this fact we can find a rich and endless symbolism. Einstein was the pure theoretician whose speculations about the physical universe unlocked the atom and became energy itself. Kafka was the ineffectual little clerk in Prague whose tender and incandescent fables taught that the hunted Jew, on trial for an unknown crime and condemned to endless punishment, was more than a Jew—was a metaphor for mankind itself. Bounded then by the vision of energy and the energy of vision, Jewish thinkers of lesser magnitude have investigated four basic themes in our century.

How do you reconcile mass murder with a benign providence?

Is religious Judaism an anachronism—along with other religions?

What is the meaning of the state of Israel?

Is our civilization still a viable concept?

The answers outnumber the questions, but they do not last long. This, too, may be some kind of metaphor for the Jew, that ceaseless questioner, that eternal target for extinction, that stubborn survivor.

David Ben-Gurion (1886–   )

You do not have to be Jewish to know about David Ben-Gurion. Anyone who has been in the habit of reading newspapers anywhere in the world during the last twenty years knows the name and surely some of the achievements of this brilliant and dynamic statesman. His many-faceted political career culminated in his service as first Prime Minister and Minister of Defense for the state of Israel.

Ben-Gurion has also made considerable contributions to Jewish thought. He is a journalist, a philosopher, a historian and an outstanding authority on the Bible.

The Meaning of Israel

Israel represents a great tradition and a universal ideal. It cannot be measured by the yardstick of territory alone. It must be seen and appreciated against the background of our thousand years of history. Viewed in this light, the creation of the State of Israel is one of the great developments in the annals of mankind. And what's more, whoever looks back at the achievements of the Jewish people while it was struggling against tremendous odds, cannot but come to the conclusion that the future of that people will not be like that of all other nations and that somewhere in the higher reaches of the human spirit it has a rendezvous with Destiny.

The new epoch inaugurated by the rebirth of the State of Israel is but the beginning of its greatness. The vision of redemption which sustained us thousands of years had as its goal the complete redemption of the Jewish people and not of the Jewish people alone. There can be no redemption for the Jewish people without the redemption of all mankind. We can go on with our great and difficult task only by remaining true to our great vision—the vision of the Jewish Prophets which will be realized in the days to come.

Chaim Weizmann (1874–1952)

*Chaim Weizmann's scientific discoveries possibly
did more to create the state of Israel than the accomplish-
ments of any one man, except for Theodor Herzl. An
organic chemist, he became director of the British Ad-
miralty Chemical Laboratories during the First World War.
His original work in the production of synthetic acetone
(used in explosives), synthetic rubber, of certain dyes and
digestible proteins was considered so great a contribution
to the war effort that it influenced Lord Balfour and his
associates toward the Balfour Declaration, allowing large-
scale Jewish immigration into Palestine—wrested by the
British from the Turks during the war.*

*Weizmann had been a Zionist for many years
by that time. In 1914, he became chairman of the London
Committee of the Zionist Movement. After the Balfour
Declaration he was recognized as a world leader. In 1919
he was one of the three Zionists who represented the movement at the peace conference. The next year he convened
the London Zionist Conference which mobilized the re-
sources of the community for work in Palestine, and was
elected President of the World Zionist Organization. In
1946, disillusioned by the failure of the British leadership
to keep its pledges to the Jews on immigration into Palestine, he left Britain for Palestine.*

*When the State of Israel was established in
1948, Weizmann became its first president. But his health
was already failing and he could take only a limited role in
the developments that followed. He died in 1952. His home
in Rehovot is now the world-famous Weizmann Institute
of Science.*

Our Unique Destiny

*(Address to the Ad Hoc Committee on the Palestine
Question, October 18, 1947)*

It is a moving experience for me to
come before this committee of the United Nations
for the purpose of summarizing the view and senti-

232

ments of the Jewish people at this turning point of its fortunes.

My mind goes back a quarter of a century to the previous assembly of nations which solemnly endorsed our program for the reconstitution in Palestine of our National Home. I came from the council room in which the mandate was ratified with the feeling that the most cherished ideals of our own history had been sanctioned by the conscience of all mankind.

Our ancient civilization, which had enriched the thought and spirit of the world, was to be given a free abode in the very cradle of its birth. Our people were to find a home—not a refuge, not an asylum, not a mere shelter, but a home with which their past memory and future hope were inseparably bound up. The Jewish people was to fashion its own political and social institutions in the image of its own character and tradition, on a level of equality with all other nations in the human family.

I can testify here that the establishment of the Jews as a nation among the nations of the world was the real purpose and motive of that international covenant endorsed by the League of Nations.

It is no coincidence that the statesmen who developed the idea of organized international cooperation as well as the leaders in the creation of the United Nations found time, amid their universal preoccupations, to plan for the Jewish State.

Despite some of the things that have been said in this debate, I retain my belief in the prospect of Arab-Jewish cooperation once a solution based on finality and equality has received the sanction of international consent. The Jewish State in Palestine may become a pilot plant for processess and examples which may have a constructive message for its neighbors as well.

Maurice Samuel (1895–   )

Maurice Samuel belongs to that rare breed among writers who can speak of matters of intellectual and moral complexity without ever slipping into pretentious dullness. While he addresses himself to profound questions about the Jew and his ordeal in the world, he does so with a kind of light-handed grace, with a wit and charm that have made him one of the most beloved among contemporary Jewish writers.

He was born in Rumania in 1895, educated in England and came to the United States in 1914. He left for Palestine in 1929 and spent the next ten years there; was a friend of Chaim Weizmann and many of those who are the leaders of Israel today. A great traveler, he has visited, in his own words, "practically every Jewish community between Jordan and the Golden Gate, between Manchester and Cape Town."

His World of Sholom Aleichem, *written in 1944, won him the Saturday Review of Literature Prize. Among his best-known works are* Level Sunlight, The Web of Lucifer, Prince of the Ghetto *and the recent* Blood Accusation, *a study of the infamous Beiliss case which tells in chilling detail of a Russian Jew accused of ritual murder.*

In The Gentleman and the Jew *Samuel describes his family's transplantation from Rumania into a startlingly alien England, and what happened to him in a British public school. His memoir is full of wit and irony, a brilliant examination of two dynamically opposed traditions intersecting upon the psyche of one bewildered boy.*

The Union Jack

(From The Gentleman and the Jew, *Chapter III)*

The homage that my elders paid to England's greatness was a pallid thing compared to the blazing loyalty that was awakened in me.

My proprietary attitude was in one sense justified: I learned English very quickly (the older generation learned it slowly and with various degrees of imperfection) and was soon reading furiously. Oddly enough, I did not feel the less English for not knowing any English people, any gentiles or Christians. Throughout my early boyhood and well into the teens all my friendships were within the Jewish colony. But we youngsters created an English colony within the Jewish colony; and like many colonials we outdid the inhabitants of the mother country in pride and love.

Our integration into England was effected by two instruments, the school and juvenile literature; and since the second was, as it seems to me, infinitely more important, I shall devote most of my attention to it. I call it the "Union Jack" literature, partly because a penny weekly of that name was, I think, the first material that I learned to read outside the school curriculum; and partly because the name itself is a summary and symbol.

The magazines were produced within the rigid framework of a folklore and outlook that were profoundly and irreproachably English. While they held the youngster spellbound with stories of adventure and high jinks in public schools (English public schools; i.e., private schools), they indoctrinated him powerfully with English ideals of fair play, honesty, respect for the throne and the county nobility, pluck, cheerfulness, loyalty, and cricket. They were Kipling brought down to semi-slum levels, as Kipling was Shakespeare's Henry the Fifth brought down to Victorian levels, as Shakespeare's Henry the Fifth was Castiglione's *Courtier* transplanted to England, and *The Courtier* was the ideal man of the classical Greeks reinterpreted by the Italian Renaissance. They were in a great and universal tradition, something that is obscured for us—for those of us, I mean, who were brought up on them—by their primitive literary quality and their peculiarly English ideological argot.

I suppose "cricket" comes nearest to summing it all up. The impact of that word on us youngsters—the little Roumanian Jewish immigrants who became little Englishmen without mingling with English boys—was overwhelming. A thing that wasn't cricket was of course shocking and shameful; but these adjectives do not convey the force or flavour of the condemnation to an outsider. That "it" was not cricket did not simply mean that it was morally wrong. Something deeper was involved: the disapproval of Harry Whartin, Tom Merry, Darrel Figgis, and all the other decent fellows of Greyfriars and St. Jim's, the right people—no, the only possible people, all other people being outsiders.

That these people never stole and never lied goes without saying. They were frank and aboveboard, just as they were fearless and full of japes. Nevertheless, when they wanted to emphasise the truthfulness of an assertion, they used the formula "Honour bright!" If you said that, it was caddish of anyone to doubt your word. "Honour bright" did not actually mean "Otherwise I am possibly a liar." It was just a reminder of one's consciousness of the code, it was a salute, a Masonic signal. "I'm from St. Jim's." "I'm from Greyfriars." Among us Jewish youngsters "Honour bright" was used as often as in the stories of Greyfriars. It was a source of deepest chagrin to us that we could not explain the phrase and all its vast implications to our parents, or to our *Rebbi* in *cheder;* and it certainly made us feel that they were irretrievably outsiders.

The code also included "the stiff upper lip," which was as tacitly a part of a decent fellow's equipment as it was unthinkable to be a bully. Bullying was among the unforgivable sins; but some sins were merely venial, hardly more than misdemeanours, like Billy Bunter's comical greediness. The genuine criminal was of two types, with a social distinction that is best brought out by a comparison between the words "poacher" and "cad." (Of course we knew poachers only from the books.) A poacher was a low-class person in both senses. Besides being dishonest, as a thief, he was in his low way subversive; not only did he steal from the squire; he showed an ugly disregard for the sporting code, which demands that hares be shot or hunted down by gentlemen at the proper season, and not trapped by ungrammatical vagrants at any time of the year. We little Strangeways Jews had a lofty disdain for poachers; however, it was nothing like the wordless contempt that the cad inspired in us.

For the cad was a horse of a different colour. A member of the lower orders could not aspire to be a cad. A cad was something more than a thief, a liar, or a sneak. One could be all of these, and even a bully to boot, and yet not quite a cad.

The crimes of a cad, like those of a poacher—but more odiously, since he, unlike the poacher, had originally been "one of us"—implied a corrupt disregard for the *structure* of things. It is the difference between the amoralist and the sinner. A cad was one who accepted a bribe to sell out the game in the great annual cricket match between Greyfriars and St. Jim's. He did not care who was the winner even when he had no special interest. He was capable of sabotaging a boat race by tampering with the oars. What these things mean, how far they go beyond the ordinary transgression that is motivated by greed, or cruelty, perhaps only a public-school Englishman, or a former reader of *Pluck* and *The Union Jack,* can feel.

The gulf widened steadily between us and our parents as we, the youngsters, sank deeper into the traditions of Greyfriars and St. Jim's. Our parents remained, till the end, incapable of understanding that a game was more than a game, and that "playing the game"—untranslatable concept! —was morality itself. They lived out their lives in England, from early middle to old age, without so much as a glimpse of the English attitude toward sports; and until the end they were baffled by the extraordinary phenomenon of grown-up, often elderly people passionately addicted to football and cricket. In those early days there was one famous cricketer, G. W. Grace, who was bearded like a rabbi. His picture once appeared in the *Yiddish Express,* which on rare occasions had a few lines about Test Matches and similar national solemnisations. My father looked long and earnestly at the bearded man in the white flannels and kneepads, posing in the worshipful attitude of a semi-genuflection before the three wickets; he looked, pondered, sighed, and gave it up. Neither he nor the other grown-ups knew what to make of this whole aspect of adult English life.

At a distance of decades the problem invites facetious treatment, or at least the light touch. Invariably it is in fact so treated. This is evasive, unsatisfying, and unilluminating. We youngsters were reconciled to the idea that our parents would always be aliens, that Englishness would never be theirs as it was ours. What wounded us was the completeness of their exclusion. For there were gradations of alienness. Hindu and French boys turned up at St. Jim's and Greyfriars, and in time came to be voted "rather decent fellows." They even acquired a special merit because they had become rather decent fellows without really having to, not being English. But their admission to this status of associate human being was always won at cricket. Even a Jewish boy (Goldwasser: I remember the name because of the mingled discomfort and pride it awakened in me nearly fifty years ago) was once permitted to score a century at the wicket. What, however, was I to think of my *Rebbi,* and of my parents, who did not know by which end to hold a cricket bat, and to whom the higher symbolism of cricket was forever inaccessible?

It might be inferred from the foregoing that I became a little anti-Semite. This was not the case. I never developed a contempt for the Jewish world, or a hostility toward it, and this still surprises me. It was a world which, apart from certain spiritual difficulties it created for me, might have become repellent by reason of its severe disciplines.

From the age of six till the age of thirteen I was "robbed" of two or three hours every day (except Friday), confined to an evil-smelling room with thirty or forty other youngsters between those ages, and compelled to learn the Pentateuch in Hebrew by translation into Yiddish.

238

Regular school took up from nine to four thirty, with a two-hour break; the *cheder* took up from six to eight or nine, depending on the age of the pupil. Saturday afternoons and Sunday mornings and afternoons were similarly preempted. So self-enclosed was our Jewish world, so little did it occur to us to compare our lot with that of gentile boys, that we accepted the discipline as self-understood. I must also remark that none of the people who went to *cheder* with me (I have kept in touch with quite a number of them) seem to be any the worse for it.

That Jewish world of thought in me should have been, I suppose, constantly at war with the English world of thought. As I have said, it was not; and I do not understand how the two failed to join issue. The mutual incompatibility of those two worlds comes back to me with peculiar vividness as I reconstruct, with inescapable certainty, the moral instruction I received in *cheder*. When I place it side by side with the moral instruction that I derived from the *Union Jack* books, I am astonished not to find myself in the care of a psychiatrist.

I will only recall that from the age of seven or eight on I had the following precepts drummed into me in Hebrew and Yiddish:

"Thou shalt love the Lord thy God with all thy heart and with all thy soul and with all thy might."

"Thou shalt love thy neighbour as thyself."

"By three things the world is sustained: by truth, by judgment and by peace."

"Keep not aloof from the congregation, and trust not in thyself until the day of thy death, and judge not thy fellow until thou art come in his place."

"Let the honour of thy fellow be as dear to thee as thine own, and be not easily provoked; and repent one day before thy death."

We also learned: "If a man puts his fellow to shame publicly, he has no share in the world to come." Likewise we were instructed: "Be exceedingly lowly of spirit, for the portion of man is but the worm."

Then there were passages with a lilt: "Who is wise? He that learns from all men. Who is mighty? He that subdues his evil nature. Who is rich? He that rejoices in his lot. Who is honoured? He that honours mankind."

At Greyfriars and St. Jim's, too, it was taken for granted that a man ought to be modest and kind, that one ought not to put on side, one ought not to be a rotter. But that was not the point, really. Where, in the *cheder* code, was the cheerfulness, gaiety, and magnanimity of life at St. Jim's? Where was the gallantry, where were the affirmations: "Carry on, carry on, carry on, till the field ring again and again!" "Play the game!" There was no hurraying in the Mishnah, no feeling of loyalty, attachment, camaraderie. There was, in short, no cricket.

Less intensely, because it did not grip the imagination like St. Jim's, our working-class school on Waterloo Road also contrasted in spirit with the *cheder*. At school we learned English history as in *cheder* we learned— though much less systematically—Jewish (mostly Biblical) history. English history was adorned with poems like *The Charge of the Light Brigade* and *The Revenge, a Ballad of the Fleet*. There was nothing like this in Jewish history and legend. We knew something about the valiant men of King David's *corps d'élite,* and something about Bar Kochba and his rebellion against Rome. Concerning the latter we were told thrilling things: that every man who enlisted with him had to cut off a finger to demonstrate his courage, and had to be so strong, and so skilful a rider, that he could at full gallop uproot a sapling without being unhorsed. And yet Jewish wars and Jewish heroes and Jewish songs of triumph failed to strike the right note.

Jewish wars were gloomy things; Jewish heroes, though impressive in their way, were without form and style; Jewish songs of triumph were too furiously triumphant. Where in Jewish history was a Hereward the Wake or a Black

Prince? Where was a Sir Francis Drake singeing the beard of the King of Spain, or gaily finishing his game of bowls on the green at Plymouth before proceeding to polish off the Spanish Armada? Samson was obviously quite a fellow, but it did not seem that he ever set about the business of killing his enemies with the gallant and modest smile which would have illumined his features if he had been an English gentleman—an old St. Jim's man.

I read very early a verse of Newbolt's:

To set the cause above renown,
  To love the game beyond the prize,
To honour, while you strike him down,
  The foe that comes with fearless eyes.

That was exactly what I meant. When Jews used to go to war, thousands of years ago, they did not kill their foes in that fine spirit. And Jews, teaching and learning their own history, did not begin to understand the deficiency. How could one convey to them the spirit in which an Englishman did his killing? It was almost not killing. It was—well, it was rather like cricket.

"A good clean fight, no hitting below the belt, may the best man win, and no hard feel-

ings": on the battlefield as in the ring. One could put these words accurately into Yiddish, but they would be gibberish. Jews looked on all fighting, private and public, personal and historic, as such a disgusting business that they could not associate it with an affirmative code; and I felt this so strongly even in my boyhood that I despaired of ever giving my parents a glimpse into the sunny combativeness of the St. Jim's *Weltanschauung*. How could I begin to reconcile it with the somber thoughtfulness of the Pentateuch and *The Ethics of the Fathers?* Where, within that subtle and perceptive discipline, could you find room for the dashing buccaneer type, who could make his prisoners walk the plank, but who, beneath everything, was something of a gentleman because he knew the meaning of "a fair fight"? And in what terms could I present to my *Rebbi* the honourable features in the characters of a Captain Kidd and Claude Duval?

For a long time I was deeply convinced that in the churches of the Christians there were wonderful prayers and rituals which expounded and expressed the code of St. Jim's; that for the gentiles there was the same congruence between their divine services and the ideal secular life as there was for us. In the church the sights would be set higher than in daily practise, even as they were in the *cheder;* but the direction would be the same. And this belief of mine was fortified by the difference in externals. How different the churches were from our synagogues, which at best looked squalid from the outside, and sometimes consisted of nothing more than a rented room upstairs in a private house. If, among our Roumanian Jews, in such surroundings, and in connection with such a prosaic moral code, the overwhelming effects of the Day of Atonement could be produced, what must be the glories of the church services, with their stained-glass windows, their organs, and, above all, the radiant possibilities of the English public-school philosophy of life?

But it is with a church service, the first I attended—the second was not to follow for many, many years—that I associate the beginnings of my understanding that the Christian world is not the simple thing I once took it for. It came about thus:

I was in love with a little Christian girl in my last class at Waterloo Road School. I had never spoken to her. One did not play with girls, or do more than exchange a few words with them, at the age of twelve: that is, if they were Jewish. How thrillingly right I found it when, one day, passing down the little street where the object of my adoration lived (a daring indulgence that I permitted myself occasionally), I saw her playing cricket on the sidewalk with a man who wore the reversed collar of a curate. I did not nod or raise my cap; nor did she acknowledge my fleeting and feverish presence. How unimaginable that my *Rebbi* should ever play cricket with one of us— much less with a girl! How unimaginable, for that matter, that any Jewish adult should play cricket with a youngster, or cricket at all! My heart swelled . . . with a loving and unuttered salutation from afar, the unenvious, ungrudging salutation of an inaccessible paradise.

I formed there and then a resolution the daring of which is perhaps as incomprehensible to a Christian as the manly jollity of *D'ye Ken John Peel?* was to my *Rebbi* and my parents. I was going to attend Sunday service in the neighbourhood church. I was going to penetrate into the forbidden place which pious Jews never passed without the prescribed muttered formula of indignant repudiation. I was going to witness exalted ceremonies that were the highest expression of the English way of life.

The incident remains in my mind after more than forty years as a great confusion whirling about a single point of astonishing clarity. I was so terrified, when I sneaked in among the last of the worshippers; I was so lost and helpless in the dim light; I was so busy trying to conceal from someone (whom?) that I was a little Jew committing a mortal sin, that I could not have given a coherent account of my general impressions ten minutes after I escaped into the sunlight. The point of astonishing clarity came toward the end;

and it became more and more vivid with the passing of the years: I was utterly confounded by the sermon preached from the pulpit. The sermon, in which the name of Jesus appeared and reappeared with—to me—terrifying frequency, had nothing whatsoever to do, in spirit or in substance, with that gay, magnanimous, adventurous and gamesome world which I had come to hear glorified. It did not proclaim, in new and unimaginably attractive phrases, the cosmic rightness of the life of Greyfriars, *The Revenge, The Charge of the Light Brigade,* and the cricket team. In a most unbelievable way it rehearsed what I had been learning in *cheder!* It appeared that among the Christians, too, the meek and the humble were blessed. It appeared that when someone hit you, you did not answer laughingly with a straight left, and you did not invite your friends to stand around in a circle while you carried on with the Marquis of Queensberry rules. Not a bit of it! You turned the other cheek! And what was my stupefaction on hearing that anyone who called anyone else a fool was in danger of hell-fire—a straight lift from *The Ethics of the Fathers!* It appeared that the peacemakers, not the soldiers, not the manly, laughing killers, were the blessed. This was not Tom Merry's world at all. It was my *Rebbi's*.

I simply did not understand. It was beyond my power of insight at that time to perceive that some sort of fraud was being perpetrated, that someone was misrepresenting something. I only felt that this English church, and so-English St. Jim's, and what we learned at school, did not go together, as I had supposed they would; and I was ready to believe that I was at fault; I assumed that I was too stupid to get at the higher unity. I did not know that this was the faltering start of a search which was to occupy me most of my life and provide the substance of many of my books.

The Burden of Faith

In The Professor and the Fossil, *Maurice Samuel addresses himself with grace and precision to profound questions about the Jew and his ordeal over the ages.*

Not in the "discovery" of God lies the meaning of the Jews, but in what they did with that discovery. For whereas many individuals in moments of brilliant insight made the discovery before and after them, the Jews alone as a people sweated out their monotheism over the millennia; they alone made it their obsession as a people and somehow or other hung on to it with unbelievable doggedness from its first emergence four thousand years ago until this day; and the record of the first half of this multimillennial torrent is that collection of books known as the Jewish Bible. One may properly say that Judaism is meaningless without the Jewish Bible, not because it tells of the discovery of God, but because it mirrors the struggle of recalcitrant man with the consequences of his discovery.

Thus we are dealing not with a discovery but with a process. The Biblical record is a continuing drama. The theme is the struggle, inspiration, defection, return, near-obliteration, rëemergence against all probability, the picture of a people possessed by a divine destiny reluctantly assumed, everlastingly repudiated, everlastingly reclaimed. One is tempted to say that the Israelites and God could neither get along together nor let go of each other.

The endurance of the Jewish people is a continuous exertion of the will in the face of adversity, of creative ingenuity in the midst of change.

We need not speak of the courage it needed to die for one's faith at the stake, or to become for its sake a wanderer in a hostile world. More impressive in its way was the ability to stand up to the choreography and decor of humiliation which the Middle Ages added to their economic and physical maltreatment of the Jew: the ghetto,

246

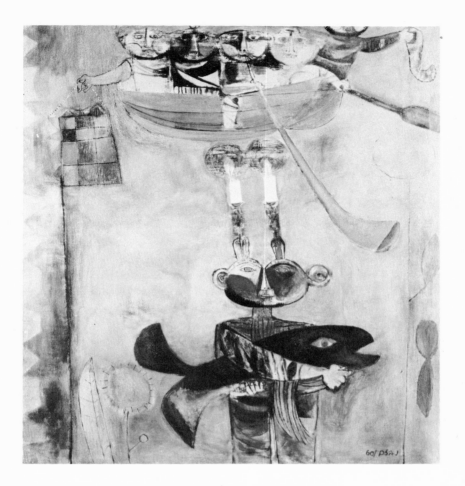

the yellow badge, the spitting ceremonials, the in-
sults, the naked foot-races, the blood libels, the
accusations of poisoning the wells. Hundreds of
thousands of little people accepted the verdict of
an ever-renewed malevolence without a thought
of purchasing security and comfort by defection.
And escape was so easy, so simple! The "racial" rejection of the Jew was unknown in the Middle
Ages. It was all a matter of belief. The Churchmen
were eager to win souls; the conversion of the Jews
was an ideal; and there were prelates of a genuine
Christian disposition who, protecting the Jews in
times of popular bloodthirstiness, made the offer
of Christianity in a spirit that was particularly
tempting. The answer of the faithful was NO! The
Jewish people had a task to complete and would
not quit in the middle.

Isaac Bashevis Singer (1904–   )

There are many Jewish writers of fiction; according to latest statistics they form the largest single occupational group in the United States. In the reception of their work the ordeal of the Jews has finally paid off. The overvaluation of this work has been a weird extension of the reparations principle into the realm of books. However, there are some authentic artists among these Jewish writers, both famous and obscure—J. D. Salinger, Leonard Cohen, Michael Seide, Grace Paley, Edward Dion—and, at the very top of the list, Isaac Bashevis Singer.

Singer writes in Yiddish—possibly the last literary artist who will do so—and, without question, he is the best writer in that defamed argot since Sholem Aleichem. There are those who consider him one of the two or three most effective of living writers in any language. One critic calls him "not a writer, but a literature. . . ." Henry Miller speaks of "The wonderful, wonderful world, a terrible and beautiful world of Isaac Bashevis Singer, bless the name!"

Most of his work centers about the rich though doomed life of the Hasids of Poland in the early part of this century. His tales are saturated with the magic of Cabala as embodied in the imps, demons and sprites that swarm his pages and charm the reader with their radiant malevolence. But there is an enormous spaciousness to his work. When the mood is on him he abandons his theological whimsies and delivers himself of some of the most powerful naturalistic stories in all literature. But even the most heartbreaking tragedies are invested with grace notes of humor and irony, a total lack of self-pity and a wry perspective, separating his work so profoundly from the pretentious kitsch of some of his contemporaries.

Among the best-loved of his books are the novel The Family Moskat, *the two collections of short stories issued under the titles* Gimpel the Fool *and* Spinoza of Market Street, *and the novels* The Magician of Lublin *and* The Slave. *His latest short-story collection,* The Seance, *includes some tales in which he first uses an American setting; they are gems.*

In My Father's Court *is another change of pace,*

glowing modest memoirs of the magistracy of his rabbi-father and of the Jews who took their disputes and trans-gressions to him for judgment. The piece printed here is not quite typical, but it offers a sardonic warm-hearted glimpse of the most successful species of charlatanism—that based on the commercialization of an ideal.

The Salesman

Things happen in life so fantastic that no imagination could have invented them.

One day the door to our kitchen opened and a man entered who looked different from any Jew I had ever seen. He wore a hat in the rabbinic style, but his alpaca jacket reached only to the knees, in the German fashion. He had a white beard, but it was too even to have grown naturally; it had been trimmed by shears. His trousers were striped, his boots glistened. But he also had white earlocks. His face was young and rosy, not at all like the face of an old man, and in his black eyes shone a youthful vitality and a strange pensiveness. His Yiddish was heavily Germanic.

"Is the Reverend Rabbi at home?" he asked.

Neither my mother nor I was used to hearing my father called "the Reverend Rabbi," but after a moment's hesitation my mother realized who was meant and indicated to the visitor that he should go into the next room.

My father welcomed the man with an open-hearted greeting, as he welcomed everyone rich or poor, and asked him to be seated. After a while he asked why he had come, but the visitor did not answer directly. It appeared that he had come simply to chat. In his Germanized speech, he began to demonstrate his familiarity with Jewish learning, and I saw that my father was impressed by his knowledge. He apparently knew the Mishnah by heart. He cited several scholarly books, and from memory recited a few lengthy passages. The conversation became more and more dense. Although my father was a scholar and the author of a number of commentaries, he could barely keep up with him. The man knew everything by heart. He even remembered the exact pages on which certain passages were to be found. He tossed quotations from Maimonides around like nutshells. He seemed to pull commentaries and laws out of his sleeves. He led the conversation around to what the Aramaic translator had said about a certain Biblical verse, and then recited passages of Onkelos and Jonathan ben Uzziel.

As a rule, my father refrained from praising a man to his face, but this time he could not hold back. "How can a man—may no evil befall you—have such a memory? You are indeed to be compared to 'a limned cistern that loses not a drop,' " he exclaimed.

"Permit me to show you some affidavits. . ."

The stranger took out a packet of letters bearing the seals of many Rabbis. Famous Rabbis called him "genius," "Prince of the Torah," "one who uproots mountains and reduces them to dust. . ." One Rabbi attested that he had examined this man and that "his hands were filled" with the Babylonian Talmud, the Jerusalem Talmud, Sifri, Sifra, Tosefta, Mehilta. Father rubbed his forehead and almost smacked his lips. He said, "It is a privilege to have you in my house!"

He sent me to tell Mother to bring tea and refreshments for his guest.

A little later he himself came into the kitchen to tell her about the visitor. Mother, herself the daughter of a renowned Rabbi, was equally enthralled. In our house, learning was looked upon as the greatest wealth. I stood with my ears cocked, so as not to lose a word. Father asked the stranger whence he came, and it turned out that he was originally from Hungary and had visited many lands. He had even studied with a Sephardic *Hacham* in one of the provinces of the Turkish empire. He had been in Palestine and had wandered as far as Damascus and Babylon. He had traversed the world and knew several languages—

Russian, Hungarian, German, and Arabic. With great deliberation, he took out an Austrian passport and showed my father the many, many visas issued by all sorts of consulates. This was the first time I heard the words "visas" and "consulates." On the whole, my father attached little value to such secular matters, but when they accompanied learning such as this, he considered it a combination of Torah and worldly glory. He called me over and ordered me to shake hands with this extraordinary man. Apparently he wanted me to have the honor and privilege of touching the visitor's hand. The man pinched my cheek and asked, "What are you studying?"

Then he recited by heart not only the

passage of the Gemara that I was studying at the time, but added to it bits of Rashi and the other commentaries.

In the meantime my mother had served tea, cookies, and fruit. She seemed almost embarrassed by this modern-looking scholar. Father told the visitor whose daughter she was, and I was pleased to hear that he knew my grandfather by reputation.

After a while he whispered something to my father, who turned to me and said, "Leave the room now."

Mother had already gone out, and after a slight demurral I slowly made my way to the kitchen. I greatly desired to listen to this man's scholarly Germanic speech, but such was the way of adults: as soon as the conversation became really interesting and every word began to draw me like a magnet, they would suddenly decide to "send the boy away." As I went out, I left the door slightly ajar, but the stranger himself walked over and closed it firmly. Obviously, he had an extraordinary secret to confide.

In the kitchen Mother began to lecture me. "How does one become a scholar like that?" she argued. "By studying, not by being idle. But, instead of studying, you read foolish storybooks, about things that never were and never will be." Then she told me a story she had read in a newspaper. A professor had a wife who never had dinner ready on time and every day he had to sit around waiting. Suddenly it occurred to him that he could utilize this time and he began to write a book. A few years later he published the work he had composed entirely in the time spent waiting for dinner. Now if scholars can show such diligence in secular knowledge—for which there is no divine reward—how much more important is such effort in the study of Torah? One could become a scholar and at the same time attain merit for the hereafter.

Mother's words made a deep impression upon me. Yet I was also filled with curiosity as to what the stranger from those faraway lands was telling my father so secretively. Through the closed door I could hear whispering, mumbling, sighs. From time to time I even thought that I heard a stifled cry. The voice was my father's, and it sounded as though he were angry at someone, barely restraining himself from erupting into a towering rage. But why would Father be angry at this man? What was going on inside? Mother, too, began to look curious, for the voices that came from the study were rising higher and higher. There was no longer any doubt that a dispute— indeed a quarrel—was taking place. Could they be arguing so heatedly about a passage from the Gemara, or over the interpretation of a law? Somehow that did not seem likely. Mother went over to the door and tried to listen. Then she said, almost resentfully, "Why is your father shouting?"

Suddenly the door was flung open and my father appeared. I had never seen him so flushed, so disheveled and upset. His forehead was covered with beads of sweat. His red beard trembled. His earlocks, which were nearly black, quivered. Confusion, dismay, and fright were apparent in his eyes. He called out to Mother: "Give me some money, quickly!"

"How much do you need?"

"As much as you have."

Mother was upset.

"But I cannot give away my last groschen!"

"I beg of you, don't keep me waiting. I don't want that vile creature in my house another minute! May his name and memory be wiped out. . ."

"Why is he a vile creature?"

"Give me the money—if not, I'll leave the house at once! His very presence defiles. . ."

Tears rose to my eyes. With trembling fingers, Mother began to search the drawer of the kitchen table. She had grown pale. I could see our visitor through the door. He stood in the center of the study, plucking at his beard and examining our oil lamp. My father returned to argue with him a while longer. Then the door of the study opened again and the stranger came out. He looked at my mother and said, in his precise, neo-German, "Good day."

A minute after he had left, Father stormed into the kitchen and cried out: "Woe is us—such a thing has not been heard of since the days of the creation! The man is a heretic—a spiteful apostate—an insolent heathen—a willful sinner! Such learning—and yet he is the lowest of curs!"

"Why are you shouting so? What did he want of you?"

"He came to sell me eternal life. . ." Father's voice did not sound like itself.

"What?"

"Yes, you heard right. He wanted to sell me his share in the hereafter for a hundred rubles."

"He must be a lunatic."

"No, he's not a lunatic. He is an atheist! A total unbeliever! An Elisha ben Abuya!"

And my father, still upset and barely able to speak, told how the man had made his offer. Since he had amassed so much knowledge in the Torah and sacred lore, he claimed he had acquired a great portion of eternal life and he had come to sell it to my father. Father argued that an unbeliever has no share in the hereafter, but the visitor had cited Talmudic passages to prove that through the learning he had acquired he had earned a share in the world to come, and that it is possible to sell one's share of eternal life. He argued that since he needed the money, and since he himself did not believe in life after death, he was willing to do business with his portion of it.

Mother looked at Father with reproach in her eyes.

"And why did you give him our last few rubles?"

"I had to get rid of him. He threatened that he would not leave the house without the money. . ."

"But how shall I prepare for the Sabbath now?"

Father did not know what to say. He

254

ran to the sink and washed his hands, as though to cleanse away the defilement of that creature. He remained standing, his head bowed, confused, almost as though he had been struck by a fist. So much learning—and such heresy! Such a scholar— and such a reprobate. Esau had given away the rights of the first-born for a mess of pottage, and this scoundrel was prepared to throw away eternal life for a few rubles. . . .

"World's end! World's end!" my father muttered to himself. "How many days are left him on this earth? He is already an old man. . ." Then he looked scowlingly at me and added, "Let this be a lesson to you!"

Soon we heard that the stranger had visited all the Rabbis, scholars, and men of substance in Warsaw. To each he had offered the same unholy business deal, and everywhere he had received at least a few rubles. This schnorrer practiced psychology on his victims: first he inspired admiration, then anger, abhorrence, and fear, and finally he let himself be paid off just for going away. It was even rumored that here and there he snared a rich fool who actually paid the hundred rubles. This, then, was his merchandise; with these wares he made his way through the world.

Albert Memmi (1920-   )

This essay, "Name-Changing," is taken from the
book The Liberation of the Jew, *by Albert Memmi, a*
French Jew born in Tunis. He has written several books,
all pivoting upon the theme of the Jews' "unlivable" fate,
and the painful stratagems they use to cope with it.

The classic devices range from small ones, like
name-changing, to big ones like assimilation. In between
are the partial strategies of conversion and mixed mar-
riages.

For a people so skilled in words the process of
name-changing has always been full of bitter humor.

Name-Changing

I was never able simply to deny my
Jewish fate. I had to accept it or reject it, fight it
or assume it, but never without misgivings or
ambiguity. When I wished to dissimulate, it was
with laborious stratagems; when I acknowledged
it, it was with passion. I preferred to push my rejection to extremes, even to a mixed marriage,
even to rupture with my people . . . free to return to them with the same violence. Appearances
to the contrary, I sincerely believe that few Jews,
whatever they say, are ever able to remove themselves from their Jewishness for very long.

Name-changing is a well-known and
much-discussed act. Its results are pitiful. It was
in Europe, in France to be precise, that I discovered its extent: the Jews from Eastern Europe,
North Africa and Asia are desperately anxious
to pass unnoticed. So are old French-Jewish families, who have realized, perhaps as a result of
some alarm, the Hebraic or Germanic consonance
of their names. Since Jewish destiny is surely one
of the most troubled in history, one can understand that this is certainly a very old and familiar
Jewish tactic. Here again my first reaction was
one of severity, until I understood the meaning of

this other disguise of the hunted man. If the idea never occurred to me in my own case, I do not wish to appear more virtuous than I am. Had I been called Levy, Cohen or some other more revealing name, who knows if, at some period of my life, I too might not have been tempted? Why wouldn't I have discarded a banner-name, a brand-name which would have immediately designated me as a member of a minority, separated?

On the other hand, I maintain without hesitation that the non-Jew's irritation or derision on this subject is either monstrous gall or an extraordinary lack of perception: that the oppressor who accuses his victim of the crime of which he himself is guilty. One of our professors at the university had what he thought was a most humorous habit. He systematically translated the names of his Jewish students: "Klein? Do you know what Klein means? In *German* it means little. You must have had a little ancestor, etc. . . ." Thus translated and illuminated by etymology Jewish names can perhaps seem comical; Blumenfeld which means field of flowers or Zilberberg which means mountain of money can be funny. In translating Klein or Blum, our witty professor literally unmasked the outsider; he destroyed his actual social being, so painfully acquired. He proved that he did not have an ordinary French name; he sent him back to his foreign origins.

I do not believe in the innocence of this little game. I am even convinced that there is no fundamental difference between this amusing manipulation of Jewish names and one of the extreme forms of anti-Semitism: pure and simple denunciation. A collection of Jewish names, enumerating their various transformations, periodically appears in French bookstores: in every case it is an attempt to prevent the victim from escaping his destiny, to mark him more certainly as a target.

Name-changing is a means of defense, a flight, almost a fraud.

On closer inspection one is amazed to find that this effort is never pushed to its conclusion. Of course, there are Jews who change their names radically; but they seem to be extremely rare. It is almost always a question of half measure.

A case in point is that of a Jewish doctor from Central Europe, obliged to relocate. Many patients, he thinks, would rather not be attended by an alien and a Jew. He therefore decides to change his name. It was Kalmanovitch; what will he be called from now on? Smith, Jones? Not at all: his decision will be charged with a significant ambiguity. After going through a great deal of red tape and money, he obtains official permission to call himself . . . Kalman. Certainly Kalman is less obvious, less exotic than Kalmanovitch; but still he will not remain completely unnoticed. In the final analysis this camouflage is but a veil through which it is easy to see if one cares to look. Thus Davidovitch is content with David or Davidson, Silverman with Silvers, etc. There were enough of these changes at the end of the war to give rise, in France, to the humorous expression: *mutilated names*.

Some decide to go beyond this simple amputation. But though they want to change their countenances completely they nevertheless choose one which is equivalent. A Jewish publicist from Morocco whose name was Benamar decides to sign himself Emmanuel. He gains a little, of course, for it might conceivably be a Protestant name, and doubt is possible. But while he was at it, why stop at a name that is half-camouflage, half-revealing? At times, the make-up is very thick, at times very superficial, but it is almost always make-up and not a true transformation. Aron becomes Nora: which is equivalent in reverse, hardly a disguise. Schwartz becomes Black, Bronstein becomes Brownstone and Grünfeld, Greenfield: an exact translation!

The translation is often very approximate. For example, when Napoleon forced the French Jews to choose a surname from among the French names, they forged themselves conventional equivalents. The Haims decided on Vidal, because

Haim means "living" in Hebrew, and Vidal comes from vitalis.

One might discover complete transformations, but accomplished in two or three stages: Block first becomes Block-Morhange, then Morhange alone; Weill-Curiel will become, I suppose, Curiel; Levy-Lebar: Lebar; Grunenbaum-Ballin: Ballin; and Block-Dassault: Dassault. (Yes, even one of the richest men in France deemed it necessary to change his name.) Then, in spite of a complete exchange, the rupture does not appear absolute.

Why these masks? Why this timidity, this half-hearted concealment? Such a transparent disguise is not without significance. It seems to be a double contradiction: self-rejection immediately counteracted by a profound resistance to this rejection. The camouflage is at the same time wished for and not wanted, decided upon but not desired.

So [the Jew] compromises: he chooses a name which might be Jewish, without having to be Jewish.

Whatever the disgrace of his condition, in every victim lies an ambiguous desire, both ardent and shameful, to resemble his persecutor. It is a legitimate temptation: for to overcome his difficulties the oppressed must often identify with his oppressor. A scandalous temptation: for this identification is relatively treasonous vis-à-vis his own people. "Really," a young Jewish doctor told me with a sigh, "they ought to force us to change our names!" He forgot that if such a decision were taken in spite of us, it would give rise to martyrs.

How do you resolve this contradiction? How do you preserve your self-esteem, that of your fellow Jews and still obey one of the imperatives of life among the non-Jews? Well, you remodel yourself in their image, you dress in the latest styles; you abandon Bronstein, because Bronstein is a symbol of oppression and because it is troublesome; nevertheless you try basically to save it: you call yourself Brownstone.

In other words, behind the new clothes, the facial contortions and the make-up, you remain the same. Better still if you give your children Christian first names, their religious names, in reality their true names, will be those of their grandparents: Moses, Abraham or Sarah. On their official documents, they will come second, behind the other, but will in secret link them to Judaism. The change of name is truly a mask, a tactical measure, and not an auto-da-fé. It is only the first step in self-rejection, but as can easily be seen, it forewarns of further difficulties and troubles.

One might object that I am drawing exaggerated conclusions from an ordinary procedure. I don't think so. On the contrary, I am convinced that a whole psychology of name relationships might be evolved. The name literally sticks to the person, and most people suffer when they hear theirs mutilated. It is doubtless the old magical fear of losing one's soul. A number of incantations, maledictions or benedictions are made, through the intermediary of the real name. It would be easy to show the affective and symbolic importance of the name in the family group. To abandon the family name is to leave the family, to break away; which is precisely what happens to girls who marry.

The fact is that the Jew never abandons his name without regret and remorse. If he finally does decide on this course of action, it is because it can aid him considerably in his difficult existence. But one cannot resign oneself to pay for his security at the terrible price of one's own destruction.

Israeli Jews furnished me with a surprising proof of this phenomenon, only in reverse, for there too people change their names; it is apparently the custom for anyone wishing to gain an administrative or political post. Now, although the *intention is exactly the opposite, the mechanisms of transformation are identical.* The Jew of the Diaspora tries to cover up the too-visible signs of his attachment to another culture since they arouse hostility in others. The Israeli Jew, on the contrary, wishes to find a spectacular way of affirming himself, to pick up the scattered pieces of his peo-

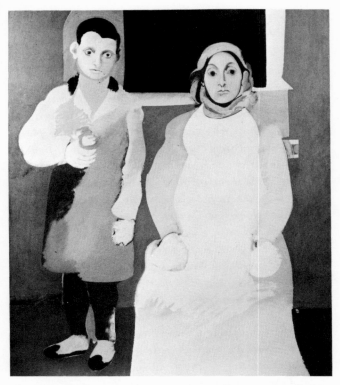

ple. Far from wanting to camouflage, to veil his
Jewishness, he accentuates it, he claims it. Therefore he too will change his name; but this time in
the opposite sense. He disdainfully dismisses the
fake name of his exile borrowed from non-Jews,
symbol of his long night of oppression. Never
again will he be a Bronstein or a Block, a Vassilo-
vitch or a Benillouche. It is then that he hesitates:
just how far can he go in this direction? The exiled
Jew he condemns, whom he definitively rejects,
was, all the same, himself—is still a part of himself.
He cannot, without unbearable loss, totally deny
the memory of his misery. So he in turn will not
dare go all the way in his transformation.

Thus, even in his new-found glory, the
oppressed does not immediately cease being one
of the oppressed. Even in the path of his liberation
which must undo what the oppression did, one can
see the mechanisms of resistance to self-rejection
come into play. Finally, whatever the case, one is
not so easily freed from so many centuries of oppression.

Edward Dion (1924–   )

Dion's comment on the opening passages of Genesis is, "Why didn't He take two weeks and do it right?"

Those who compile anthologies usually play it safe. They select from that which the judgment of time has selected for them; they honor the famous and confer recognition upon the recognized. However, there is another possible road the anthologist can take, at least on occasion. He can anticipate fame and honor himself by introducing an obscure author of great talent.

For those fortunate enough to know his work, Edward Dion casts a brilliant light among contemporary writers. The few things he has published are absolutely startling in their originality. His style is vivid, powerful, polished; he displays a scalding wit, uncanny perception and passion without sentimentality. Refusing the easy way, he never affects stylistic mannerisms; he avoids the macabre, the monstrous. But his prose vibrates with natural sensuality, and the love encounters that occur in his work are more erotic than anything since D. H. Lawrence.

He views Judaism as "Neither religion nor nationality, but a hereditary neurosis—a triumph of involuntary affiliation"—and then goes on to say of himself, "As has been said of an even more irritable and self-conscious minority, it takes one to know one."

For the past years he has been working on an enormous novel to be called Raskolnikov in Oz *and has been kind enough to allow the editor to print some excerpts here. We have selected those passages which bear most directly on Judaism.*

"We Must Choose"

We must understand time to accept revelation. We are beginning to learn again through the evidence of instruments what Abraham first knew in a blinding flash of recognition— the sense of our smallness and God's power. We know now, our instruments tell us, that this earth, this self-important locale, is a tiny speck in the firmament. This huge earth is literally less in the scheme of creation than a single grain of sand among all the sands of all the seas. And this speck of reflected light is a billion years old. Recent among the specks. And man is a million years old, or one thousandth that time. And tool-making, cave-dwelling man is twenty thousand years old. And man in his contemporary consciousness, five or six thousand years old. So that three thousand years is only the space between words when God speaks slowly. And the pronouncements made to Abraham are still being uttered to us. It is the same sentence.

While he is saying that we Jews are forbidden to practice usury, generations of comprehension and noncomprehension rise and fall. And we do not only commit usury, we become identified with its practice. And our spirits are rotted by it. And we become an offense to our neighbors. And a watchword of loathing. And are punished. And undergo the whole experience even while the edict is being pronounced.

What was meant by the idols we were forbidden when our identity began? From these grossly hewn images of stone man sought sanction for bestiality. At their feet, savagery was certified. Therefore the edict: "Do not bow down to stick or stone." Do not celebrate the image; seek for the idea.

What were these image-worshippers? Who were these men of Ba'al? What did they do? They ate filthily. Bloody entrails, slugs, worms, snakes. They moved their bowels where they ate, pissed in their beds. They fornicated with their own children, with other children, with their parents, with other men—with sheep, goats, horses, and dogs. Their spirit was a dull glimmering in a blubber of bestiality. They lived in a glut of undifferentiated sensation, of appetites without gradation. Their thoughts could not shake free, their language could not come clear. They were brutish, foul-smelling, clogged. They stopped at the image.

Jews did not precede the Idea. The Idea preceded Jews, and defined those who avowed it. Abraham first recognized the Idea, which burned with this strange luster—the further possibilities of man. And so Abraham was promised manhood, and his seed after him. And he broke the Chaldean images, and went out of Ur to this place, where the Idea chose to utter itself.

What was the nature of Abraham's God? He was immanent, incorporeal, almighty.

And even as he is saying Ye Shall Not Bow Down to Stick or Stone, even as he is warning us of disinheritance by Esau's charade of gluttony —generations are born and generations die, generations of belief and disbelief, of observance and defiance. Even as the warning against idolatry is being pronounced, we disown the Idea, and worship the God of Things. We become a byword for selling. We become the merchant race. The Traffickers, the Exemplars of Esau. The commercial race. And God puts his finger on us, making a costume of flesh for our desires. Greedy beaks, mouths like purses, hands like hooks, eyes like pennies. Our shoulders cringe. Our voices wheedle. Even as he is pronouncing the words of warning, we observe them, and forget them, and disobey, and rationalize disobedience—until our souls rot, and our bodies become deformed, and we undergo the utmost agonies of humiliation. . . .

He warns those who do not obey his commandments: "I will send a faintness into your hearts in the land of your enemies. And the sound of a shaken leaf shall chase you, and you shall flee as fleeing from a sword, and shall fall where none pursue. . . ." And even as he is pronouncing these words, the generations are born and die; the people flourish and sin and are dispersed; generations rise and fall—remembering, obeying, forgetting, disobeying, rationalizing the disobedience, remembering the forgetting, and forgetting again. And even as the words are being pronounced, the shameful faintness grows in our hearts. Fear turns us into vermin, and we are incinerated by the sanitary German—and all that is left is ashes, and a few live coals, and a few witnesses to the flame.

The tortured history of the Jews is the

grammar of God's rhetoric. Our ordeal is a metaphor of man's dilemma. A labored metaphor. The
Lord tends to exaggerate when he speaks Hebrew.
Perhaps because he is aware of diminishment. For
Hero and Adversary have declined together. God
becomes a myth, the firmament is a formula, and
the Devil is a clerk. Fierce and gorgeous Nebu-
chadnezzar, in his stallion madness wrenching the
hillside grass, has become—what? An Eichmann. A
frightened tallowy little man, more like a Jewish
accountant than a warrior for Wotan. When the
victims are merchants, and the executioners are
clerks, and they confront each other with the same
fright—it little matters who will die. They are
both dead.

God uses what is to hand. As he had
taken the filth-eating Egyptians, and the cow-
connubial Philistines, so he took up those poor
German sticks and scourged his people once again.
Most frightfully. For the Jews had sinned beyond
compare—again denied the living God and chosen
Ba'al. They had known the light and disowned
it. They had blinded the eyes of their soul. They
had become cowardly. They had sought refuge in
weakness, in the world's spurious humanity. After
four thousand years of bitter experience, they tried
to delude themselves about man's humanity, and
sought safety in it. They had become tamed. So
tamed, so softened—they had begun to putrify.
And so God took the most mechanical nation and
used it as a blowtorch to incinerate the illusions
of his people—of his frightened and separated
people. For what is fear, but absence of God? A
unique kind of emptiness. A primal alienation.
Fear, father of all the sins. Which the fat timid
soft Jews glorified, addressing the God of Battles
in petitions for their own safety.

The German tool was rotten in itself.
A scourge in God's hand as long as he chose to
scourge. But then he let it fall; its fire died. For,
once again, he had preserved a remnant of his
people for the Blessing. And the Germans—now,
themselves, soft fat happy humanistic melioristic
apologetic guilty rational—are being prepared for

the slaughter. Fattening themselves for the slaughter. That fat land will burn richly on the Day of Fire. And our hearts will rejoice.

Rejoice, rejoice—for the penalty has been paid, the experience has been suffered, the time of choice has come, and we must choose.

Immanent, capricious, almighty, incorporeal. The All-Visitor. Light of the sun and light of the glowworm. Juice of sap, and juice of the blood, and great lymph of the sea. Recognizing itself in tidal wave and tear. Uttering tarantulas, lilies, wolves—uttering Jews, tigers, roses, rain. He has honored us once again with the perilous distinction of choice. The time has come. We must choose. And we have chosen. . . .

David Daiches (1912–)

David D. Daiches was born in Scotland in 1912. His grandfather, his father and his uncle were all rabbis, but he chose to become a writer. He has taught at the University of Sussex and at Cambridge, as well as at several universities in this country.

Author of various books and articles on English literature, Daiches has also written a delightful autobiography, Two Worlds, *from which this episode is taken.*

Reaching Across

The change which resulted in my life when I left school and entered Edinburgh University was enormous, and had far-reaching consequences. At school I had done my work and gone home, taking no part in sports or other extracurricular activities. But the university was different. There was a great variety of social and intellectual life outside the lecture room, and it was not mostly confined, as nonacademic school activities were, to Friday night and Saturday; I found myself joining societies, writing for the student magazine, making friends among my non-Jewish fellow students. I discovered, to my delighted astonishment, that my fluency in speech and facility in turning verse, which had helped to amuse the family at home but which I had not till now thought to be in any degree out-of-the-way qualities, made me a popular and sought-after figure at the university, and Lionel, too, found that his oratorical gifts and genius as a raconteur gave him an important place in student life. I remember, after taking part in the annual Associated Societies Debate early in my undergraduate career, I was congratulated by the chairman, who remarked: "I suppose at school you must have run the Literary and Debating Society singlehanded." I merely smiled in reply. I did not like to tell him that at school I was never able to attend the Literary and Debating Society because it met on Friday nights, nor did I admit that this was my first appearance at a public debate. In due course I became senior president of the English Literature Society, junior·president of the Diagnostic Society, and literary editor of *The Student*. I found myself being continually surprised that I was actually taking a prominent part in such activities.

The sense of liberation was intoxicating. I had not realised before how narrow and indeed lonely my life had previously been. There was, of course, the family circle with its loyalties and affections; but in my last years at school, when my literary interests were growing and I was going through a phase of romantic introspection, I had no one to discuss these things with, and got into the habit of going for long walks alone. I even grew for a while apart from Lionel, with whom I had grown up in closest association, for as we became older our interests came to differ. And I had no close friends at school—at least none whom I saw anything of outside school hours. But now I was free of a new and richer world, and not only free of it but sought after by it.

At first this had no effect on my Jewish feeling. I was, in fact, aggressively Jewish, taking every opportunity of pointing out my background and, I am afraid, rather snobbishly insisting on its superiority. When, in my first year at the university, I fell sentimentally in love with a fellow student (it was an extraordinary calf-love affair: I had hardly spoken to a girl except my sisters before that) we exchanged passionate avowals and then decided to part forever because my being Jewish made any further relationship impossible. (The decision, I should add, was mine, not hers. It never occurred to *her* that there was a barrier.) I had a broken heart for almost a year after that. I also did some serious thinking. To my father, it was inconceivable that I should even take a non-Jewish girl out to tea. Indeed, it was inconceivable to him that Lionel or I should take *any* girl, even one of deep Jewish orthodoxy, out to tea or anywhere else. The Daiches boys didn't do that. We were the rabbi's sons, and known, and we were not to be seen going about with a girl. When the time came, we would be introduced to beautiful, intelligent, and perhaps also wealthy Jewish girls from cities which had larger Jewish populations than Edinburgh, and we would then doubtless fall in love and get married. Or, if we did not fall in love with the first one provided, there would be others. Here again, my father's innocence was shattering. He was bitterly angry as well as puzzled when he once met Lionel walking with an extremely respectable Jewish girl in an Edinburgh street. This was when I was having my first romantic love affair with the non-Jewish student, and it occurred to me that if my father felt this way when Lionel went for a walk with a Jewish girl from an orthodox family, what would he have said had he known that every day I had been walking my girl home from the university?

Oddly enough, my father never made any objection to our going to university dances, whatever his private misgivings might have been. But it was unthinkable that we should take a girl to a dance we attended; we went alone, or as a member of a large party where the couples were not paired off. What my father thought we did at these dances I cannot imagine. The difficulty, if not the sheer impossibility, of going to a dance alone never seems to have occurred to him. Lionel, always more enterprising than I was in these matters, once arranged to take to a university dance the daughter of a highly respected member of the Edinburgh Jewish community. When my father found out that he intended to take this girl to the dance, he was thunderstruck. An enormous storm broke, and the upshot was that Lionel went to the dance alone. Fortunately, he went in his capacity as business manager of the university society that was running the dance, so he had an excuse for breezing in by himself, as though to see how things were going.

Deceit was forced on me by degrees. My father knew that I was a member of several university societies attended by both sexes. He

knew that girls attended the university lectures. Presumably it was all right if I got into conversation with a girl after a lecture or after a society meeting. Was it all right to walk a few steps while talking with her? If so, how many? The position was, in fact, ludicrous. I began to ask myself whether this "so far and no further" attitude between Jews and non-Jews was healthy or desirable or even, over any length of time, possible. And when I found that I made friends at the university to whom I could talk more freely and satisfyingly than to any Jewish friends or relations, the problem became more acute still. No one had warned me of the possibility that I might find some non-Jews were more *sympathique* than any Jews I knew. This was a most disturbing revelation to me, and it made toeing the invisible line imposed by the policy of Jewish self-segregation not only physically almost impossible but a great strain psychologically. It was all very well for my father to speak to enthusiastic gentile audiences at Burns clubs or anti-Hitler protest meetings; he was a rabbi, with his status, his mission, his publicly recognised position as a Jewish leader. My position was very different: I was exploring friendship for the first time in my life, and I found the invisible line increasingly illogical. The first time that I took a girl to a dance was at the end of my first year at the university when, secretly and with every kind of precaution against being found out at home, I took the fellow student I was in love with. (Let the psychologists say what they like about the sense of guilt, but the fact is I had a wonderful time. I was a poor dancer; most of the time we sat in a corner and talked.) The second time was some years later, when I had matured considerably both intellectually and emotionally: I took then another fellow student, who was to become my wife.

Thus it was that a policy of anguished reconsideration of the relation between my Jewish background and my non-Jewish environment was forced on me: It was a long, difficult, and painful process, which was not complete until the end of my years as a research student at Oxford. My deep affection and admiration for my father never altered, but I had a sense of living on the edge of a precipice. I would come home from a walk on the Pentlands with a group of my university friends (or with only one of them), to find, say, preparations for Passover in progress, and I would feel as though I was walking from one century into another. My non-Jewish friends made things as easy for me as they could. They knew I ate no meat at their houses; they knew that Friday night and Saturday were impossible times for me; when I was asked to take part in a play put on by one of the university societies, the performance was arranged for the evenings of Tuesday, Wednesday, and Thursday instead of the usual Thursday, Friday, and Saturday. But though this saved me inconvenience it only increased my sense of living in two worlds, and sometimes in an abyss between them.

Simon Wiesenthal (1908–)

When Allied troops reached the Mauthausen concentration camp in May, 1945, they found rooms full of corpses. In one room, however, one of the corpses still breathed, and the medical officer could distinguish a very faint pulse. This survivor was taken to a field hospital and nursed back to health. His name was Simon Wiesenthal. And if there was one prisoner in that camp whom the Nazis, for their own sake, should have been careful to kill, it was he. For Simon Wiesenthal, since the war, has made himself a one-man Nemesis. Operating out of a tiny office in Vienna, with no funds at first, obstructed by the authorities, working night and day and almost alone, he began to hunt down those Nazis responsible for atrocities.

He was implacable, moved not only by the memory of his own ordeal, but by the disappearance of his wife, and by the loss of his family who had been incinerated in the ovens.

As he began to find the criminals in their hiding places and to amass the documentation and the word-of-mouth testimony needed to bring them to trial and to secure their convictions, he did attract helpers and some funds; most significant though, survivors of the camps began to come to him with their stories and their memories and their passion to identify those responsible for wrecking their lives.

From the time he started until now, Wiesenthal has brought almost a thousand Nazis to justice. But he is not exclusively an avenger. A gentle, studious man, he has also helped many of those accused of war crimes if he found evidence that they were not responsible. His most famous quarry, of course, was Adolf Eichmann, whom he tracked down in South America, after a sixteen-year search. He caught the Nazi official who had sent Anne Frank off to camp—found him right in his own town, a member of the Vienna police force.

In The Murderers Among Us, *edited by Joseph Wechsberg, Wiesenthal tells his unforgettable story, in which the crimes of Dr. Mengele are only one episode. We are reprinting the chapter in its entirety here because it tells the crimes of a Nazi doctor with such ghastly effectiveness that it cannot be abridged or synopsized.*

The Man Who Collected Blue Eyes

The Nazi regime succeeded in corrupting members of every profession in Germany, including physicians—men who had sworn the Hippocratic Oath. The Hitler regime had created its own kind of medical science. Invalids and others unable to work were sent to the gas chambers; prisoners showing symptoms of contagious diseases were shot, as were others who had had contact with them. When a trainload of prisoners arrived at a camp, a doctor stood by, arbitrarily separating those who looked healthy from those who did not, signaling those who looked well to one side—a temporary reprieve—and those who did not to the other side—the crematorium. Worst of all, the camps became weird laboratories where mad scientists used human beings instead of white mice and guinea pigs. Much has been written about the tests that were carried out with incredible callousness not only by doctors but also by chemists and experts from many leading German drug companies. In Auschwitz there was a special "experimental block" where prisoners had to submit to tests ordinarily made only on animals.

After the war, I met a young Jew whose left arm looked like a multicolored chessboard. The doctors in Auschwitz had put some stuff on a two-inch square of his skin. After a few day of terrible pain, the skin became dark-blue. The doctors cut out that piece of skin and put something else on another part of his arm. This time the reaction was yellowish and the pain was worse. The experiments were continued for months.

I met another boy whom the scientists of Auschwitz, after several operations, had successfully turned into a woman. He was then thirteen years old. After the war, a complicated operation was performed on him in a West German clinic. The doctors restored the man's physical masculinity, but they couldn't give him back his emotional equilibrium. Also at Auschwitz, a group of

doctors and chemists worked on a new, simplified
method of sterilization. They wanted to find "an
act of surgery" that would be so easy to perform
that quacks and barbers could do it; the new
method would be used on the Slavs and other peoples whose procreation was not in the interest of
the Nazis.

It is no secret that some of these doctors are still practicing medicine—in Austria,
Germany, Egypt, Africa, South America. We have
a file of their names and some of the addresses.
Perhaps the worst of the lot is Dr. Josef Mengele,
the former chief doctor at Auschwitz, who spe-
cialized in what he called "the science of twins"
and who tried to artificially create children with
Aryan features and blue eyes.

The name of Dr. Josef Mengele was
known to all former concentration-camp inmates,
even those who had never been in Auschwitz.
Mengele had thousands of children and adults on
his conscience; in 1944 it was he who determined
which of thousands of Hungarians at Auschwitz
would live or die. He particularly hated gypsies
(perhaps because he looked like one) and ordered
thousands killed. I have the testimony of a man
who had seen Mengele throw a baby alive into a

fire. Another man testified that Mengele once killed a fourteen-year-old girl with a bayonet.

In 1959 I asked my friend Hermann Langbein, general secretary of the International Auschwitz Committee, with whom I had worked on several cases, whether he happened to know Mengele's address. Langbein said: "In 1954 Mengele filed a suit for divorce against his wife in Freiburg, Breisgau, their last place of common residence, and exchanged several letters with his lawyer, Dr. Hans Laternser. I got his address in Argentina at the time—don't ask me how."

I learned from various sources that in the past years Dr. Josef Mengele has used these assumed names: Helmut Gregor-Gregori, Fausto Rindon, José Aspiazi, Ernst Sebastian Alvez, Friedrich Edler von Breitenbach, Walter Hašek, Heinz Stobert, Karl Geuske, Fritz Fischer, Lars Ballstroem.

At the time of his divorce, Mengele was practicing medicine in Buenos Aires under the name of Dr. Helmut Gregor-Gregori. He had since been married again—to the widow of his older brother Karl, who had been killed in action in the war. I asked Langbein whether the West German authorities had tried to get Mengele.

"On July 5, 1959, the Freiburg prosecutor issued a warrant for his arrest. Then the Bonn Foreign Office asked Argentina for his extradition. The Argentinians claimed that Mengele could not be found at the address indicated. We must try to get his latest address."

Langbein had known Mengele in the concentration camp and described the doctor to me—a small, swarthy, dark-haired man with a slight squint in the left eye and a triangular cleft between his upper front teeth. He stood five feet six.

Mengele is a Doctor of Philosophy (University of Munich) who studied Kant's *Critique of Pure Reason* and simultaneously swallowed the racial rubbish of the Hitlerian philosopher Alfred Rosenberg. He is a Doctor of Medicine (University of Frankfurt) who sacrificed thousands of childen—twins from all over Europe —by using painful injections to try to change the color of their brown eyes to blue. (Both universities have deprived Mengele of his academic degrees.)

Mengele had a theory that human beings had pedigrees, like dogs. He was convinced of his mission to breed a super-race of blue-eyed, blond "Nordic" people, and of his duty to kill "biologically inferior specimens." In Auschwitz, his surgical ward was impeccably clean, his syringes always sterilized. He often used the syringes for injecting phenolic acid, benzine, or air, which killed his patients within a few seconds. Mengele was the perfect SS man; he would smile at pretty girls while he sent them to their death.

The West German government offered a reward of sixty thousand marks (fifteen thousand dollars) for him. Next to his friend Martin Bormann (one hundred thousand marks—twenty-five thousand dollars), Mengele is the Nazi fugitive with the highest price on his head.

After talking to Langbein, I contacted a friend in Buenos Aires to whom I gave the doctor's last two known addresses. On December 30, 1959, my informant in Buenos Aires notified the German Embassy there, at my request, that Mengele was now residing under his own name at Vertiz 968, Olivos. He apparently no longer thought it necessary to hide his identity.

I gave the new information to Langbein, who called up the prosecutor in Freiburg. Files were exchanged between the embassies, the foreign ministries, the ministries of justice, and the prosecutor's office. Early in January 1960 an urgent official request—the second—for Mengele's extradition was cabled from Bonn to Buenos Aires. A few weeks later the German Embassy in Buenos Aires was informed that the Argentinian Procurador de la Nación might raise the objection that Mengele's offenses could be considered political rather than criminal. Most countries, especially in Latin America, do not extradite people for political offenses.

Traditionally, most Latin American

countries have a strong conception of political sanctuary. The political situation in these countries sometimes changes abruptly; political leaders may have to run for their lives—usually by applying for sanctuary in the embassy of another Latin American country. Many of these leaders believe that by granting demands for the extradition of Nazi criminals they might create a dangerous precedent. The example of Mengele does not mean that there is widespread sympathy for the Nazis throughout South America, but that there is widespread antipathy toward extradition.

Meanwhile, Mengele had been informed by his relatives in Germany that a warrant for his arrest was being issued in Freiburg. In May 1959, eight weeks before the Freiburg indictment was published, Mengele went to Paraguay, where he had made friends during an earlier visit. One of these friends was Baron Alexander von Eckstein, a Baltic Russian who is said to be close to Paraguay's German-descended President, General Alfredo Stroessner. Eckstein sponsored Mengele's naturalization as a citizen of Paraguay.

A few days after his naturalization Mengele returned to Argentina. There he learned that the West German government had made the second urgent demand for his extradition.

Mengele was not certain that his brand-new Paraguayan passport would protect him. He thought it might be safer to leave Buenos Aires. He went to Bariloche, a beautiful resort in the lake district of the Andes, where many wealthy former Nazis have elegant villas and large estates. Bariloche is conveniently close to the frontier of Chile, another favorite refuge of many Nazis.

A mysterious incident occurred in Bariloche. (I cannot give the source of my information, but I can vouch for its reliability.) Among the tourists in Bariloche at the time was a Miss Nora Eldoc from Israel, who was visiting her mother. The two women had been in Auschwitz, where Miss Eldoc had been sterilized by Dr. Mengele. It was mere coincidence that she came to Bariloche at a time Mengele was there. She was

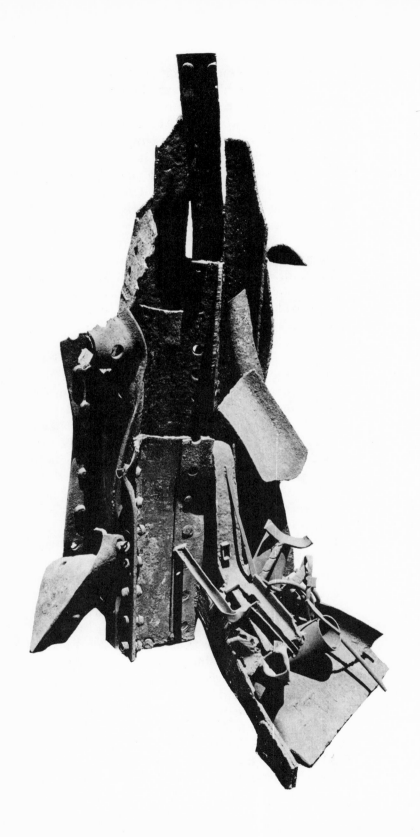

then forty-eight, still attractive, and had many friends in town. One evening, in the ballroom of a local hotel, she suddenly found herself face to face with Mengele. The local police report does not say whether he recognized her. Mengele had "treated" thousands of women in Auschwitz. But he did notice the tattooed number on her lower left arm. For a few seconds the victim and the torturer stared at each other silently. Eyewitnesses later testified that no word was said. Miss Eldoc turned and left the room.

A few days later she did not return from an excursion into the mountains. The police were notified. Several weeks later Miss Eldoc's bruised body was discovered near a crevasse. The police made a routine investigation and ascribed her death to a mountain-climbing accident.

After Eichmann's abduction, the irate Argentine government complained, claiming that it would have handed over Eichmann voluntarily. This seemed doubtful, to say the least, and I informed the wire services and the leading newspapers of the world what had happened in the case of Mengele. These revelations may have convinced some people in Buenos Aires that something would have to be done about Mengele. At any rate, in June 1960 a warrant was issued for his arrest by the Argentinian authorities. It came too late. On the day of Eichmann's capture, Dr. Mengele had slipped across the Brazilian border and disappeared once more. Not for long, though. One day in April 1961, a man I'll call Johann T. came to visit me. Johann is an elderly German who once was a member of the Nazi Party and still keeps in touch with his former *Kameraden*. Yet Johann, whom I have known since the end of the war, has on several occasions given me information that has proved accurate and useful. I know that Johann does not help me because of a sense of guilt or because he wants to atone for the crimes committed by the Hitler regime. He is not particularly fond of Jews, but he is a man of character. Although he is still an ardent German nationalist, he has a very personal reason for his attitude toward the Nazis. In 1942, his niece Linda, a pretty, blond, blue-eyed girl was taken against her will to a so-called *Lebensborn* castle—an official Nazi breeding camp where young Aryans, male and female, were brought together to produce super-Aryans—precisely the sort of place Mengele might have invented. There Linda gave birth to a baby whose father she couldn't identify, since he could have been any one of a dozen young SS man who had been with her in accordance with the program. Johann never got over this insult to human dignity. He once told me he would never stop hating the Nazis for their perverted race theories. When he came to see me in 1961, I hadn't seen him for years. His hair was white now, but his feelings were unchanged.

"I've got good news for you," he said. "I know where Mengele is. I hope you catch him. His trial would open the eyes of many people." He looked at me. "Last week I met two Germans; one is an old acquaintance. They had just returned from Egypt, where they saw Mengele a few weeks ago."

"Johann, so far as we know, Mengele is still somewhere in South America," I said.

"He *was* there, but he left last month. It seems he was getting worried. He had the feeling that he was being followed by Israeli agents."

"And how do the Egyptians feel about him?"

"They gave him the cold shoulder. Nasser wants to stay on good terms with both the United States and the Soviet Union. Perhaps he is worried about adverse publicity if it became known that Egypt was sheltering a man like Mengele. At any rate, the Egyptians suggested that Mengele should leave the country as soon as possible. The German group in Egypt, under a former *Obersturmbannführer* Schwarz in Alexandria, who handles such delicate operations, rented a yacht and took Mengele and his wife to the Greek island of Kythnos."

"Is Mengele going to stay there?"

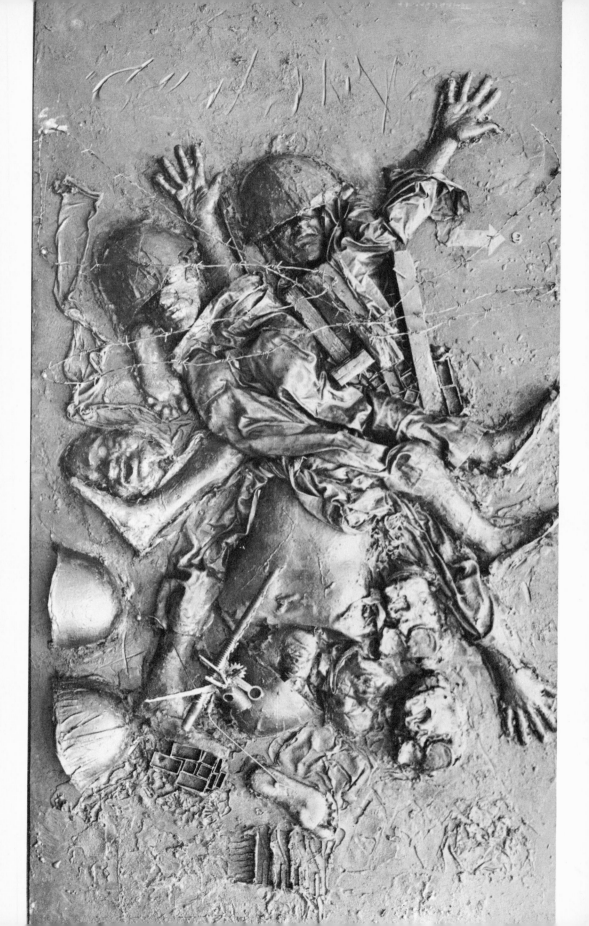

"The Germans promised to have him and his wife taken off the island as soon as it could be arranged. You haven't got much time, Wiesenthal. If you move fast, you might get him on Kythnos."

I was about to leave for Jerusalem to attend the Eichmann trial. If I notified the Greek authorities through normal diplomatic channels, several weeks would be lost. I called up the editor of a large illustrated magazine in Germany. The magazine wanted the story; I wanted the man. Through Langbein we called Athens to contact a Dr. Cuenca, a noted scientist who had been forced during the war to work in Auschwitz as a "medical attendant" under Mengele. It was decided that a reporter from the German magazine would go to Kythnos by way of Athens. If he found Mengele in Kythnos, he would telephone Cuenca, who would come there and identify the doctor. If he was the wanted man, Cuenca would notify the Greek police. Everything would be strictly legal. The Greek authorities would certainly extradite Mengele.

The reporter arrived in Kythnos by boat forty-eight hours later. There were only two large buildings on the island, a monastery and a small inn near the harbor. The reporter entered the latter and asked the innkeeper whether he'd had any guests lately.

"A German and his wife. They left yesterday."

"But there was no passenger steamer yesterday," said the reporter.

"A white yacht came into the harbor. The German and his wife went aboard and the yacht left again, in a westerly direction."

So they had been twelve hours late.

Later, when I met Johann again, I asked him whether Mengele might have been warned that the German reporter was coming to Kythnos.

"I don't think so."

"Who went to fetch Mengele in Kythnos?"

"Some Spanish friends. This man has friends everywhere. I don't know who they are, but I know they brought him to Barcelona. Do you know that he once even dared to go back to Germany?"

"To Germany? But there is a warrant out for his arrest."

"Mengele has *very* good friends in Germany. I know that he came to Günzburg some time in 1959 to attend his father's funeral."

"And no one went to the police to denounce him?"

"In Günzburg, everybody depends, one way or the other, on the Mengeles. I am sure the police did not know he was there."

When it became known that Mengele had been in Günzburg in 1959, Public Prosecutor Rahn told a press conference in Frankfurt that the town of Günzburg "acted like a group of conspirators to help the Mengele family."

Günzburg is proud of its lovely Renaissance castle, its Rococo church, its market square with its old houses, and its largest enterprise, the farm-machinery factory of Karl Mengele & Sons. Mengele's father had founded the firm about the turn of the [present] century. The family had become wealthy; the Mengeles had long been Günzburg's first citizens. A considerable percentage of the town's inhabitants are employed, directly or indirectly, by the Mengele firm. In Buenos Aires, after the war, Mengele & Sons acquired a fifty percent interest in Fadro Farm KG, SA, a new local assembly plant for German-made tractors. The Argentine company was founded with a capital of a million dollars.

In 1962, some months after Mengele had given us the slip on Kythnos, I learned that he had returned to South America. His wife and son remained in Europe. Frau Mengele lived in Kloten, near Zurich, Switzerland. I got in touch with a Swiss lawyer, who learned that she had rented a small house at 9 Schwimmbadstrasse—close to the airport. Not a very quiet place (the planes came in over the roof of the house), but convenient for her husband, who could be home a few minutes after arriving at the Zurich airport, without the risk of being seen by many people. I wanted to go there and find out more about the couple, but the Swiss police don't like inquisitive foreigners in their bailiwick. I therefore asked a Swiss friend to visit Frau Mengele.

He later told me that the house was an inconspicuous brownish villa in a modern development. He'd rung the bell. A small woman, about fifty and "rather pretty," opened the door.

My friend explained that he came from the insurance company. "The policy for your house is due. The premium must be paid."

"I am a new tenant. I know nothing about this policy." Frau Mengele tried to shut the door. My friend quickly put his foot in the aperture.

"Excuse me, Madame, aren't you Frau Vogelbauer?"

"No. She's the woman who rented the house before me. Better go and see the landlord."

"I'd just like to take a quick look at your place to find out for my company whether any repairs are needed."

The German *Hausfrau* in Frau Mengele became alive. She told my friend there was a leak in the bathroom and asked him to come in and take a look.

That night I met a Swiss official in Zurich, told him of our investigation, and asked him to inform the Swiss police. I didn't want to harm Mengele's wife. I only asked that her house be watched so we would know if Mengele happened to drop in. Probably as a result of my intervention, the Swiss federal authorities expelled Frau Mengele from Switzerland several weeks later, in July 1962. The Swiss didn't want to have the problem of extraditing a Nazi criminal, nor did they want to become involved in a war-crimes trial. Frau Mengele left Zurich and moved to the lovely town of Merano in the Italian South Tyrol. She still lives there, in a secluded house, comforted by the presence of many former Nazis.

By now Mengele had gone back to Asunción. He would have preferred to live in Buenos Aires, but the warrant for his arrest was still out there. From the family firm's branch, though, he received enough money for a comfortable life.

Mengele had good reason to feel safe in Paraguay. Today there are more than thirty thousand people of German descent in the country. The population is now almost two million, but the influence of the German minority is considerably greater than its proportion of the population. Germans have key positions in Paraguayan commerce and trade. The President, General Alfredo Stroessner, is the grandson of a Bavarian cavalry officer. Stroessner himself was born in Paraguay, but he seems to be attached to his German heritage. His presidential guard consists of goose-stepping six-footers.

About a thousand Jews now live in Paraguay. One of them is an old friend of mine from the Mauthausen concentration camp. He had been in Auschwitz, and had known Mengele. I met him in Milan in 1964 and talked about Mengele. He seemed apprehensive.

"Please don't do anything drastic, Simon," he said. "The leaders of our Jewish community in Asunción have received many anonymous letters. If Mengele should be kidnapped, the letters threaten that 'not one Jew in Paraguay will survive.' That may be a stupid joke—but some of our people are worried, and I don't blame them."

"What about the police?"

"An outsider who doesn't know Paraguay won't understand how very strong the German influence is in our country. The Nazi ideology of 1933 is still very much alive there. So is the old Nazi principle of *Sippenhaftung* (racial discrimination). The Jews of Paraguay would collectively be made responsible for anything that happens to Mengele."

286

"That's silly," I said. "We've known for years all about Mengele's second wife, and his son Karl-Heinz. He is a nice, serious boy. I know where he lives, whom he sees, what he does. It wouldn't occur to me to make him responsible for the crimes of his father."

"Of course you wouldn't. We don't do such things. But that doesn't mean that they might not do them."

He said goodbye to me and went off, a deeply worried man. I thought of him for a long time. Twenty years after the end of the nightmare there were still people for whom the nightmare still existed.

In July 1962 the Bonn government had asked the Paraguayan authorities to check on Dr. José Mengele, living at Fulgencio Morena 507 in Asunción. Several months later, the authorities notified the West Germans that Mengele was a citizen of Paraguay with "no criminal record."

Mengele didn't stay long in Asunción. His friends told him that he would be safer in one of the German colonies on the upper Paraná River, in an area where Paraguay, Brazil, and Argentina border one another. The river that forms the frontier is lightly patrolled. It is easy to cross it and enter Brazil. Mengele moved to an estate near Encarnación belonging to Alban Krug, a wealthy farmer in his sixties who has been described as a man with a violent temper and violent political ideas. On his journeys Krug is escorted by four heavily armed bodyguards. Mengele stayed two years at the Krug estate, under the alias Dr. Fritz Fischer. Late in 1963 he became restless again.

I knew that it would be impossible to trace all the movements of a man who was protected by so many people in various parts of the world. Instead, I decided to watch the movements of the people closest to him—in this case, his wife and his son. Shortly before Christmas 1963, a letter mailed in Montreux informed one of my friends in Austria that Karl-Heinz Mengele had just gone to Milan, where he would stay at a certain hotel. He

had told his classmates he was going there to meet
some relatives from overseas. I took the first plane
to Milan. At the hotel I was told that a man carrying a Spanish passport in the name of Gregor-
Gregori had stayed there. He had left two days
earlier.

The third round occurred a few months
later, one night in March 1964. Mengele was
spending the weekend at the Hotel Tyrol near
Hohenau, a prosperous German settlers' colony in
eastern Paraguay.

It was a hot, dark night. Half a dozen
men had trailed "Dr. Fritz Fischer" to Suite 26
of the hotel. I later met some of them. They had
formed a Committee of Twelve; they were twelve
survivors of Auschwitz. Some had become wealthy,
and had donated considerable money for the purpose of bringing to justice some of their former
torturers. Unfortunately, the committee's methods
were not as good as its intentions.

I was later told what had happened: six
committee members had drawn the assignment of
going to South America. They were to seize
Mengele alive and bring him to Frankfurt am
Main, where preparations for the Auschwitz trial
were being made. A few minutes before 1 A.M.
the men entered the lobby of the Hotel Tyrol, ran
up the stairway, and broke open the door of bed-
room number 26. It was empty. The hotel owner
informed them that "Herr Dr. Fischer" had left
in a hurry ten minutes earlier, after getting a telephone call. He had been in such a hurry that he
hadn't even bothered to take off his pajamas. He
had put his suit on over them, raced down the
stairway, and disappeared into the night.

Mengele was still odd man out.

The Auschwitz trial was to begin in
Frankfurt in 1964. Dr. Fritz Bauer, the chief prosecutor, told the press that "José Mengele," believed
to be somewhere in Paraguay, was identical with
the former concentration camp doctor. The Bonn
government made a last determined effort to get
the chief defendant extradited. On July 16, 1964,
Eckhard Briest, the German ambassador in Asun-

ción, once more presented a formal demand for Mengele's extradition during an audience with President Stroessner.

President Stroessner became furious and banged his desk. "If you continue with this," he shouted, "I shall break off diplomatic relations with the German Federal Republic!" Briest explained that he had received specific instructions about Mengele from Bonn. The President said: "Not another word, Mr. Ambassador! I shall not tolerate such things any longer!"

An account of the meeting appeared several weeks later in the German news magazine *Der Spiegel*. After Stroessner read his airmail copy of the issue, he realized that he might have gone too far. He consulted his advisers. Foreign Minister Raoul Pastor urged the President to get rid of Mengele. Pastor pointed out that Paraguay had just obtained a three-million-dollar development loan from Bonn, and might get more. It would be unwise to antagonize the West German government.

For a week, Mengele's fate was in the balance. He came to Asunción, and shortly afterward an inscription in black paint appeared on the wall of the German Embassy: JEWISH EMBASSY! HANDS OFF MENGELE! THIS IS AN ORDER!

Perhaps it was. Once again General Stroessner decided to keep *his* hands off Mengele. It was decided that Mengele should return to eastern Paraguay. He would live in a heavily guarded area into which no foreigners were permitted. In Caracas, Venezuela, the case of Mengele was later discussed at a conference of Interpol, the international police group. Dr. Frederico Nicholas Fernández, Interpol director in Rio de Janeiro, said he'd been informed that Mengele was hiding in the jungle near the Paraguayan border. But Paraguay is not a member of Interpol, and direct intervention was impossible, he said. Dr. Fernández was right. Mengele now lives as a virtual prisoner in the restricted military zone between Puerto San Vincente on the Asunción-Sao Paolo highway and the border fortress of Carlos Antonio López on the Paraná River. There he occupies a small white shed in a jungle area cleared by German settlers. Only two roads lead to the secluded house. Both are patrolled by Paraguayan soldiers and police, who have strict orders to stop all cars and shoot all trespassers. And just in case the police should slip up, there are four heavily armed private bodyguards, with radios and walkie-talkies. Mengele pays for them himself.

The West German government still wants Mengele, and there is still a reward of $25,-000 for him.

Lenny Bruce (1922–1966)

In one of his best monologues, comedian Lenny Bruce is a sleazy, brash Broadway agent talking long distance to the Vatican, trying to persuade the Pope to fill a guest spot on television. The Pope apparently agrees and the agent shouts joyously, "Don't forget, wear the big ring."

This joke tells something about Lenny Bruce. He was obsessed with religion. The tension between its present eunuch code and the spiritual flame of its origin provided him with some of his best routines. They said he was obsessed by sex; he was obsessed by it in the same way that D. H. Lawrence was. He saw it as the great force of the human relationship and behavior and could not bear the way it was hounded, sterilized, made into a dirty little sneer. In this respect, his alleged sickness was health.

You get a marvelous picture of this funniest and most profound of all modern comedians in his autobiography entitled How to Talk Dirty and Influence People. *For those unfortunate enough to have missed seeing him in a night club and watching the blistering concepts being born on the spot as the small, dark, elfin-looking man was swept into a kind of erotic ballet of improvisation, this book is the next best thing. In fact, it is the only way to know him now. You cannot see him in any night club. He died a few years ago. His last years were tormented, the police hounded him, he was hardly able to make a living, and the manner of his death shamed the society that would not let him live.*

Lenny Bruce was a Jew in the great tradition of dissent; the tradition that compels certain of these people to become irritants, antibodies against hypocrisy and injustice. He was a Jew, very consciously so. He loved the Yiddish language and used it like a caustic, profane street poet. Three selections from his autobiography—which is richly larded with his comic routines—display the superb fusion of humor and moral passion that marked his best work.

What's Jewish and What's Not

Perhaps at this point I ought to say a little something about my vocabulary. My con-

versation, spoken and written, is usually flavored with the jargon of the hipster, the argot of the underworld, and Yiddish.

In the literate sense—as literate as Yiddish can be since it is not a formal language—"goyish" means "gentile." But that's not the way I mean to use it.

To me, if you live in New York or any other big city, you are Jewish. It doesn't matter even if you're Catholic; if you live in New York you're Jewish. If you live in Butte, Montana, you're going to be goyish even if you're Jewish.

Evaporated milk is goyish even if the Jews invented it. Chocolate is Jewish and fudge is goyish. Spam is goyish and rye bread is Jewish.

Negroes are all Jews. Italians are all Jews. Irishmen who have rejected their religion are Jews. Mouths are very Jewish. And bosoms. Baton-twirling is very goyish. Georgie Jessel and Danny Thomas are Christians, because if you look closely on their bodies you'll find a boil somewhere.

To trap an old Jewish woman—they're crafty and they will lie—just seize one and you will find a handkerchief balled up in one of her hands.

I can understand why we can't have a Jewish President. It would be embarrassing to hear the President's mother screaming love at the grandchildren: "Who's Grandma's baby! Who's Grandma's baby!"

". . . And this is Chet Huntley in New York. The First Lady's mother opened the Macy's Day Parade screaming, "Oy, zeichint mine lieber' and furiously pinching young Stanley's cheeks . . ."

Gentiles love their children as much as Jews love theirs; they just don't wear their hearts on their sleeves. On the other hand, Jewish mothers don't hang gold stars in their windows. They're not proud of their boys' going into the service. They're always worried about their being killed.

Involvement

Come on down to the West Coast and visit the *schuls*. There are no *schuls*. Yes, there is a reform temple where the rabbi—no, it's a doctor, he is a doctor of law. His beard is gone . . . "You know, someone had the *chutzpah* to ask me the other day—they said, 'Tell me something, Doctor of Law, is there a God or not?' What cheek to ask this in a temple! We're not here to talk of God— we're here to sell bonds for Israel. Remember that. A pox upon you, Christ and Moses . . ."

Christ and Moses are confused. They go to New York. . . . Saint Patrick's Cathedral. There is Bishop Sheen, played by Ed Begley. Cardinal Spellman, played by Hugh Herbert— "Wooo, wooo, terrible, terrible, terrible." Christ and Moses standing in the back of Saint Pat's. Confused, Christ is, at the grandeur of the interior, the baroque interior, the rococo baroque interior. His route took him through Spanish Harlem. He would wonder what fifty Puerto Ricans were doing living in one room. That stained-glass window is worth nine grand! Hmmmmm . . .

The Sell

And now we go to the headquarters of Religions, Inc., where the Dodge-Plymouth dealers have just had their annual raffle, and they have just given away a 1958 Catholic Church. And seated around the desk are the religious leaders of our country.

We hear one of them. He's addressing

the tight little group in Littletown, Connecticut (Madison Avenue is getting a little trite). "Well, as you know, this year we've got a tie-in with Oldsmobile. Now, gentlemen, I don't expect any of you boys to get out there in the pulpit and hard-sell an automobile. That is ridiculous. But I was thinking now. What do you say to this? If just every once in a while, if we'd throw in a few little terms, just little things like, uh, "Drive the car that He'd drive"—and you know, you don't have to lay it on, just zing it in there once in a while and then jump maybe to the Philistines."

Paul Goodman (1911–   )

Paul Goodman is an aging enfant terrible *who has kept his infantilism and his terribleness working profitably for him as he continues to goad the Establishment of which he is now willy-nilly a part. Dubbing himself an "anarchist," he is on the record against all forms of totalitarianism, although exhibiting more tolerance to those on the left than on the right—which gives him legitimacy in the psychopolitical syndrome shared by most Jewish writers. But his insights are often better than his conclusions. He is a most effective critic of our schools and of certain time-encrusted values of American society. Warm advocate of homosexuality as life style and of civil disobedience as social therapy, he has developed of late into a sought-after campus guru and spends more time lecturing than writing. For all that he remains a more graceful practitioner of prose than most of those coarsened by a series of causes. His best-known books are* Growing Up Absurd *and* Compulsory Miseducation.

Skeptical Survivors

Some intelligent Jews nowadays lay all their stress on survival, having survived. The Jews are those who have survived, and modern Zionism is not a return to sacramental glory but the engine of survival. *Is* this the way to survive? It seems to me that one in fact survives by having an idea which—surprisingly, but one was not thinking about survival—outlasts the roundabout forces of destruction; it proves to be a stronger way of organizing energy. To work at survival as such is like trying to be happy as such. Not that the "idea" is to be taken at face value, nor that survival isn't more important evidence. But to use survival pragmatically is bound to make it boring and we'll destroy ourselves just for spite. To boast of surviving tempts Nemesis, our deeper impulse.

The tenacity of the Jews to persist in America, though the "religion" continues to decline, is indeed significant. But the attempt to make of this persistence a social-cultural idea, like Ahad-Ha-Am and his "reconstructionist" followers, seems to me to be strangely anti-Jewish. It seems to me that the essence of the persistence is not, mainly, to be other than the Gentiles, except as a response to anti-Semitism, but just simply that the Goyim and their *goyim nachus* are not worthy of emulating and being assimilated. It is not that the Jews have the answers, but that we, by our historical good fortune, such as it is! are able to be skeptical and a little disengaged from some of the gentile foolishness. We are befuddled, but not that befuddled, in our thirst for paradise.

It is not a "Jewish" idea that animates Jewry—such a notion confuses everything; it is the society of justice and the culture of paradise, which belong to all mankind, but for historical reasons the Jews have often been less confused about them. And so far as, among the existentialists, there has been a small "religious" revival, this *has* been its content.

Already in the 18th century, the Protestants had become Catholic, and the emancipated Jews took over as Protestants. Now in America Jews have become Establishment and people the Rand Corporation. But we were taught *not* to put our faith in princes, and to dwell as if in tents.

(1966: And now there is a revival of spirit among the existentialist Protestants and the *aggiornamento* Catholics; but the suburbanite Jews have sunk into spiritual degradation.)

Leslie Fiedler (1917–)

Leslie Fiedler, critic and novelist, is a highly talented writer whose warmth and wit contrast intriguingly with the rigidity of his ideas. Bitten early by Freud, he refined and subtilized the crude literary theories of the Freudians and ingeniously adapted them to a study of American literature. In his construct, classic pieces emerge as a series of homosexual fantasies—Huck is in love with Jim; the narrator of Moby Dick has carnal notions about Queequeg; Cooper's leather guides and trappers are caught in a love-hate relationship with Indians; and there are others. And these journeys downriver, into the sea and into the woods are desperate escapes from women into the embrace of a savage male lover.

Fiedler's idea of the Jew in all this is interesting. To him the Jew is a metaphor of modern man, sterilized by rationalism, twisted by urban tensions, tormented by the special breed of guilt known only to victims—who must turn to Negro and Indian for a kind of psychic relief. Particularly fascinating to him, therefore, is the spectacle of Negro anti-Semitism—a complex and tragic phenomenon which has inspired some of his most perceptive writing.

The Last Taboo

What chiefly exacerbates relations between Negroes and Jews, as far as Jews are concerned, is the persistence among them of the mythology of Liberal Humanism. This troublesome myth-system, derived in part from Old Testament sources, most highly developed in modern Anglo-Saxondom, and picked up again in that world by emancipated Jewish intellectuals, includes the following articles of faith: that all men desire freedom and full human status and deny that freedom and status to others only when it has been refused to them; that equality of opportunity leads to maximum self-fulfillment, and social well-being; that the oppressed and the injured have

been so ennobled by their oppression and injury that they are morally superior to their masters; that all men desire literacy and suffrage—and can exercise those privileges equally well when granted them; that all the foregoing are not the parochial belief of a tiny minority of mankind over a minute span of time, but what all men have always believed, or would have believed given the opportunity. The Jews have felt especially righteous in respect to the application of these principles to the Negroes in the United States, since they are well aware that they were not as a group involved in the enslavement of the Negro, and they know themselves to have long been involved in Civil Rights Movements in numbers all out of proportion to the percentage of the total population which they represent. No Negro ever died for a Jewish cause, Jews tell themselves; but some of our boys have died for Negro rights.

How utterly unprepared they have been, therefore, to find a growing number of Negroes rejecting not only their credo but them in particular as its messengers—spurning in short the whole body of "Jewish Liberalism." "Hear our message and be saved," they cry only a little condescendingly, and are dismayed to hear in return: "All we want from you white mothers (or alternatively, Jew mothers) is to get off our backs and out of our road!"

Yet worse, much worse, is the fact that the Negroes, whatever their avowed credo, challenge by their very existence a basic article of the Liberal Faith: equality of opportunity will not grant very many of them, brutalized by long brainwashing and bred by a kind of unnatural selection, a decent life or the possibility of prosperity. What they demand, not so much by what they say as by how they are, how they test, how they perform, is *special privilege* rather than equality if they are to make it at all in the very world in which the Jews have so pre-eminently flourished. And what a shame and embarrassment that some men (i.e., most Jews) have done so well under conditions in which certain fellow-humans seem bound to do ill.

What can survive of liberal mythology in the face
of this?

Marxism, especially in its more brutal
Bolshevik version, has long offered an alternative
mythology to that of liberalism; but so many intellectual Jews now sufficiently advanced into middle

age to have become its spokesmen have been there before. Some, indeed, are alive and articulate at the moment who have lived through the loss of three religions: first Orthodoxy itself, then Stalinism or Trotskyism, finally enlightened liberalism; and for them, what lies ahead but despair?

Sometimes I feel this way and am tempted toward desolation; until, looking out into the streets, the schoolyards, the coffeehouses, I find my heart leaping up at the sight of young couples linked arm in arm. And I think our daughters will save us, love (not big theoretical, but small sexual love) will save us.

What sunders us may not be first of all but is last of all a sexual taboo; and that taboo is every day being broken, with or without benefit of clergy, Christian or Jewish; and its breaking is the beginning (though *only* the beginning) of the end.

I sat the other day eavesdropping on the conversation of a group of very young white girls—most of them pretty, blond daughters of Jews with black boyfriends, discussing what they would do when the first race riots broke out in Buffalo. And one of them suggested that they march between the two opposed packs, Black and White, carrying signs which read: MAKE LOVE NOT WAR. It was elegant and vain as the loveliest dream; and I am old and cynical enough, after all, to know it.

To make matters worse, I had just been reading a statement by a Negro poet that Jewish girls only married Negroes in order to emasculate them. And I was aware that it was his paranoid and sinister mythology which operated in the tensions that made headlines day after day; but I knew that the counter-mythology of those young girls had power to move men, too.

I, at least, prefer to live in its hope rather than the Negro poet's despair, convinced of its superiority to all the weary mythologies of mere politics. The disillusionment it will inevitably breed at least still lies ahead, and (if I am lucky) I may not live so long.

Abraham J. Heschel (1907–   )

It is only fitting that the final word should be said by Professor Abraham J. Heschel, of the Jewish Theological Seminary in New York City—one of the most important Jewish thinkers in the United States today.

Judaism

Judaism is the track of God in the wilderness of oblivion. By being what we are, namely Jews; by attuning our own yearning to the lonely holiness in this world, we will aid humanity more than by any particular service we may render.

We are Jews as we are men. The alternative to our Jewish existence is spiritual suicide, disappearance, not conversion into something else. Judaism has allies, partners, but no substitute. It is not a handmaiden of civilization but its touchstone.

Index

Photo Credits

p. 17—**Kneeling Figure, Humbert Albrizio.** Courtesy Kraushaar Galleries, New York.

p. 18—**Examination of Jewish Boy by Rabbi, Menkes.** Harry G. Friedman Collection, The Jewish Museum, New York.

p. 20—**Untitled—Ovadia Al-Kara.** Courtesy America-Israel Cultural Foundation.

p. 23—**Fragments, Rina Rotholz.** Courtesy America-Israel Cultural Foundation.

p. 26—**Mother and Child, Sir Jacob Epstein.** Collection The Museum of Modern Art, New York. Gift of A. Conger Goodyear.

p. 38—**Pottery Mask of a Bearded Man.** Courtesy America-Israel Cultural Foundation.

p. 40—**Ancient Tablets, Rina Rotholz.** Courtesy America-Israel Cultural Foundation.

p. 45—**Light of the Sun, Leonard Delonga.** Courtesy Dr. and Mrs. Eli Scheer.

p. 52—**Three Standing Figures, Leonard Delonga.** Courtesy Mr. and Mrs. George Perutz.

p. 55—**Despair, Hugo Robus.** Whitney Museum of American Art, New York.

p. 60—**The Twelve Tribes, Rina Rotholz.** Courtesy America-Israel Cultural Foundation.

p. 64—**Moses and Tablets of Law, Ben Zion.** The Jewish Museum, New York.

p. 68—**Torah Wrapper, German, 1750.** The Jewish Museum, New York.

p. 73—**Men on Horses, Leonard Delonga.** Courtesy Mr. and Mrs. William F. Oliver.

p. 86—**Basalt Bust of a Roman Emperor.** Courtesy America-Israel Cultural Foundation.

p. 97—**Etching by Elias M. Grossman.** The Jewish Museum, New York.

p. 103—**Warrior Group, Leonard Delonga.** Private Collection.

p. 108—**L. Pilichowski.** The Jewish Museum, New York.

p. 116—**Spinoza, Moissaye Marans.**

p. 129—**Adam and Eve, Shalom of Safed.** Courtesy America-Israel Cultural Foundation.

p. 133—**Repentant Sinners, Boris Schatz.** The Jewish Museum, New York.

p. 160—**Dust Storm, Bernard Arnest.** Courtesy Mr. and Mrs. Dante Cerza.

p. 165—**Masked Figure, Ralph Dubin.** Courtesy Kraushaar Galleries, New York.

p. 167—**The Zodiac (mosaic),** from E.P.A., New York.

p. 175—**The Struggle, Arie Kilemnik.** Courtesy America-Israel Cultural Foundation.

p. 177—**Testing Grain, H. Grabe.** Harry G. Friedman Collection. The Jewish Museum, New York.

p. 186—**Time, Joe Lasker.** Courtesy Mr. Charles H. Renthal.

p. 190—**Evan's Corner, Joe Lasker.** Courtesy Mr. and Mrs. Benjamin Tell.

p. 198—**Newborn, Ralph Dubin.** Courtesy Kraushaar Galleries, New York.

p. 214—**Six Standing Figures, Leonard Delonga.** Courtesy Mr. Charles H. Renthal.

p. 217—**Casa Emma Lou, Joe Lasker.** Courtesy Tupperware private collection.

p. 220—**Trees, Leonard Delonga.** Courtesy Mr. James F. Duffy, Jr.

p. 231—**The Lesson, Moissaye Marans.**

p. 241—**Two Boys, Joe Lasker.** Private Collection.

p. 242—**Kids Running, Tom Hardy.** Private Collection.

p. 247—**Coming Back, Napthali Bezem.** Courtesy America-Israel Cultural Foundation.

p. 251—**Day Dream, Ovadia Al-Kara.** Courtesy America-Israel Cultural Foundation.

p. 255—**Plaster, Ralph Dubin.** Courtesy Kraushaar Galleries, New York.

p. 261—**The Artist and his Mother, Arshile Gorky.** Gift of Julien Levy for Maro and Natasha Gorky in memory of their father. Collection of the Whitney Museum of American Art, New York.

p. 266—**Pillar of King Solomon's Mines, Moshe Castel.** Courtesy America-Israel Cultural Foundation.

p. 270—**Reader, Russell Cowles.** Courtesy Kraushaar Galleries, New York.

p. 272—**By Yigael Tumarkin.** Courtesy America-Israel Cultural Foundation.

p. 275—**By Yigael Tumarkin.** Courtesy America-Israel Cultural Foundation.

p. 279—**Crematorium, Yigael Tumarkin.** Courtesy America-Israel Cultural Foundation.

p. 282—**By Yigael Tumarkin.** Courtesy America-Israel Cultural Foundation.

p. 287—**The Synagogue, Hyman Bloom.** Collection The Museum of Modern Art, New York. Acquired through the Lillie P. Bliss bequest.

p. 291—**The Prodigal Son, Auguste Rodin.** Allen Memorial Art Museum, Oberlin College.

p. 293—**Twin Heads, Alfred Maurer.** Gift of Mr. and Mrs. Hudson D. Walker. Collection of the Whitney Museum of American Art, New York.

p. 294—**Portrait de Ma Mère. Myriam Bat-Yosef.** Courtesy America-Israel Cultural Foundation.

p. 299—**Across the Tracks, Ralph Dubin.** Courtesy Kraushaar Galleries, New York.

p. 301—**By Yigael Tumarkin.** Courtesy America-Israel Cultural Foundation.

p. 302—**Passions, Arie Kilemnik.** Courtesy America-Israel Cultural Foundation.